# The UKCC Code of Conduct

## of Conduct

### A critical guide

**Irene Heywood Jones**

MSc, RGN, RMN, DipN(Lond), ONC(Hons), RNT

First published 1999 by Nursing Times Books
Emap Healthcare Ltd, part of Emap Business Communications
Greater London House
Hampstead Road
London NW1 7EJ

Printed and bound in Great Britain by Drogher Press

Typeset by KAI, Nottingham

British Library cataloguing in Publication Data
A catalogue record for this book is available from the British Library.

ISBN: 1 902 499 123

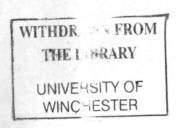

# Contents

# Preface

The UKCC Code of Professional Conduct for the Nurse, Midwife and Health Visitor is a valuable statement, which sets out what the public can expect from professional practitioners. It provides a set of guiding principles to enable the practitioner to serve the public. Of necessity, it consists of several principles, to make it equally appropriate to the vast array of traditional and emerging practitioner roles in a wide variety of working environments.

Within these complex and diverse circumstances, practitioners are confronted by all manner of practical and ethical dilemmas in caring situations. Ideally, they should be able to turn to the Code as a guide to enable them to reach the best judgements in their patients' interests in any situation.

Unfortunately many practitioners work in less than favourable circumstances. Many factors militate against the ideal practice that is required and many are beyond the practitioner's control: staff shortages, increased workload, bed shortages, unresponsive managers, uncooperative colleagues and violent patients are just a few of them. Faced with intolerable pressures and perceiving a lack of power, practitioners may become apathetic, demoralised and frustrated that patients are only getting necessity-based care. At the grassroots many practitioners function at a level of constant crisis intervention and struggle to fulfil their professional obligations amid the grim reality of parlous circumstances, financial constraints and a deaf management.

How do professional practitioners reconcile the ideals of the Code with the requirements of their employment contract when they both appear to conflict? Just as nurses have a duty to their patient, the organisation has a duty to its employees, to provide a healthy and safe environment and sufficient resources.

It is the practitioner's professional responsibility to flag up concerns and inadequacies, and spell out clearly, both verbally and in writing, how they relate to protecting the public — putting the onus back on the manager. If practitioners work with the Code of Professional Conduct as a living document and adhere to its recommendations, then they can live with their decisions at the end of the day.

This book aims to throw open challenges from practice to provide a thorough exploration and examination of the Code. It will examine and expand on each clause to get a more complete and detailed understanding of the Code's guiding principles and their application.

It is true that the Code is used to advise on conduct and is therefore also a measure for misconduct. But it would be a pity if this negative, defensive view dominated the practitioner's thinking. We hope the information in this book will enable practitioners to interpret the Code in a positive light which will be useful within each unique context that confronts them in their daily work.

We ask the reader to note that any mention of a nurse implicitly includes a midwife and health visitor, and the term practitioner will convey all three. The many varying terms for the recipient of care will be interchangeable; patient, client, service-user, customer.

It is to our advantage having a variety of experienced and highly qualified contributors, each of whom has an interest in the clause they have chosen to examine. We welcome the differing perspectives and styles of presentation in this collection.

Quite fortuitously this is a most timely publication, reaching nurses precisely when the statutory bodies and the Code itself will be the subject of close scrutiny and review.

As editor, I hope that this book serves our practitioners well in their pursuit of excellence in care in the changing and challenging health provision of the next century.

The professional reader is advised to use each chapter, combined with reflective practice from his or her own field of work, to complete study hours for the PREP requirement.

*Irene Heywood Jones*

# Foreword

I joined the General Nursing Council for England and Wales as its deputy registrar shortly before its demise. This followed publication in 1972 of the report of the Committee on Nursing which was chaired by Professor [now Lord], Asa Briggs. This report recommended a significant number of changes in the way that nursing was regulated, one of which was the introduction of a single United Kingdom Council, which heralded the end of the organisation I had just joined. Several more years were to pass before most of the changes favoured by government were to reach fruition.

Although my knowledge of the way my profession was regulated was probably greater than the average registered nurse, I was surprised by both the limited range of powers of the statutory body and the fairly minimalist approach it took to exercising the powers that it had.

For example, although hearing complaints alleging misconduct against nurses, and frequently removing them from the register for misconduct, the GNC provided no advice or guidance about what it regarded as appropriate conduct. This was equally true of its fellow Nursing Councils for Scotland and Northern Ireland. This failure extended even to situations in which individuals, finding themselves in unusual and challenging practice situations, sought advice. The justification for this seemed to be that 'The Act (the then current edition of the Nurses Act) doesn't say you can do that.' My response was to say that the same Act did not forbid you from giving advice when it was sought, and that it infringed no other law were such advice to be given. Thereafter, whenever my advice was sought, I gave it to the best of my ability, operating from the basis of my own professional experience, some knowledge of the ethics of professional practice generally and, I hope, the application of at least a modicum of common sense.

While this caused me no sleepless nights, it seemed to be a source of some aggravation and anxiety to my employers. In due course, that concern was put to good use. The sense and logic of providing advice, and not only to those who actively sought it, was accepted. Second, the Council pressed for its statutory regulatory body to be given that power and responsibility.

During the development of what eventually became the Nurses, Midwives and Health Visitors Act, 1979, the senior civil servants principally concerned kept the text of the proposed Bill a close secret until it was published and moved rapidly into the parliamentary system. It is not possible, therefore, to establish an exact cause and effect relationship between the pressure exerted and the ultimate result. It is a fact, however, that when the Act of 1979 passed into law in April of that year it was, for all its defects, very different from any UK nursing legislation that had preceded it.

This Act of Parliament, through the words of its first section, established the United Kingdom Central Council for Nursing, Midwifery and Health Visiting [UKCC] and the four National Boards. It then proceeded to define the functions of the council. Using positive language it stated that:

> 'The principal functions of the Council shall be to establish and improve standards of training and professional conduct for nurses, midwives and health visitors.'

The words 'principal', 'shall' and 'improve' all contained in one sentence seemed almost to smack of revolution! Sadly, although some progress has been made in subsequent years, I fear that neither the Council, nor the profession as a whole, has yet to come to grasp the full significance of that short sentence in the law and respond to its challenge and opportunities. The Act then moved, to my great pleasure, to one of the means by which that might be achieved, and eliminated some of the earlier doubts, stating that:

> 'The powers of the Council shall include that of providing, in such manner as it thinks fit, advice for nurses, midwives and health visitors on standards of professional conduct.'

Unfortunately, an election led to a change of government immediately after the 1979 Act received royal assent, and it seemed to be put on the shelf and allowed to gather dust. Pressure, from both the profession and the Council, eventually led to the dust being blown away. Shadow Council and Boards were created early in 1982, subordinate legislation was prepared after a great deal of consultation with nurses, midwives and health visitors, and the appointed day on which the new bodies would become substance rather than shadow was set as 1 July 1983.

So it was that in May 1983, by filling the post called Director for Professional Conduct with the shadow UKCC, while sitting at home convalescing from minor surgery, and being mindful of the Council's declared intention to have Code of Professional Conduct for the Nurse, Midwife and Health Visitor prepared for it first day of real life, I wrote the first draft of the first edition. It was taken to the next meeting of the Council and, to my amazement, approved for printing with relatively little discussion or amendment. To that, however, was attached the condition that the text be reviewed and, if deemed necessary, revised after a year.

In preparing that text for the consideration of the Council I read numerous documents that I considered relevant. Recognising the shadow UKCC's requirement that a succinct text was required, my main sources of influence were the *'Code for Nurses'* [sub-titled 'Ethical concepts applied to nursing'] in the amended version approved by the International Council of Nurses in 1973, and the 1976 version of the *'Code for Nurses with Interpretive Statements'* of the American Nurses Association.

A significant feature of the first edition of the UKCC Code of Professional Conduct was that it set out supplementary notes. One of these emphasised that it was the responsibility of every practitioner to join with the Council in keeping the Code under review and invited contributions. As a result of this invitation and the fact that, during the first year, I addressed numerous meetings in many parts of the UK to introduce and debate the code, when the time came for the promised review I had received almost 4,000 letters. It was now possible to bring to the review a range of views much broader than that of the then 45 Council members.

Each of the organisations representing registered nurses, midwives or health visitors had submitted its views and these were, without exception, helpful and constructive. So also, for the most part, were the many responses from individual practitioners or from groups who had met and offered a collective view. There were, of course, exceptions. These included the sceptics and cynics whose views betrayed an abysmal ignorance of any concept of ethical or even vaguely responsible practice, and others who argued that the Code was inadequate in that it did not tell them, in every situation, precisely what they should do. Included in the latter category was the lady who wrote to me almost monthly to press her case for the revised code to declare that people on the Council's register should never exceed the speed limit when driving, never be overweight, never drink alcohol or smoke, and so on.

The second edition of the Code, prepared with these comments and suggestions firmly in mind, was subjected to more robust scrutiny. Once again it fell to me, as the relevant Council officer, to prepare a draft. That draft text was then debated at a meeting that ran deep into the night. It was a pleasure to share in this stimulating discussion with Council chairman Dame Catherine Hall, Council members Margaret Green, Ruth

Schrock and Mary Uprichard, and my professional staff colleagues of the time, Peta Allan and Ann Bent. The council, at its meeting the following day, endorsed the text we had prepared, and so the second edition of The Code of Professional Conduct for the Nurse, Midwife and Health Visitor was released in November 1984.

This edition would appear to have influenced professional thinking in a number of occupational groups in the UK, and also among nurses in a number of countries, since there is evidence of its text being copied with relatively minor amendments. If it is the case that imitation is the sincerest form of flattery, there were many who deemed us to be declaring the right principles in the right way. The document also received a warm welcome from organisations representing consumer interests. After its release in the UK the flow of letters commenting upon the text and making recommendations for change slowed to a trickle which, unless it is evidence of disturbing professional apathy, I take to indicate a reasonable level of satisfaction with the finished product.

Although the regular annual reviews of the text continued and were informed by the contributions I had received and summarised, no strong feeling of a need to revise the text was felt by the Council until 1992. The main criticism made by my correspondents, particularly from about 1990 onwards, was the wording of what was then Clause 6. This required the practitioner to *'Take account of the customs, values and spiritual beliefs of patients and clients.'* To 'take account', some argued, was much too soft. More specifically, there was written criticism that the wording did not emphasise the practitioner's responsibility to care for people irrespective of their personal attributes or ethnic origin. The response to this – in my view the most significant change between the second and third editions – was the new Clause 7 which, linked with its stem as all clauses should be, now states that:

> *'As a registered nurse, midwife or health visitor you are personally accountable for your practice and, in the exercise of your professional accountability, must recognise and respect the uniqueness and dignity of each patient and client, and respond to their need for care irrespective of their ethnic origin, religious beliefs, personal attributes, the nature or their health problems or any other factor.'*

At the time that this book is being prepared, the third edition, dating from 1992, remains the definitive text.

Meanwhile, during the intervening years, a number of comparable texts have emerged which are worthy of consideration and should, I believe, be studied closely before any further revision of the UKCC Code or preparation of its replacement by a successor statutory regulatory body. For example:

- The American Nurses' Association published a new edition of its 'Code for Nurses with Interpretive Statements' in 1985;

- The New Zealand Nurses' Association published its 'Code of Ethics' in 1988;

- The Australian Nursing Council Incorporated published its 'Code of Ethics for Nurses in Australia' in 1993;

- The Canadian Nurses Association published its 'Code of Ethics for Nurses' in 1985.

The second, third and fourth of these are significantly longer than the UKCC text and the International Council of Nurse' Code, but the subject matter is essentially the same. What differs is the approach. For instance, both the Australian and New Zealand texts are constructed in such a way that they present a 'Value statement' [Australia] or 'value' [New Zealand]. For example, 'Value statement 1' in the Australian text is that 'Nurses respect persons' individual needs, values and culture in the provision of care', and expands upon it with three 'Examples of behaviour'. I find this approach very interesting, but still have a preference for a brief and succinct document that can, where required, be elaborated and developed in other texts.

In one sense the wheel has come almost full circle for me. As I have indicated, one of my major sources of reference and influence in preparing the UKCC's first edition of the Code was the 'Code for Nurses' of the International Council Of Nurses. Now, as I conclude this foreword, I am serving as the sole UK member of an eight member advisory group convened by the International Council of Nurses to assist the review of that very same text.

I therefore find the decision of NT Books to publish a text which explores the Code of Professional Conduct in some depth both timely and constructive. From the vantage point of having read the text before writing these words, I contend that it has the capacity to assist reviews both nationally and internationally. I congratulate the respective chapter authors for their thoughtful and often challenging contributions.

One of the substantial features of my career has been the preparation, review, revision and promotion of the Code of Professional Conduct for the Nurse, Midwife and the Health Visitor. Depending on the view you take of that document, I must therefore take either a substantial part of the praise or blame. I have certainly felt priviliged to have been so heavily and directly involved with this document that I regard as highly important.

I conclude, however, with a cautionary word, borrowed from the writings of Australian nurse-ethicist Megan-Jane Johnstone. With her usual clarity and wisdom, she states that

> 'Nurses around the world would be well advised to be cautious in their use of formally stated and adopted codes or ethics, and to be especially vigilant not to fall prey to"worshipping the code" at the expense of being ethical - and not to fall into the trap of treating the prescriptions and proscription of a code as absolute, and as ends in themselves, rather than as prima facie guides to ethical professional conduct.'[1]

Those of us who, as staff or members of UKCC, have been involved in the construction of the three different UKCC Codes since 1983, have certainly endeavoured to adopt and hold to that approach. I am pleased to note that most of the chapter authors in this book seem to have seen it in that light.

## Reference

1. Johnstone, M-J (1994) *Bioethics: a nursing perspective* [2nd edition] Marrickville, New South Wales: W.B. Saunders/Bailliere Tindall.

# List of contributors

**Chris Bassett, BA, RGN, RNT,** is a lecturer in nursing at the University of Sheffield. He has written widely in the nursing press and his main interests are practice development and the use of research; he has edited practice-focused texts on clinical supervision and nursing research which will be published by *NT Books*.

**Patricia K. Black, MSc, SRN, RCNT, Further Education TeachingCert, Family Planning AssociationCert,** is a clinical nurse specialist in stoma care affiliated to the Hillingdon Hospital NHS Trust, Mount Vernon and Watford Hospitals NHS Trust and Harrow and Hillingdon Healthcare Community NHS Trust. She qualified as a nurse and midwife at Hammersmith Hospital in 1969, then spent two years on the renal transplant unit at St Mary's Hospital, London. Later she worked in family planning and agency occupational health nursing, followed by work on surgical wards, where she became a clinical teacher. Patricia took up her current post in 1985. In 1992 she completed an MSc in medical anthropology and is currently researching the rehabilitation of ethnic minority patients after enterostomal surgery. She is also interested in the rise of sponsorship. Patricia lectures on stoma care, publishes in the medical and nursing press and has spoken on radio.

**Jacqueline Docherty, MBA, RGN, DipManagement Studies, CertHealth Economics,** is the executive director of nursing at King's College Hospital, London. After qualifying and working as a registered general nurse in Scotland Jacqueline moved south. She was a theatre sister at the Royal United Hospital, Bath, and a senior sister at the Royal Free Hospital, London. On returning to Scotland her jobs included nursing officer at Glasgow Royal Infirmary and deputy director of nursing at West Lothian NHS Trust. She was a member of the management executive at the Department of Health in the Scottish Office before becoming director of nursing at King's College Hospital. In 1987 Jacqueline was awarded the British Institute of Management Prize, and the Devro Award for Creative Thinking and Innovation.

**Jane Eastland, BSc, RGN, Dip. Professional Studies in Nursing** qualified in 1990 at Durham College of Nursing Studies. She is a sister on the combined intensive/coronary care unit at Wansbeck General Hospital,

Northumberland, and her special interests are education and clinical supervision.

**John Eastland RGN, Dip. Higher Education Nursing Studies,** qualified in 1992 at Mid Northumberland College of Nursing Studies. He is a staff nurse on the combined intensive/coronary care unit at Wansbeck General Hospital, Northumberland, and his special areas of interest are coronary care and research.

**Jill Fardell, RGN, RM, Midwifery TutorDip**, is chief executive of the Disability and Rehabilitation Education (DARE) Foundation, which became a registered charity in July 1998, following *The Case for Action Report*, a national survey of education needs relating to disability and rehabilitation of health and social service professionals. The Foundation promotes the active involvement of clients/service users in planning, delivery and evaluation of their care and services and educating service providers. Its ultimate aim is to enable disabled people achieve quality of life on their terms. Jill is also a family carer.

**Ray Field, MPhil, RGN, RMN, DipNursing, DipCommunity Psychiatric Nursing, CertEd, RNT,** is director of nurse education and professional development at St George's Healthcare NHS Trust, Tooting, south London. He has a background in community mental health and education purchasing. His current interest is in PREP and professional development and how nurses are meeting their professional requirements.

**Sarah Furlong, PhD, BSc,** qualified as an applied biochemist in 1992, and, after a period researching the genetic origins of breast cancer at the Royal Marsden Hospital, London, did a PhD while conducting research for the British Heart Foundation. She worked in the pharmaceutical industry and became interested in the social implications of disease. She took part in nursing research at Glenfield Nursing Development Unit, a King's Fund-supported nursing development unit, where she explored the implications to patients of primary nursing and Orem's self-care philosophy. After a period teaching research methods at De Montfort University, Sarah returned to the King's Fund to research nurses' changing roles for the Department of Health.

**Deborah Glover, BSc, RGN,** qualified in 1983 at University College Hospital, London. Clinical areas she has worked in include care of the elderly, oncology, ITU and HIV. Over the past few years she has been involved in practice and professional development roles and has brought her clinical and development experiences to her role as clinical editor for

*Nursing Times*. Deborah's main passion is the development of practice that retains the values and principles of nursing.

**Chris Green, BA, RGN, RMN, DipLaw, DipLegal Practice,** is a general and mental nurse and also a qualified solicitor. He has worked in the legal department of the Royal College of Nursing, representing nurses in a variety of legal matters, most recently in the Fallon inquiry into Ashworth special hospital.

**Diane Haddock BSc, RGN, Dip. Higher Education, Occupational Health NursingDip,** works for Aintree NHS Trust as occupational health nurse adviser. In the past five years she completed a BSc degree at Lancaster University, followed by OHND at Manchester Metropolitan University. Diane works as a named nurse for Aintree NHS Trust for several public and private occupational health contracts, advising on risk management and health and safety. To keep clinically up to date she does extra bank work as a staff nurse at weekends, also within Aintree NHS Trust.

**Irene Heywood Jones, MSc, RGN, RMN, Orthopaedic NursingCert, DipNursing, RNT,** has a long and varied career within nursing and nurse education, including clinical and teaching roles in general, psychiatry, orthopaedics and elderly care. As a mature student she took a master's degree in medical anthropology at Brunel University and found the social and cultural aspects of health and healing put a lifetime of caring into a new perspective. Irene has published articles in the nursing press and several books including the first major text on the Code of Conduct in 1990. She feels most comfortable writing about 'life as she finds it'.

**Graham Johnson, RGN, Occupational Health NursingCert,** has worked in occupational health nursing for more than 22 years. In 1990 he took up his present post, managing a team of occupational health practitioners serving four NHS trusts and other public and private sector clients. Graham is a former chairman of the Royal College of Nursing Occupational Health Nursing Society and is secretary to the Scientific Nursing Committee of the International Commission of Occupational Health Nursing. He is a member of the *Occupational Health Journal* editorial board, an expert referee for *Nursing Times* and *Nursing Standard*, and has had many articles published. He has an interest in latex allergies and recently conducted a survey of UK health-care employees.

**Malcolm Khan, LLB, Barrister at Law,** is principal lecturer in law at University of Northumbria, Newcastle. He is the co-author of the book,

*Medical Negligence* (Cavendish Press, 1997), and of various articles on medical law.

**Carolyn Mills, MSc, BSc, RGN, PGAEC,** is assistant director of nursing at Hillingdon Hospital Trust. Before her present post, she spent most of her nursing career in critical care. Her last post was project leader/clinical nurse specialist in intensive care at Chelsea and Westminster Hospital.

**Mandy Pullen, BSc, RGN,** works at Hillingdon Hospital NHS Trust as a colorectal nurse. Mandy has addressed conferences and written in the nursing press on colorectal nursing issues. She has also published a patient booklet and written for her local newspaper. Mandy and other members of her team are currently setting up a fast-track screening clinic for colorectal cancer.

**Michelle Robson, LLB, Solicitor,** is senior lecturer in law at the University of Northumbria in Newcastle. She is the co-author of various articles on medical law and of two books, *Medical Negligence* (Cavendish Press, 1997) and *LPC Case Study: Civil Litigation* (Blackstone Press, 1998, 5th ed).

**Ron Steed BSc, RGN, CertEd** has been nursing since 1985. He trained in America but emigrated to the UK in 1989 because he wanted to work in a health-care system that catered for all people, regardless of their status. He is currently a freelance back care adviser/manual handling trainer and expert witness for the company Back to Safety, and also holds a full-time position in a large south London hospital.

**Martin Vousden** is projects editor for the Nursing Times. He trained as a RMN in Kent and was a psychiatric nurse for 12 years before becoming a journalist, first with the *Nursing Mirror* and later with *Nursing Times*. In between, he worked for six years on golf magazines and says that, tough as it is to understand the Code of Professional Conduct, it is a lot easier than trying to get an interview with Nick Faldo.

# Introduction: On being professional

**Irene Heywood Jones**

> 'Each registered nurse, midwife and health visitor shall act, at all times, in such a manner as to:
>
> ► safeguard and promote the interests of individual patients and clients;
>
> ► serve the interests of society;
>
> ► justify public trust and confidence;
>
> ► uphold and enhance the good standing and reputation of the professions.'

The preamble which introduces the Code of Professional Conduct for the Nurse, Midwife and Health Visitor (UKCC, 1992) is an overarching statement that reflects the collective commitment of nursing professionals to the community which they serve. The profession is confirming its contract with members of the public and intending to meet their expectations for safe and competent practice. It emphasises how it will honour, respect and protect the rights and values of individuals, thereby aiming to maintain the confidence of those people entrusted to its care.

This part clearly guides practitioners to consider their professional behaviour and their relationship with clients, both on and off duty, indicating an obligation to a performance that may reflect upon the corporate body of the profession.

In their book on nursing ethics, Thompson, Melia and Boyd write: 'Becoming a nurse is not simply a matter of learning particular knowledge and skills, or adopting forms of behaviour appropriate to particular contexts. It is also a matter of assimilating the attitudes and values of the nursing profession, in a way which can profoundly influence the thinking, personality and lifestyle of the individual concerned.' (Thompson, Melia and Boyd, 1994).

Beyond the obvious ethical implications, safety is paramount where the public is concerned and the full measure of law controls the practice of nursing, midwifery and health visiting. It is through the Nurses, Midwives and Health Visitors Act of 1997 that the United Kingdom Central Council (UKCC) is charged with managing this function, and it is a privilege that nursing is allowed to be a self-regulating profession using peer evaluation.

A review of the legislation and organisation of the statutory bodies has just been undertaken, and may result in changes in the near future.

The legal management and control of the profession is currently entrusted to the UKCC, on the understanding that nurses are best placed to discern how professional standards and practice can be maintained. Let there be no misunderstanding that in the case of all three professions, the UKCC's prime objective is to serve and protect the public. To ensure this is successfully fulfilled, the UKCC has a number of statutory obligations which are spelled out in the 1997 act. It must:

- establish and improve standards of training and professional conduct;

- set standards for admission to and the kind, content and standard of training;

- maintain a register of qualified practitioners;

- make provision for the kind, content and standard of post-registration education;

- provide advice to nurses, midwives and health visitors on professional standards;

- determine the circumstances in which a practitioner may be removed from the register for misconduct or unfitness to practise.

Let us examine how these roles relate to the defining characteristics of a profession, if indeed it is agreed that nursing is a profession or aspiring to be one.

Nursing has made a long and determined struggle to shake off its historic legacy as a vocation and its subservient position to medical colleagues. It has struggled to demonstrate that it has an equal standing with other health-care professional groups, so that the patient may expect to be cared for by a multiprofessional team. Various team members may demonstrate distinct roles but their contributions have equal merit and equal status in health-care delivery.

# WHAT IS A PROFESSIONAL PERSON?

Many characteristics contribute to professionalism, which deserve closer examination.

## Learning and specialism

A professional person is someone engaged in a learned profession, with a specialised body of knowledge, and this often involves a long and intensive preparation.

Perhaps the most compelling plea for an all-graduate profession — and the urge to pursue degree status for nurse training — has been the desire for parity with other health-care disciplines, such as medicine and professions allied to medicine (PAMs), which include occupational therapists and physiotherapists. There is also a cultural pressure within modern society to see undergraduate training generally as an academic benchmark, as more and more school leavers continue into higher education.

Nursing has been haunted by difficulty in defining its role, finding explanations of holistic and humanistic care rather less convincing than tasks and technological skills. Certainly within the last few decades an explosion of academic work has defined nursing as a discrete discipline, with the development of nursing degrees and an increasing body of research work on nursing matters.

The UKCC's role in relation to pre-registration admission, training and assessment can reassure the public that nurses receive appropriate preparation before being considered competent to meet the standards required for admission to the register, when they formally become members of the profession.

## Competency and increased knowledge

Professional development for nurses means continuing to maintain competency and increase knowledge in their chosen field. Professional education continues beyond initial preparation and qualification with post-registration training. All practitioners are also updated through the Post-Registration Education and Practice Project (PREP) initiative. The need for the PREP process was recognised when the profession was alerted to the fact that practitioners could complete their training and remain on the register for their whole working life without evidence of furthering their professional knowledge or competence.

PREP requires a mandatory period of updating to qualify for periodic registration, ensuring that the UKCC maintains a 'live' register, with nurses who maintain and improve their knowledge base and expertise.

It is debatable whether this process actually does improve competence, for as a profession matures, it should expect the maintenance of competence to be an implicit condition of practice. *The Scope of Professional Practice* (UKCC, 1992) probably addresses this area more appropriately by enabling practitioners to develop practice to meet the needs of patients and to remain competent and accountable within their sphere of responsibility. The moves towards evidence-based practice or care based on research are important tools to demonstrate that the practitioner is offering the very best and currently researched service to patients.

## Identity and belonging

A strong professional identity and belonging to a corporate body are other aspects of being a professional person.

Professionalisation develops a group consciousness. Members cannot exist in isolation and are, by necessity, collectively assembled within an organisation that can represent the profession's standing. A corporate body must support the profession's aims and its members, have strict criteria of admission and retention, and the power to eject those unworthy of the profession. This ensures a form of quality control for the public.

The UKCC is legally placed to dictate admission through training and assessment, retention through the maintenance of a live register, and removal of members proved unworthy of remaining in the profession.

While members gain and retain entry to a profession by adhering to specific requirements, a further feature of membership is that any practitioner can represent and influence the profession from within. The UKCC consults its registrants on changes and is responsive to comments from them. However, nurse practitioners appear to be notoriously poor respondents and turn-outs in UKCC elections are low — for example only 18% of members voted in the 1992 UKCC elections.

Does this reflect apathy, a lack of interest in professional matters or a belief that nurses are dictated from on high, that their views do not count or that the UKCC has little impact on day-to-day practice? The UKCC does its best to circulate information to members via the quarterly publication *Register* and holds a number of well-attended open days to explain its functions.

## Autonomy, accountability and independence

Professional activity involves a relatively high degree of autonomy, accountability and independence in practice. The notion of accountability means nurses will accept responsibility for actions they take to provide care. As we see later, it forms the stem of the Code of Professional Conduct and is implicit in all nursing activity, central to the integrity of the professional nurse's role.

The Scope of Professional Practice gives nurses the freedom to engage in practices for which they have been adequately prepared and have proven competence. Practitioners decide when they are ready to take on new duties, but accountability for that action and its consequences also lies squarely on their professional shoulders. To be able to say 'no, I am not able to do that' is more professional than saving face and trying to achieve something beyond their professional capability, which may constitute dangerous practice. The 'have-a-go syndrome' should be discouraged.

Professional autonomy means that nurses are empowered, articulate agents for change. They can have control over clinical decisions and speak up about poor care and unacceptable conditions, wherever these are detected. As nurses are increasingly becoming involved in independent practice, collaborative practice and new developments in care delivery, they must be clearly guided by the standards of their professional behaviour and no longer be compliant, submissive partners.

## Serving the public

Professional activity is largely altruistic and for the benefit of the public.

Serving the public is the key, and that is why the UKCC, in speaking for the nursing profession, emphasises its primacy for the patient above all else. The public can be assured that the ethos of the professional relationship is based on serving the patient's interests and not the quest for self-aggrandisement or corrupt gain by the practitioner.

The UKCC is constantly refining its performance to provide a better service to practitioners and the public. It is currently reviewing pre-registration training for the 21st century, looking at advice for working in secure environments and guidelines to improve the prevention, detection and management of abuse. At the time of writing, a major review of the Code, the Scope of Professional Practice and the Guidelines for Professional Practice was underway.

The recent appointment of a professional officer specifically for consumer issues, in October 1998, is timely, as questions of quality and clinical governance come to the fore. And it has always been the function of the UKCC to be a professional advisory service, responding to the needs of practitioners in the field who may have concerns over professional issues covering relations with the public.

The disciplinary proceedings now have consumer participation and the professional conduct committee is an open hearing which allows access to the public.

## Ethical standards

A professional person conforms to high ethical standards and follows a code which guides members in the execution of their practice.

Ask anyone what they mean by 'professional' and their struggle to find some definition will probably elicit phrases such as 'knowing how to behave correctly', 'doing the right thing' or 'acting in the right manner'. While perhaps not being able to quote specific principles, we are able to gauge instinctively the type of standards that would be expected from a lawyer, doctor, social worker or accountant.

Certainly the public would expect any professional to behave in a non-judgemental and non-prejudicial way, equally and fairly, and act in the best interest of the client, not a self-serving interest. Additionally there would be no violation of trust and no exploitation by virtue of the special relationship which involves a less knowledgeable and vulnerable client.

The need to state some tangible ideas to guide behaviour and practice emerges as a code of conduct. This code is formulated by the governing organisation, which in the case of the UKCC is a statutory body, although details of the code are negotiated by the members to reflect their agreement.

These are statements requiring members to uphold the reputation of the profession and implicitly to refrain from misconduct. Members pledge themselves to conform, and by adopting a code of conduct will gain the confidence of the public they serve. A code of conduct is a declaration by the members to the community, who can expect a professional person to perform in a certain fashion and to a certain degree of competence. A code reflects agreed ethical standards for the members.

In reiterating the question, 'What is a professional person?', having a code of conduct is clearly the hallmark of professional status.

# WHY A CODE OF PROFESSIONAL CONDUCT?

The Code of Professional Conduct came about in response to the requirement by the Nurses, Midwives and Health Visitors Act (the original Act was in 1979, revised in 1992 and the most recent update in 1997, which is currently under review) for the UKCC to 'establish and improve standards of training and professional conduct'. The Act states that 'the powers of the Council shall include that of providing, in such a manner as it thinks fit, advice for nurses, midwives and health visitors on standards of professional conduct'. It is a guide for practitioners in their professional practice and conversely provides a way of assessing misconduct within those parameters.

The Code cannot be prescriptive, it must consist of guiding principles, with sufficient versatility to meet the needs of nursing practice found in so many varying fields of employment and circumstances, as widely diverse as school nursing, the practice nurse in a GP surgery, occupational health, a nursing home environment or independent practice. The key is to 'translate' the principles, adapting them to meet nurses' needs in individual practice scenarios.

However, in its role as adviser to practitioners, the UKCC has recognised the need to expand on certain areas of the Code and give greater clarification in particular areas of practice. This has resulted in the publication of additional advisory documents to supplement the Code, such as: *Standards for the Administration of Medicines* (1992, and under review); *Guidelines for Mental Health and Learning Disabilities Nursing* (1998); and *Guidelines for Records and Record Keeping* (1998).

Earlier documents on Advertising, Confidentiality and Exercising Accountability have been superseded by an all-encompassing document which gives greater guidance on the clauses of the Code, in Guidelines for Professional Practice (UKCC, 1996).

The Code must be able to respond dynamically to changes in society, within health-care delivery and within the profession, both in practice and education. It must take into account social changes, such as ethnic diversity, lone parenting, travelling communities, teenage pregnancy, refugees, same-sex partnerships, and increasing elderly and frail population.

The power base is changing within the professional relationship. Patients are no longer quiet, accepting, unquestioning, grateful recipients of professional attention. Practitioners are encountering changing public attitudes, values and aspirations.

Easy access to freely available information from the media and the Internet means that patients may ask some very challenging questions (Heenan, 1999).

With an increasing consumerist and rights-orientated approach patients, or customers, or service-users, know their entitlements as enshrined in *The Patient's Charter* and statements of intent issued by some health-care organisations. Individuals and communities are invited to contribute and participate in decisions about local health service arrangements.

The introduction of clinical governance is a move to promote professional responsibility for quality of care. The results will be public knowledge which can inform arguments and bargaining efforts. Clinical governance will hopefully become a useful lever for nurses to persuade intransigent managers that quality issues are now everybody's business. It should assist their demands to improve resources for patient care. In an open and responsive service consumers' comments are welcomed, and they are invited to complain.

The spectre of litigation within health care also keeps practitioners mindful of their duty of care and their need to work closely within professional parameters.

The scale of changes in the health service will impact on individual practitioners. Such changes include: super hospitals requiring high technology input; the impetus of greater care within the community; increased day care and early discharge arrangements; developing services within the GP surgery; and the bureaucratic changes of NHS reforms.

Certainly the power and control previously held by the medical profession was effectively curbed with the introduction of the internal market and purchaser-provider split, which gave greater control to those who managed the money.

While nurses find their jobs are being altered, they are also helping to push back the boundaries of traditional nursing by pioneering new roles such as: surgeon's assistant, endoscopy nurse, manning telephone helplines for *NHS Direct*, consultancy roles, nurse specialist, nurse prescribing, nurse-led clinics and increased management and advisory positions with trusts and primary care groups.

To accommodate all this dynamism within health care, the Code needs to retain a broad-brush approach and not be prescriptive. And it must support nurses effectively when they challenge the system and not prove to be a paper tiger.

## CHANGES WITHIN THE CODE

Several modifications took place between the original Code and the current one, drawn up in 1992. There was some tinkering with semantics and some alterations to reflect evolutions within society and the profession.

The use of 'you' and 'your' when referring to the practitioner obviously makes the message more direct and personal then the distant 'his' and 'hers'.

The wording in relation to professional updating was changed from 'taking every opportunity to improve professional knowledge and competence...' to the more peremptory 'maintain and improve professional knowledge and competency...', reflecting the PREP initiative.

An addition to the clause on the abuse of the privileged relationship within nursing care was modified to include 'access to the person' to the original's 'access to property, residence or workplace'.

There has been much disquiet within the profession because of the many cases appearing before the UKCC Professional Conduct Committee that focus on the abuse of clients or patients and of inappropriate relationships between practitioners and their clients. This area of concern is currently being examined and will result in recommendations from the UKCC.

The clause which originally mentioned respect for 'customs and values and spiritual beliefs' has been expanded to recognise ethnic and religious diversity, in addition to 'respect for the uniqueness and dignity for patients with different personal attributes and health problems and other factors'. This firmly outlaws any racist attitudes or bigotry within the profession, reinforcing the ethos of equity and equality.

It also gives guidance on instances within caring which are especially challenging or may be seen to pose a threat to practitioners and their families. Nurses cannot discriminate on personal grounds and refuse to care for any patients, whatever their individual circumstances or the nature of their health problems. Perhaps the most illuminating example was during the AIDS scare, when some nurses were reluctant to care for people affected by HIV and AIDS.

As explained by Bridgit Dimond (1990): 'The employee could not refuse to treat an AIDS patient simply because he has AIDS. There are no statutory grounds for refusing to take part in such care, as is provided by the Abortion Act.' She continues: 'The guidelines of the UKCC have made it clear that it would regard the refusal by a registered nurse to treat an AIDS patient as professional misconduct.' Other clauses in the Code ask nurses to press employers to provide a safe working environment for practitioners in such circumstances.

Perhaps the most striking addition is the clause that expects practitioners to 'work in an open and cooperative manner with patients, clients and their families, foster their independence and recognise and respect their involvement in the planning and delivery of care' (Clause 5). It seems curiously late to include the notion of involving patients in their own care, although we can only believe this was previously implicit in nursing care which puts patients' interests at the centre of their practice.

It is more likely to indicate the move from a paternalistic health service to one that is patient-led and emphasises patient participation and consultation. It shows a move from telling the patient to 'do as I say' to 'this is my advice on how best you can be helped'.

The Code must be sufficiently comprehensive to meet the needs of practitioners as they create new ways of caring and provide the correct backdrop to innovative professional practice.

# WHO BENEFITS?

The Code of Professional Conduct has three-fold benefits: to the public, the UKCC registrants and the organisation.

The public is safe in the knowledge that the Code of defining principles is a declaration by the profession of how practitioners can be expected to behave, standards they will uphold and competence in practice. It aims to justify public confidence by that declaration and endeavours to protect the public by agreeing on principles of conduct. Adherence to the Code ensures a type of quality control for care, while acting as a yardstick to censure those who disobey the standards.

Perhaps a profession's most distinguishing feature is a code of conduct that indicates the value members place on their professional integrity and their contract with consumers.

If both the individual action and collective representation make members of the public feel confident, they will place greater trust in professional people and hold them in greater esteem.

Practitioners who take pride in belonging to their profession will want to maintain a healthy, respectable corporate identity. The Code is a great unifying statement, decided by the registrants, for the registrants and on behalf of the public. It can help identify the practices of less scrupulous practitioners, outlaw their practices in common agreement with the body of the profession, and become a tool to correct or eject practitioners unworthy of belonging.

The reputation of the organisation that produced the Code is also enhanced, as it meets the expectation of the public to serve their needs and provide a certain openness and accessibility. Professional secrecy is to be discouraged.

If practitioners are assured of backing and support from the organisation, this will stop managers and employers putting undue pressure on individuals or requiring them to act in an unethical manner. Reference to the Code enables the practitioner to quote their professional position and area of responsibility.

Pippa Gough (1998) clarifies the new professional paradigm in respect of changes to the NHS and the culture of health care, presenting new opportunities for nurses.

She explains that nursing must reject notions of professional status based on exclusivity, authoritarianism and mastery. This requires them to redefine professionalism as founded on a knowledge base that is:

- dynamic rather than static;
- developed in collaboration with patients, communities and other professional groups;
- born of reflection in, and on, practice;
- strengthened by being shared rather than guarded;
- derived from a commitment to lifelong learning.

The service ethos must be based on public participation and empowerment rather than exclusion and be defined by a move away from paternalism and professional protectionism.

# REMEMBER THE STEM

> As a registered nurse, midwife or health visitor, you are personally accountable for your practice and, in the exercise of your professional accountability, must:...

The stem of the Code must accompany each of the subsequent 16 clauses. Accountability, as we have already discussed, is a defining feature of professionalism. It means that nurses alone are personally responsible for their actions, and indeed omissions, and that they must be able to justify those decisions. Every nurse is also accountable for the actions of those to whom they delegate care. This reinforces the obvious necessity for practitioners to maintain and improve competence in order to remain secure in the exercise of their professional accountability.

There is no excuse for acting on someone else's orders unless you agree that this is in the interests of the patient and adheres to the Code's principles. There would be no support for a nurse who acted blindly on a manager's or doctor's instructions if it was questionably against the patient's interest.

To be truly accountable, nurses must have the freedom to exercise their competence and independent judgement as befits their training and sphere of responsibility. This type of autonomy and professional self-determination in practice bestows power on the individual. Accountability should be matched by the necessary authority to control the care environment. This is a new position and poses a threat within many bureaucracies because nurses can flex their power to challenge failures that compromise patient care.

When nurses get political they may face conflict, with their own ethical stance opposing the pressures within an administration which has financial constraints or a different agenda.

For the sake of good patient care nurses may ask for safety equipment, specialist training, extra staff or closure of beds in certain circumstances.

Here is where the Code can help nurses to insist on improved services or facilities, or complain about a colleague's poor practice, if they can argue that there may be deleterious effects on patient care.

Used in a professional, constructive way the Code will empower and support nurses who have right on their side. Indeed, those who fail to champion improvements or collude with sub-standard practice will put their own professional standing in jeopardy.

But no one is suggesting this is easy. Some nurses may have become complacent, ground down by the daily toil or repeated refusal of reasonable requests too many times and have had job satisfaction eroded from their working life.

Occasionally it can be seen as the nurses' own fault if there are limitations on their power and freedom to make decisions. Many nurses may still be locked in the culture of obedience, the traditional victim role of subservience, compliance and passivity, and do not perceive they have the power. Much has to do with being confident, assertive, questioning and challenging, and understanding that the modern professional nurse can be influential in bringing changes to the system in which they work.

To sum up, in the words of Reg Pyne, a key collaborator on the original Code (Kershaw, 1990): 'You — not someone else acting on your behalf or whose instructions you may have followed — can be called to account for what you decide to do, for what you fail to do and for matters at the very heart of our professional accountability. The Code is a document, the words of which are no sinecure. It is a document which you ignore at your peril.'

# References

Dimond, B. (1990) *Legal Aspects of Nursing*. Hertfordshire: Prentice Hall.

Gough, P. (1998) The future is yours. *Nursing Times*; 94: 26, 30.

Heenan, A. (1999) The Internet: a perennial resource for clinical practice. NT Clinical Monograph no. 9. London: NT Books.

Kershaw, B. (1990) *Nursing Competence*. London: Edward Arnold.

Thompson, I., Melia, K., Boyd, K. (1994) *Nursing Ethics*. Edinburgh: Churchill Livingstone.

UKCC (1992) *Scope of Professional Practice*. London: UKCC.

UKCC (1996) *Guidelines for Professional Practice*. London: UKCC.

## Recommended reading

Catalano, J. (1996) *Contemporary Professional Nursing.* Philadelphia: F.A. Davis Company.

Chadwick, R., Tadd W. (1992) *Ethics and Nursing Practice.* London: Macmillan Press.

# Clause 1: Being there

## Sarah Furlong

> '…act always in such a manner as to promote and safeguard the interests and well-being of patients and clients.'

The UKCC Code of Professional Conduct fosters a move away from the paternalistic style of caring that is a feature of the medical model, where the health care professional is dominant over the patient or client.

The Code advances an approach in which patients and clients are actively involved in negotiating their care and it highlights the importance of the nurse-patient relationship in achieving this end. It is written to advise nurses, midwives and health visitors on how to promote and ensure a holistic approach to caring, with the health-care practitioner working in partnership with patients and clients. The patient is often dependent upon the nurse in a caring relationship and is, by definition, therefore the weaker partner. It would be easy for nurses to sustain a paternalistic approach in which carer knows best.

To avoid a return to the past and introduce balance into the caring relationship, practitioners are charged with the responsibility of putting their patients' interests before their own or other health-care colleagues and this is a recurrent theme throughout the entire Code.

It is addressed specifically, if somewhat obliquely, by Clause 1 and this chapter will attempt to explore its meaning in relation to the registered practitioner's role and relationship with the patient or client. It will also examine the associated concepts of empowerment, accountability and responsibility, which underpin modern nursing practice. Finally, it will explore how these concepts can be applied in practice, together with the potential for Clause 1 to impact on a nurse's legal responsibilities, professional accountability to the patient and contractual responsibilities to the employer.

## EMPOWERMENT AND A PARADIGM SHIFT IN NURSING PRACTICE

People enter the health-care system when they need help, care or treatment from health-care professionals. They become patients or clients by virtue of this need and, by definition, health-care professionals will generally have the upper hand in any partnerships between themselves and patients or clients.

Clause 1 addresses the power balance, and potential imbalance, of these relationships. It identifies that nurses, midwives and health visitors are perfectly placed to provide support to their patients and in doing so, it is asserted, nurses will be able to ensure that patients are able to voice their needs and desires to them. As a consequence, ideally patients and clients will be able to participate fully in any decisions concerning their health and care. Implicit in Clause 1 is the registered practitioner's role as patient advocate. In other words, they are required to support their patients or clients publicly and intercede on their behalf where necessary.

The concept of empowerment, that is 'the process of helping people to assert control over the factors which affect their lives' (Gibson, 1991), stands as a precursor to the partnership approach to caring and the roles of both partners. Patients or clients are unable to make informed choices until they are empowered too. Moreover, nurses cannot act as advocates and help patients to be more fully involved in making decisions until they, too, are empowered. However, empowered nurses will not necessarily act to empower patients or clients (Skelton, 1994).

Traditionally the nurse has been viewed as the doctors' handmaiden. In this old, hierarchical approach, doctors oppressed and exerted power over nurses, senior nurses oppressed and exerted power over junior nurses and all nurses oppressed and exerted power over patients. Although this system is now, thankfully, in decline, its legacy remains. Arguably, health-care institutions bear some responsibility for perpetuating it, but many nurses do continue to exert power over their patients and clients (Trnobranski, 1994). This is manifested in nursing language, such as the seemingly innocuous 'my patient' or the use of terms of endearment in order to 'mother' and thus control patients. It is also apparent in the largely routinised and task-oriented way in which many nurses still practice (Hewison, 1995; Holden, 1991).

Many nurses may behave in this way because they do not feel empowered themselves (Hewison, 1995). They claim power in their working lives through reassuring daily routines, such as the early-morning drug round, the mid-morning observations, and in attempting to get as much as possible of 'the work' — meeting the needs of patients and clients — done before the late shift comes on duty. These approaches do not take into account the true needs or desires of patients. For example, the nurse may wish to bathe Mrs Jones in order to clear some of the work that she needs to do in a particular morning. But Mrs Jones may not want to be bathed. Instead she may want to talk to the nurse. Listening to patients is a major part of the nurse's role as advocate, but taking time to talk to patients also leaves less time for the other tasks that need to be done while on duty. Such divergence of needs is a potential source of conflict and there is evidence that nurses actively coerce patients into doing what they, rather than the patient, want (Hewison, 1995).

A holistic approach to care, which underpins the nurse's role as patient advocate, therefore requires a paradigm shift in both thinking and doing. Indeed, this has already begun with nurses asserting their right to recognition as a profession. Approaches to organising nursing care, such as primary or team nursing, focus more on the needs of individuals than on the health-care institution. Adopting new nursing philosophies which promote patient involvement has enabled nurses to reclaim a legitimate and important role in supporting and interceding on their behalf.

Nurses now seem more sure of their unique role, and are better equipped to enter into participatory relationships with patients. This has, arguably, been strengthened by graduate nurses and those with diplomas. Although there are undoubtedly flaws in such academic approaches, their strength lies in the fact that these nurses become empowered during their training. Nurses who feel more powerful themselves are more able to share power with patients, and so fulfil the professional responsibilities of advocate laid down in Clause 1.

# ADVOCACY: INFORMED CHOICE OR GENTLE PERSUASION?

In theory, practitioners are ideally placed to develop a partnership with patients and clients, to empower them and therefore to act as advocates on their behalf. The goal of being a patient advocate is to develop empowered patients who are fully informed and are, thus, able to negotiate well with other members of the multidisciplinary team (UKCC, 1996). In this way the patients, rather than health-care professionals, can determine and achieve the care and treatment that is best for themselves. The reality of patient advocacy is, however, much less straightforward.

The partnership approach is underpinned by the belief that patients and clients have a fundamental right to be more than passive recipients of health care (Ashworth et al, 1992). Implicit is an assumption that patients and clients want to be actively involved. However, this may not always be the case (Biley, 1992). Patients may not always enter willingly into a health-care partnership (May, 1995) and may be unwilling, or feel unable, to express a preference or take responsibility for decisions about their care or treatment.

As advocates, nurses must safeguard and promote the patient or client's interests and well-being and this responsibility can place them in a difficult situation. There is a danger that patients unwilling to take responsibility for their own care or treatment will manipulate the nurse, turning his or her responsibilities as advocate to their advantage. Nurses may unwittingly collude with patients who do not want to take responsibility for negotiating their own care with medical practitioners and end up negotiating with other health-care professionals on the patient's behalf.

Conversely, nurses are in danger of manipulating patients who feel unable to take responsibility for their care or treatment. In such circumstances it is possible that nurses would impose their own will, by assuming that if they were in that patient's situation, their desires would be the same as the patient's unexpressed wishes (Smith and Draper, 1994). A patient's consent to care or treatment is generally given passively, either by implication through cooperation or by verbal agreement, rather than by formal, written consent. Withdrawal from, or refusal of, treatment or care often happens in the same passive way. As advocates, nurses are bound to support the patient or client and respect their decision, whatever it might be.

However, two major factors may prevent this. First, patients may not feel sufficiently empowered to raise concerns about their care or treatment with direct care-givers. Many patients worry that they will suffer in some way if they directly challenge health-care professionals. Rather than confront the practitioner, they may agree to care or treatment that they do not really want.

Second, nurses themselves are in this front line as carers and are therefore unable to be fully impartial. Nurses, possibly unwittingly, regularly appear to coerce patients into participating in their care and treatment (Waterworth and Luker, 1990). Rather than acting as advocates, nurses are occasionally in danger of manipulating patients and clients into becoming involved in decisions or agreeing to care and treatment that they would not necessarily choose for themselves. It is therefore arguably not possible for nurses to be true patient advocates, as they have a professional interest in health-care provision.

# ETHICAL DILEMMAS

Today's nurses are increasingly autonomous professionals who are necessarily responsible and accountable for their own actions. The sentiment expressed generally in the Code, and specifically in Clause 1, effectively means that nurses may have different professional and legal responsibilities to the patient or client. Professionally, as an advocate, nurses are accountable for their actions to patients or clients, which, by definition, will have been carried out after negotiation. Legally, nurses owe patients and clients a duty of care, based on the 'neighbour principle' (Donoghue v Stevenson, 1932) (see Clause 2). This happens by virtue of the relationship that they both enter into. It means that each nurse has a particularly onerous responsibility; they need to weigh up the interests of patients and clients in complex situations, using their professional knowledge, judgement and skills to help the patient or client to come to the best possible decision regarding care needs.

Nurses may find themselves in situations where their attempts to act as a patient advocate actually come into conflict with their legal and professional responsibilities to provide care. A competent adult is legally able to make an informed judgement and refuse treatment, even when refusal will shorten their lives. Although there may be ethical dilemmas for the nurse, they would be upholding their professional and legal responsibilities by supporting these patients.

However, there is a caveat to their responsibilities as advocates.

Nurses, often along with their professional colleagues, are responsible for deciding when patients or clients are 'competent' and, therefore, whether they are capable of making informed decisions about their treatment and care. Therefore nurses' responsibilities as an advocate may occasionally conflict with their legal duty of care, which is not absolute, but varies according to situation (Powers and Barton, 1995).

For example, how does the nurse act as advocate in the case of the Jehovah's Witness who has refused blood in a life-threatening situation? Does the nurse decide that the patient is competent and support their decision, putting the patient's interest before the nurse's or professional colleagues' interest? What about the midwife whose client has refused a Caesarean section, where the prevalent medical opinion is that the unborn child will die without the operation? To give blood or to conduct an operation in cases such as these would constitute a criminal offence and, indeed, the UKCC (1996) emphasises the nurse's responsibility to observe Clause 1 and support the patient, even where refusal of treatment may be life-threatening.

In law the nurse does not always have to act as advocate. The health-care professionals can decide that the patient is not competent to make an informed decision and seek a court order to override the patient's wishes. How does the nurse or midwife act in such a situation? Do they side with their professional colleagues and decide that the patient is not competent, or with the patient? Nurses who side with their professional colleagues and become involved in treatment or interventions determined by a court order are acting in a legitimate manner and fulfilling their duty of care. They may be acting to safeguard the well-being of their patients or clients, but they are not necessarily safeguarding their interests and are certainly not acting as advocate to their patient or client. So has the nurse or midwife contravened Clause 1?

What if the health-care professionals have made the wrong decision? In theory, the patient in this case could sue the nurse or midwife for negligence. If such a case were to be found in favour of the complainant, the nurse or midwife could also be placing their professional registration at risk.

The situation becomes more complex when we look at suicide and euthanasia. A decision to commit suicide may be a sane and rational act for patients and clients in certain circumstances, for example, where a patient has an incurable disease and is afraid of becoming dependent on others. If suicide is indeed in the patient's best interests, then the nurse, as advocate should support the decision. However, there would be considerable ethical and moral difficulties in doing so. Nurses are placed in a potentially more difficult situation should patients or clients ask them to assist them with a suicide attempt. Such a decision may be in the patient's best interests and the current opinion in the UK seems to have swayed in favour of voluntary euthanasia. But UK law prohibits any deliberate attempt to hasten someone's death and the nurse would find herself in an impossible situation by acting as an advocate in such circumstances.

The legal caveat to the nurse's professional responsibilities is important and necessary, but the sometimes divergent responsibilities of the nurse raise profound ethical questions, since they impact on the balance of the nurse-patient relationship. In theory, the relationship is a partnership, and at its heart lies mutual trust and respect. Yet it is doubtful if this can ever be achieved, since there is always a legal opt-out for the nurse and so there will always be conflict between a nurse's professional and legal responsibilities to patients and clients.

## MANIPULATING THE INFORMATION

As advocates, nurses have a responsibility to ensure that the patient or client receives clear information at every stage of their care (Barton, 1995). This places nurses in a position to determine the way in which information is given to patients and clients and, consequently, to influence treatment decisions (Skelton, 1994). There are major issues to address in relation to the timing and manner in which information is given (Redelmeier et al, 1993). Value judgements by practitioners may lead them to present positive or negative data in order to influence their decisions. For example, surgery to treat lung cancer is less attractive to patients presented with mortality data than to those presented with survival data (Redelmeier et al, 1993).

Albeit unconsciously, the nurse may decide that they know what is best and provide information to support particular treatments or modes of care. Equally, manipulation of the way that information is given could easily be used to 'persuade' patients and clients to adopt healthy lifestyles. Patients must know the implications of their actions and take responsibility for them.

# INDIVIDUAL RIGHTS AND COLLECTIVE NEED

By putting the patient's interests before their own or those of their professional colleagues, nurses may come into conflict with their contractual responsibilities to their employer. Contractually they may be bound by local codes of conduct, policies and procedures drawn up to deliver finite health-care resources equitably. They may also come into conflict with evidence-based approaches to health care and, in the future, with clinical governance.

At times the individual's needs and desires may diverge from the needs of the general population. Take, for example, a man with multiple sclerosis, who is well informed about the condition and has concluded that treatment with beta interferon may have a positive impact on his quality of life. He has negotiated with his team of health-care professionals but they are unwilling to prescribe the drug as they feel that any potential benefits are far outweighed by its potential side effects and, more importantly, the cost implications for a health care system with finite resources (Muir Gray, 1998). What is the nurse's role in respect of Clause 1 in this situation? The nurse may well be torn between obligations to the patient, those to health-care users in general, personal beliefs and obligations to the employer. What would promoting or safeguarding the patient's interests actually mean in this situation? Can, or indeed, should the nurse act as advocate?

Conversely, the nurse may be caring for a young woman whose gynaecologist is advocating a D&C to relieve excessively heavy periods, despite there being a considerable evidence to suggest that this approach is ineffectual (Moore, 1996). As an advocate, the nurse could ensure that the patient was well-informed about the consequences of the proposed treatment. This would enable the patient to make an informed choice about the proposed procedure. However, the patient may then face an impossible situation. Her opportunity to make a choice is likely to be limited to deciding between agreeing to or rejecting the D&C. She may not have been given true choice, for example to have a procedure likely to have a more positive outcome.

Helping patients to make informed choices presupposes that patients have choices. This may not always be the case.

# CONCLUSION

The health care environment is a fluid and multi-dimensional world in which professional practice and decision-making are often difficult. At the end of the millennium, the focus of health care relationships has moved on from the rhetoric of a holistic approach to the realities of what this means at the coal face to the every day practice of nurses and to the health care experience of patients and clients. The Code of Professional Conduct lays down a set of principles by which nurses, midwives and health visitors are expected to govern their professional lives.

While there is no suggestion that the Code should be more prescriptive, greater clarity is needed, since Clause 1 is open to a variety of interpretations and possible contradictions. It places an onerous and sometimes confusing responsibility on practitioners.

The oblique way in which the principles of Clause 1 are presented means the nurse not only has to apply them in practice, but to interpret them first. To this end, the UKCC provides a translation in the *Guidelines for Professional Practice* (1996) for registered practitioners to ensure they understand that promoting and safeguarding the patient's interests and well-being actually means they should act as advocates. The changing face of health care means nursing practices must to be adjusted not only to meet the needs of individual patients and clients, but also to meet changing circumstances in the wider health care environment. The Code is the standard against which professional conduct is judged. If the lack of clarity inherent in the language of Clause 1 means that it can be interpreted in different ways, then this must surely undermine its robustness as a standard.

The professional responsibilities laid down in this clause may also conflict with a registered practitioner's contractual and legal responsibilities to care. This means that it is not always possible or desirable for a nurse, midwife or health visitor to act as advocate to their patients or clients. There will never be balance in the nurse-patient relationship. Since patients will always depend on health care professionals and the nurse's vested interest in health care provision, it is difficult for nurses to be true patient advocates. Similarly, the contractual and legal responsibilities incumbent upon registered practitioners mean that they may not always be able to cope with the consequences of empowering patients, nor will they always be able to act in the patient's best interest, since even empowered patients may not have real choices to make.

# References

Ashworth, P., Longmate, M., Morrison, P. (1992) Patient participation: its meaning and significance in the context of caring. *Journal of Advanced Nursing*; 17: 12, 1430-1439.

Barton, A. (1995) Who decides? The prudent patient or the reasonable doctor. *Clinical Risk;* 1; 1, 86-88.

Biley, F. (1992) Some determinants that affect patient participation in decision-making about nursing care. *Journal of Advanced Nursing;* 17: 4, 414-421.

Donoghue v Stevenson [1932] AC 562.

Gibson, C. (1991) A concept analysis of empowerment. *Journal of Advanced Nursing*; 16: 3, 354-361.

Hewison, A. (1995) Nurses' power in interactions with patients. *Journal of Advanced Nursing*; 21: 1, 75-82.

Holden, R. (1991) Responsibility and autonomous nursing practice. *Journal of Advanced Nursing*; 16: 4, 398-403.

May, C. (1995) Patient autonomy and the politics of professional relationships. *Journal of Advanced Nursing*; 21: 1, 83-87.

Moore, W. (1996) Lives in the balance. *The Guardian*, 22 May, 2.

Muir Gray, J.A. (1998) Evidence-based policy making. In Haines, A., Donald, A. (eds) *Getting Research Findings into Practice*. London: BMJ Books.

Powers, M., Barton, A. (1995) Introduction to medical negligence law. *Clinical Risk*; 1, 37-39.

Redelmeier, D.A. (1993) Understanding patients' decisions. Cognitive and emotional perspectives. *JAMA*; 270: 1, 72-76.

Smith, R., Draper, P. (1994) Who is in control? An investigation of nurse and patient beliefs relating to control of their health care. *Journal of Advanced Nursing*; 19: 5, 884-892.

Skelton, R. (1994) Nursing and empowerment: concepts and strategies. *Journal of Advanced Nursing*; 19: 3, 415-423.

Trnobranski, P. (1994) Nurse-patient negotiation: assumption or reality? *Journal of Advanced Nursing*; 19: 4, 733-737.

UKCC (1996) *Guidelines for Professional Practice*. London: UKCC.

Waterworth, S., Luker, K. (1990) Reluctant collaborators: do patients want to be involved in decisions concerning care? *Journal of Advanced Nursing;* 15: 8, 971-976.

# Clause 2: To do or not to do?

**Deborah Glover**

> '…ensure that no action or omission on your part, or within your sphere of responsibility, is detrimental to the interests, condition or safety of patients and clients.'

Clause 2 of the Code appears to be based on a legal judgement, which perhaps explains the tortuous wording! Defining a duty of care in Donoghue v Stevenson (1932), Lord Aitken said:

> You must take reasonable care to avoid acts or omissions which you can reasonably foresee would be likely to injure your neighbour. Who, then, in the law is my neighbour? The answer seems to be persons who are so closely and directly affected by my act that I ought to have them in contemplation as being so affected when I am directing my mind to the acts or omissions which are called in question.

This judgement concerned a woman suing a drinks manufacturer as she found a decomposing snail in her ginger beer. It was judged that the manufacturer had a duty of care to the consumer.

But back to the reality of nursing. In real terms, Clause 2 means that we are accountable for what we do, what we fail to do and for what happens within our sphere of influence, and to make sure this has no adverse effects. No variables, external or internal influences or human nature are allowed.

'The Code of Professional Conduct for the Nurse, Midwife and Health Visitor is the Council's definitive advice on professional conduct to its practitioners,' says *Exercising Accountability*, the UKCC Advisory Document (1989).

The Code is considered to be:

- a statement to the profession of the primacy of the interests of the patient or client;

- a statement of professional values;

- a portrait of the practitioner which the Council believes to be needed and it wishes to see within the profession.

Unfortunately, over the past 15 years or so, the Code's clauses have led to much confusion and angst among practitioners. Even with the UKCC publication in 1996, *Guidelines for Professional Practice*, which was designed to give guidance on all 16 clauses, nurses are finding that interpretation and application is becoming increasingly difficult in the health-care setting as we enter the 21st century.

This does create problems for nurses practising in the real world as opposed to the Utopia which the UKCC appears to believe we work in. It means that we frequently have to break or bend the Code to survive, even knowing that we could be called to account for our actions. This chapter will outline who the nurse is accountable to and illustrate where conflicts may arise between legal and professional responsibilities. Because the Code is considered to be more a set of themes and principles, it is not possible to cover all aspects of practice and give definitive answers to the issues which practitioners may face when considering Clause 2. However, I hope to give the reader some food for thought, helping to clarify reasoning and raising some questions which will lead to debate and reflection.

# WHO IS THE PRACTITIONER ACCOUNTABLE TO?

## The law

Legally, a duty of care is owed to a patient once the health care organisation has accepted them for treatment. If they are harmed by treatment provided by a nurse they might bring an action for damages for negligence through the law of tort. For the action to succeed they must prove that:

- the nurse owed him a duty of care;
- the nurse was in breach of the duty (failed to provide care of an adequate standard);
- the patient suffered harm as a result of that breach.

As the organisation owes the patient a duty of care once they have been accepted for treatment, the first point is easily proved. The standard of care required is that set by what is commonly known as the Bolam test (Bolam v Friern Hospital Management Committee, 1957).

> *The test is the standard of the ordinary skilled man exercising and professing to have that special skill. A man need not possess the highest expert skill at the risk of being found negligent... it is sufficient if he exercises the skill of an ordinary competent man exercising that particular art.*

And the standard is acceptable if the practitioner: 'Acted in accordance with a practice accepted as proper by a responsible body of medical men skilled in that particular art.' The law then appears to be in harmony with Clause 2. If what you do (or do not do) is accepted practice, then you are unlikely to be sued for negligence or be in breach of the Code.

However, what happens if what you do is accepted practice but is detrimental to the patient's interests? For example, most anaesthetists will instruct a patient not to eat or drink for at least six hours before a procedure, and this is accepted practice. But there is a wealth of evidence to prove that this is excessive and can be potentially harmful to vulnerable patients such as young and elderly people. Unless you discuss this with the anaesthetist, you are breaching Clause 2 as you know that this outdated practice could be detrimental to some patients.

So, legally, accepted practice in this instance may not lead to a successful negligence claim by the patient. Nevertheless you should bear in mind that the UKCC's Professional Conduct Committee (PCC) could find you guilty of misconduct if, according to the criteria in the Code, you fail to care properly for a patient or client, even if they suffer no harm.

## Your employer

You are accountable to your employer through your contract, which obliges you to give care in a safe and competent manner, and adhere to policies and procedures and resources properly. However, conflicts do arise.

Whatever your grade, you can identify a sphere of responsibility – whether you are in charge of a ward, a group of patients or a department or clinical area. Clause 2 requires you to ensure that the physical environment is safe, that staffing levels are acceptable and that resources are available for care to be given and for staff to undertake their duties. You have to inform a higher authority, in writing if necessary, if you feel that the safety and interests of your patients is being compromised because any of the above conditions are not being met (see also Clauses 11 and 12).

What if you are the manager and have a resource management aspect to your role? You cannot go over budget — you have to manage with your allocation or run the risk of being seen as incompetent and losing your job. How do you reconcile what is the 'policy' or requirement of your employing organisation with Clause 2? Perhaps this is where the Code can be seen as a lever for nurses to 'get political' and to challenge inadequacies. Understandably it is not a simple or comfortable position.

## The public

Practitioners have to provide the service for which they are employed and use the resources available appropriately because people (in effect, you) pay for them through taxes.

However, in an attempt to use resources wisely, the cheaper option is often the only one available. For example, many organisations have limited their prescribing lists. This may mean that patients are not necessarily getting the best treatment for their needs, but you have to ensure that this is not detrimental to your patient's interests or safety. The best way around this, and to satisfy your professional requirements, is to try to argue that 'it may be more expensive but the patient gets better more quickly'. Accountants are more likely to be persuaded by an economic slant than a 'caring' one.

Apparently you have a responsibility to ensure that those involved in policy-making and financial control have an accurate picture of the importance and consequence of the decisions they make. For junior members of staff, of course, this is not always easy. But it *is* necessary.

## Patients/clients

The most important people you are accountable to are your patients and clients. You have both a legal duty of care and a professional duty to care for them and for practice which is of a 'reasonable' standard (see the Bolam test). This care has to be delivered by a practitioner who has been taught and assessed as safe and to the accepted standard.

Clause 2 refers specifically to this duty of care. However, your status is no excuse for delivering care below that standard. Neither the law nor the UKCC will accept that as a junior or inexperienced practitioner your care can be below the standard of 'the ordinary skilled man'. So if you are a newly qualified D grade, you must meet the standard expected of your status as a registered practitioner.

This was clearly demonstrated in the Wilsher v Essex Health Authority (1986) negligence case, where a junior doctor inserted a catheter into a vein of a neonate and the baby was given excess oxygen. The catheter had been checked by a senior registrar. The baby was blinded as a result. Initially, the defence stated in court that it was unreasonable for the junior doctor to deliver the same standard of care as the senior. This was overruled in the Court of Appeal, which said that if there was not a uniform standard of care inexperience would frequently be used as a defence against negligence.

The more eagle-eyed among you would see that as well as personal duty here, a junior would be included under your sphere of responsibility in Clause 2, so you need to be vigilant on both counts.

## The profession

Although our primary concern must be to our patients and clients, we are also accountable to the profession as a whole. The preamble to the Code states that we must not do anything to bring the profession into disrepute as we are accountable for our actions whether engaged in current practice or not, and whether on or off duty.

For example, this means we should not come on duty with a hangover, because this may affect our actions or our judgement and could be detrimental to the patient. In reality, it just reinforces the fact that the UKCC and, in some instances, the public do not want to believe that we are human and may fall by the wayside on the odd occasion. I am not saying that we should not have a professional approach to our work. It is just that sometimes we do not feel on top of the world and we may not give of our best. But it does not mean that we should be shot at dawn, either.

## AREAS FOR DISCUSSION

### Specialist practitioners

There are an increasing number of clinical nurse specialists, nurse practitioners and specialist nurse practitioners within the profession. Indeed, the UKCC is currently considering adding a 'specialist' recordable qualification to the register. What does this mean in terms of standards of care? According to Khan and Robson (1997), the position is clear. If you knowingly (or unwittingly) hold yourself up as being more experienced than another, as possessing that degree of skill and knowledge, and have accepted the responsibility and undertaken that (specialist) training, you must reach that standard.

Clause 2 would require you to ensure that your actions as a 'specialist' will not harm your patient. This is illustrated in *Guidelines for Professional Practice* (UKCC, 1996), which gives examples of what duty of care would be expected of a skilled intensive care nurse in different situations. Here are three:

▷ Situation 1: The nurse is on duty on the intensive care unit when a patient has a cardiac arrest. Here the UKCC would expect the nurse to care for the patient as competently as any other experienced intensive care unit nurse.

- Situation 2: The nurse is walking along a hospital corridor and finds a woman giving birth. Here the UKCC would not expect nurses to care for the woman as a midwife would, but would expect them to call for a midwife and stay with the woman until appropriate help arrives.

- Situation 3: The nurse is walking along the street and comes across someone injured in an accident. Nurses do not have a *legal* duty to stop and care for the injured person. But if they do stop, they then take on a legal duty to care for them properly, to the best of their skill and knowledge. They do, however, have a *professional* duty to stop and care for the person.

## Managers

Nurses, midwives and health visitors who are also managers cannot limit their application of Clause 2 to what they may do or omit to do personally. They are responsible for how their staff apply Clause 2 and for knowing the environment in which care is being delivered. They should, therefore, actively seek the advice and views of the staff working within the environment, and if necessary use their professional skills and knowledge to influence others who may make decisions regarding that environment.

All practitioners on the register have a duty of care even if they are not directly involved in patient care. Consider the following case heard by the PCC:

Mrs R B was a 52-year-old registered general nurse and at the time of the incident was a nursing officer. It was alleged that, as a nurse manager, she failed to investigate or take other action on an alleged incident of patient abuse. She admitted the facts, but denied misconduct. The committee found the facts proved (UKCC, 1993). Quite clearly, the nurse had failed to adhere to Clause 2 as the incident took place within her sphere of responsibility.

Another example given by Pyne (1992) was of a night sister in a general hospital. The complaints against her included inappropriate behaviour in patient areas which could damage trust and confidence, serious errors in the administration of drugs and attempts to blame her mistakes on junior staff.

However, there are other instances where it is less clear. In one incident where a nurse was removed from the register due to incompetence, the employing organisation was found to be culpable as they had no framework for assessing the ongoing training needs or any continuing education programme for the night staff. In this case the director of nursing was seen to be breaking Clause 2 as the nursing staff were within her sphere of responsibility and this issue was known to her.

## Delegation

You are accountable for your decision to delegate and to ensure that the action has been undertaken. You must ensure that the person you have delegated to is able to do the work and if you omit to check on their ability, or to supervise where necessary, you will breach Clause 2.

You also have to bear in mind that you are delegating after being delegated to. Legally the doctor has responsibility for the patient. While ensuring the continuity of care he or she can, according to the Terms of Service for Doctors (NHS, 1992), delegate to a person whom 'he has authorised and who he is satisfied is competent to carry out such treatment'. If it is you the doctor has deemed competent to carry out the care, then you are obliged morally, if not legally, to ensure that you can delegate on to someone who is competent. But of course, by the same token, if the doctor has delegated a task which will be detrimental to the patient's interests, safety or condition, you are quite within your rights to refuse to accept the task, or refuse to carry out the treatment.

While on the whole you are accountable for delegating, there are instances where total accountability would be ridiculous. For example, if you asked a student nurse to run a bath for a patient and she filled the bath with boiling water and put the patient in it, you could not be expected to be accountable for that. This is an issue of common sense. One would hope that the personnel responsible for selecting her for training would have ascertained that she had some degree of knowledge and understanding of the role she was to enter into. Additionally you would assume that everyone knows boiling water is going to burn.

When dealing with common-sense tasks, accountability lies with the person undertaking the task. If it is a task that needs to be taught, then the registered practitioner must be satisfied that person is competent to undertake it.

## Agency staff

Do you check every agency nurse's PIN card and identification? If you omit to do this and there are subsequent problems, you are accountable. It is also sensible not to assume that just because they are qualified they are necessarily competent to undertake the work you assign to them.

## Custom and practice

It is easy in a busy clinical area or within a patient's home to carry on with the same habitual customs and practices because it does not create waves or upset the routine. However, this can be detrimental to patient interest or even dangerous. Take this real example from practice:

The ward was a busy oncology unit. Although the nursing staff had tried to individualise patients' analgesia times, custom dictated that intramuscular analgesics were given after the main drug rounds. As there were so many injections, two nurses checked the drug chart and the drug in the treatment room. After the first injection was drawn up, one nurse took it to the patient and administered it, the other stayed in the treatment room to draw up the next injection. The first nurse returned, both nurses signed the controlled drug register, and then the process was repeated.

When the time came for a student nurse to be assessed for her management module, she followed the same routine. She was failed immediately. Why? Because the time-saving routine not only contravened hospital policy, it had the potential to affect the safety of the patients.

## Poor practice

Let us be honest. I am sure we have all colluded with poor practice to a certain extent, whether as a student or junior nurse noticing it in a more senior colleague, or as a manager, who hoped that the guilty party would move on quickly. If they were not dangerous, it was easier to let them get on with it. Another real-life example is of a student nurse at a major teaching hospital. All the members of her set knew she was hopeless. They joked about her and some of the more conscientious ones expressed their concerns to the school of nursing. But nothing was done until she actually endangered a patient's life. The patient had arrested. The ward sister began resuscitation and asked this particular student to call the crash team. She came back after a minute or so, casually saying: 'They were engaged, I'll try again in a minute.' Her training was finally terminated.

It is difficult to challenge poor practice, especially if practitioners are more senior, or if nursing is their whole life and their only job. But by omitting to do so we have failed in our personal responsibility and breached Clause 2. And we can be called to account for that, putting our own registration status in jeopardy. It is a common area of concern and the UKCC is looking at a mechanism that can address professional incompetence.

# WITHDRAWING CARE

Is it ever right to withdraw care? Clause 2 would suggest not, as doing so would be both an action and omission which may be detrimental to the patient's safety, interests or condition. However, the UKCC does acknowledge that there are exceptional circumstances where this may be possible, for example, where the practitioner fears physical violence.

## Violent patients

Unfortunately, dealing with violent patients is becoming an increasing phenomenon that practitioners have to face in their duties. No one, apart from boxers, willingly chooses an occupation which may expose them to physical or verbal abuse. Why should nursing staff have to? And if they are abused, why should they not have the right to refuse to care for the perpetrator? Even taking into account the reasons (or excuses) given for violence, such as long waiting times, pain, fear, lack of knowledge about what is happening to them, to be forced into feeling that you have to give care unless you really cannot avoid it, and then having to justify the withdrawal of care, is unfair.

Should the UKCC be sanctimonious about this? Management has a responsibility to address this issue and, fortunately, many organisations are implementing policies which both safeguard staff from violence and support those who wish to prosecute their assailants.

## 'Horrible' patients

Consider also the patient you do not like. Clause 7 of the Code requires us to care for all patients irrespective of 'ethnic origin, religious beliefs, personal attributes, the nature of their health problem or any other factor'. In all honesty, it is impossible to like every patient we come across. Often, we cannot even explain why we dislike them. Almost every practitioner will have a story to tell of such a patient. Indeed, some are disliked by the whole team. So what do you do?

You are likely to be in breach of Clause 2, if not Clause 7. Your 'actions and omissions' will take the form of either complete avoidance (that is, the patient you delegate to the junior staff), or your interventions will be short and efficient. You will not 'care' for them. So in reality, is it not better to acknowledge that you are human and admit your dislike? Ideally, if an alternative nurse is available then the patient can be fully cared for by someone who does not share your feelings. This does address the very heart of professionalism, to be able to give non-judgemental, unbiased care to each and every patient.

## CONCLUSION

Nurses are not superhuman and their personal foibles must be managed in line with professional responsibility. Perhaps the time is right for the UKCC, or any body which may supercede it, to revise the Code of Professional Conduct as the present clauses do not guide practice so much as dictate what a nurse is supposed to be. While it is understood that the purpose of the UKCC is to protect the public, it is time that the paternalistic thrust of the Code, particularly Clause 2, is revised to reflect the diverse and changing health-care settings within which professional practitioners work.

Nurses, midwives and health visitors are much more confident and articulate professional practitioners than in the days of 'handmaidens'. We acknowledge and appreciate that self-regulation is not a right. But we can, and should, work within a framework of standards for the protection of the public, which have been formulated in consultation with them.

I would suggest the UKCC makes the Code, if in the future it is called a Code of Conduct, something that guides and informs the practitioner rather than being seen as a sword of Damocles hanging over their heads.

# References

Bolam v Friern Hospital Management Committee [1957] 1 WLR 582, in Khan, M., Robson, M. (1997) *Medical Negligence.* London: Cavendish Publishing.

Donoghue v Stevenson (1932) (House of Lords) AC 562.

Khan, M., Robson, M. (1997) *Medical Negligence.* London: Cavendish Publishing.

Pfizer Corporation v Ministry of Health [1965] AC 512; [1965] 2 WLR 387 in Khan, M., Robson, M. (1997) *Medical Negligence.* London: Cavendish Publishing.

Pyne, R. (1992) *Professional Discipline in Nursing, Midwifery and Health Visiting.* 2nd Edition. Oxford: Blackwell Scientific.

The National Health Service (General Medical Services) Regulations SI (1992) 1992/635 Schedule 2: Terms of Service for Doctors (regulation 3 [2]). London: Department of Health.

UKCC (1989) *Exercising Accountability.* London: UKCC.

UKCC (1993) *Professional Conduct — Occasional Report on Selected Cases 1 April 1991-31 March 1992.* London: UKCC.

UKCC (1996). *Guidelines for Professional Practice.* London: UKCC.

Wilsher v Essex Health Authority [1986] 3 All ER 801.

# Clause 3: Keeping abreast

**Chris Bassett**

> '...maintain and improve your professional knowledge and competence.'

Working as a safe, competent and expert nurse, midwife or health visitor has never been more difficult (Power, 1997). The requirement for the practitioner to always do the right thing, and always make the right decision in a wide variety of situations and settings is increasingly challenging. The public has become more aware than ever of their rights, while their expectations have never been higher. It is therefore essential that nurses, midwives and health visitors continue to keep up to date in their field of practice.

This chapter will explore this requirement and provide information which will enable the practitioner to understand more fully the legal responsibility upon them and, in doing so, protect them from litigation.

It will consider the key issues surrounding PREP and profiling. It will also provide an example of how the independent practitioner can remain informed and safe to practise expertly. Finally it will help practitioners to work in a more reflective manner and provide guidelines for personal and professional growth that hopefully will continue throughout a career.

Keeping updated should ensure that the nurse, midwife or health visitor will provide competent and improved care for the patient or client.

# THE GROWTH OF LITIGATION IN HEALTH CARE

All people are bound by the law. Nurses, however, are also subject to professional rules (Dimond, 1995). The Code of Professional Conduct, which we are all obliged to follow, guides us as professional people. The law impacts upon us in many ways. Nurses are expected to be knowledgeable and aware of the most current legislation and, of course, know about any new research in their particular area of practice. Remaining constantly updated on new research and current developments is a considerable burden. However, as professional people who are bound by a code of conduct, it is a requirement that we ignore at our peril for we may be called to account to prove that we have made the correct professional judgement with any type of care. This is the foundation of evidence-based nursing.

Patients and clients have never been more informed about current health issues, helped by expertly-made television programmes covering all aspects of medicine and health. Any new medical breakthroughs are also reported in magazines and newspapers, and excellent information is accessible from the Internet. Consequently the public have a growing knowledge of health and what they might reasonably expect when they or a loved one access treatment or care. This is a good thing and equally, any practitioner would want the best for themselves or a loved one.

Influencing factors for keeping up to date are:

- the law;
- the Code of Professional Conduct;
- Post Registration Education and Practice (PREP);
- The *Patient's Charter*;
- individual hospital/trust standards;
- colleague expectation;
- patient expectation;
- the desire to do a first-class job.

# POST REGISTRATION EDUCATION AND PRACTICE (PREP)

PREP is a scheme designed to ensure that all nurses, midwives and health visitors keep up to date with their practice (midwives will have their refresher courses phased into PREP). Its purpose is to improve standards of patient and client care, both directly and indirectly (UKCC, 1995).

In 1995 all practitioners were notified of the new requirements as they renewed their registration. By April 2001 all practitioners, regardless of circumstances, must meet all the PREP requirements for periodic registration. This entails a minimum study time collectively adding up to five days or equivalent every three years, the preparation of a personal professional profile and completing a notification of practice form at the point of re-registration.

The UKCC (1995) offers the following five categories to help the practitioner focus on areas of study:

- Patient, client and colleague support. Examples include counselling techniques; leadership in professional practice and supervision of clinical practice.

- Care enhancement. Examples include new techniques and approaches to care; standard setting; empowering clients and consumers of the service.

- Practice development. Examples include visits to other units or places of interest relevant to your role and practice; personal research/study; examining aspects of service provision.

- Reducing risk. Examples include identifying health problems; health promotion and screening.

- Education development. Examples include exchange arrangements; personal research/study and teaching and learning skills.

No course of study, certificate or self-directed learning scheme is approved by the UKCC. This would be impossible to achieve because of the huge variety of courses and study days available. The UKCC states that you as an accountable individual practitioner are personally responsible for your learning. In other words only you know what you need to know and must meet those needs in the most appropriate manner. There is such diversity in practice today that no prescribed menu of learning could ever hope to meet the needs of the modern practitioner.

# How PREP can be achieved

There is a popular misconception that you must achieve your PREP activity by attending study days, which might be expensive. You can certainly meet your learning needs by going on courses and study days, but there are a number of other ways available to remain updated in practice that do not entail excessive travel or cost.

## Professional dialogue

The first source of information, which is usually the easiest to obtain, is to listen to and share knowledge and information with colleagues. It may not just be nurses, midwives or health visitors with whom you share information. All health-care professionals have a duty to keep informed and abreast of research, and often physiotherapists, occupational therapists, pharmacists or others will provide us with useful and relevant information. In turn, these practitioners will also find much nursing research helpful to them in developing their roles. It is vital that nurses maintain and develop interprofessional dialogue to help improve and integrate health provision across the care continuum as a whole.

## Visits

You may decide to arrange a visit to another area, perhaps a private nursing home, clinic or hospital ward where you know there is an innovative practice or approach to care. It may be useful to accompany or shadow a clinical nurse specialist to find out more about their work. Ward managers may be able to help arrange an exchange visit as it will give them a chance to share their knowledge and skills with others.

## Study days, conferences and courses

Study days, conferences and courses are useful ways of gaining education and keeping updated. Most now give a certificate of attendance which is useful evidence to add to your personal profile, but you will also need to document how this has benefited your practice. A vast and bewildering array of opportunities is on offer for this type of professional development. Enlightened nursing agencies and independent care homes often arrange study days or sponsor employees, as it is in their interest to keep their staff updated within their professional requirements.

Conferences allow individual delegates to question speakers, who are usually leaders in their particular field of nursing. Nurses may feel in time that they too would like to present projects and innovations that they and their team are involved in to a conference. Preparation and delivery would count for PREP hours, as does writing for publications and giving teaching sessions.

Conferences, which are advertised in journals and by direct mail, usually incur a cost but can provide a stimulating and uplifting chance to share views and experiences. Delegates will hopefully emerge feeling empowered and better informed.

Study days, publicised in journals, by direct mail or in the local press, are often organised by local trusts, universities, and professional groups. Those organised or sponsored by commercial companies may be free or reasonably priced. These events are usually very specific and state clearly what the subject will be. If well organised and focused, study days can really inform and stimulate nurses. However, a word of warning. Some private training companies provide study days and seminars that are not up to scratch. Before handing over hard-earned money, ask questions about content and course aims and about the possibility of a refund if the course has not been satisfactory.

Recognised education courses from universities or distance learning programmes would obviously be acceptable in fulfilling the PREP requirements.

## Professional journals

The media, and nursing journals in particular, are a very rich source of information. In the UK there are journals to cover most aspects of caring specialities.

Those on sale in newsagents usually have a very broad focus and explore general nursing issues. They also provide interesting and stimulating health-related news and opinion, as well as accessible and clear research reports covering many key areas of study for nursing and midwifery. All nurses and nursing students should read these journals to keep abreast of general developments in the profession.

The more specialist journals provide a much sharper focus and are aimed at practitioners working in areas such as general practice, theatre, ITU or midwifery. These are available on subscription, either personal, or institutional via a ward or unit or through hospital libraries.

Several professional journals provide learning material for which they allocate points or a suggested time needed for study. The learning activity is an excellent way to manage private study. Nurses should be aware that the UKCC does not recognise 'points' though it would acknowledge the study activity itself, which should be included in the personal profile.

## Libraries

Everyone can get to a public library and may be able to use a hospital library, but university libraries usually have restricted access. With the growth in electronic information technology, even the most computer-illiterate person, with the help of a friendly librarian, can soon access important information from the Internet or search the literature using one of the many databases (CD ROMs) covering health care. Once you have obtained references appropriate to the area of study you can collect them from journals or books on the shelves, or via the inter-library loan service.

After reading articles, or completing courses, visits or study days, nurses need to continue their systematic and considered approach to learning. The next step is evaluation.

## Evaluation

This stage requires a careful and critical period of reflection that explores the following questions:

- Did your study or visit meet your expected objectives?
- How will your new knowledge help you to care for your patients more effectively?
- Has your search highlighted any further areas that you feel you need to explore?
- How will you share your new knowledge with others?

Finally, you need to record what you have learnt for inclusion in your personal profile. As an accountable practitioner, the UKCC expects that you will be honest when documenting your study in your profile and there is no need for anyone else to confirm these details.

## PROBLEMS WITH ACCESSING STUDY DAYS, CONFERENCES AND COURSES

In many ways it is easier for practitioners employed in a hospital or community trust to gain access to the increasing number of courses designed specifically for them. The course may be run by their employers who have an interest in them attending. They may be granted study time and/or have the events' fees paid for them by the trust. It is generally easier for those employed in an established role to meet the needs of professional development, although many agencies and non-NHS employers do recognise the need to support updating for their professional staff.

Many nurses work independently or semi-independently, either through an agency or on the bank of nurses at a local hospital. Enlightened nursing agencies and independent care homes often arrange study days or sponsor employees, as it is in their interest to keep their staff updated so they can fulfil their professional requirements. But how can the important group of nurses who work, for example, in a nursing home that does little or nothing to support further study, meet their professional development needs?

## SCENARIO

Registered nurse Jane Adams qualified five years ago. She has decided to work for the local nursing agency while her children are still young. This allows her maximum contact with her children while still earning and keeping her career going. She works at a variety of local nursing homes and occasionally at the local hospital, usually in the care-of-the-elderly unit. Recently she has become concerned that she will not be able to meet her PREP needs and feels that she is not keeping abreast with developments in the profession. But she has little spare money to fund her professional development. A colleague has mistakenly told her that she must get on study days to be able to practise following her re-registration in a year's time.

Jane needs to be clear about PREP and its requirements and that whatever activity she undertakes must be relevant to her professional practice and role.

As she works mainly with elderly patients both in nursing homes and hospitals, she clearly needs to focus her professional development in this area. This speciality is particularly demanding and also very wide in its scope, with subjects such as nutrition, wound care, rehabilitation and dementia all needing a clear understanding.

There is no shortage of potential areas which Jane could study. She needs to do a Personal Training Needs Analysis, a somewhat grand title for a simple process that enables the nurse to determine the most suitable and important areas of study.

She will need to consider the following:

- Does the study enhance her main area of practice?
- Does the subject stimulate and interest her?
- If she works as part of a team, is there an area of expertise that is not covered by the team?
- What materials are available covering her particular area of study need?
- What can she access easily?
- Is there currently a course that covers the subject?

# PLANNING PERSONAL DEVELOPMENT

There are several stages involved in planning personal development.

## Reviewing competence

Nurses need to look at their strengths, weaknesses and areas for personal development.

Jane always found demented patients hard to care for and felt that she did not know enough about dementia and its associated problems. She felt her understanding was inadequate to give the patients the full level of care they deserved.

## Setting learning objectives

Nurses need to examine what they want to achieve.

Jane decided to explore the issues surrounding the care of a patient with Alzheimer's disease. She was concerned about those who tended to wander and the danger to them. She felt this area of study would fall within the category of care enhancement in that she would learn about new approaches to care provision, reducing risk and patient support.

## Making an action plan

Nurses should address what learning activities will help meet their needs.

Jane was aware of a short course on caring for the demented patient at her local further education college. She read the course contents and met the course tutor, and felt this would explain the condition in a structured way. But the £650 price was too high for her and neither the nursing home nor the agency would pay.

However, Jane knew of a sister nursing home for elderly, mentally ill people where she negotiated an exchange with one of their nurses who wanted some experience of physical nursing. This was perfectly adequate for both their PREP requirements, and considerably cheaper.

## Implement the action plan

The next stage is for nurses to discuss their action plan with their manager and negotiate terms.

Jane was able to combine a visit, work experience, professional dialogue and in-depth reading.

## Evaluate what happened

Next, nurses need to examine whether the plan met their objectives.

Jane felt she had benefited from the total experience and was able to influence care within the nursing home and share her knowledge with other staff.

## Record study and outcomes

The final stage is to make an accurate record of the study activity and learning outcomes.

Jane was able to document the learning activity and outcomes back with her client group and colleagues, and to complete her PREP hours of study within her profile.

## A PERSONAL PROFESSIONAL PROFILE

A personal professional profile (PPP) is a vital part of your learning and professional development as a practitioner on the UKCC register. Again, much confusion and concern surrounds this document, which is really quite simple. The profile is a tool to enable you to systematically chart and manage your professional and personal growth.

Certainly when you start using your PPP it will seem strange and possibly tiresome, but you should remember this is one of the requirements that you as a professional must maintain to remain registered.

Your profile is a flexible, up-to-date and growing account of your professional development. It should contain historical information about yourself such as qualifications from both school and nurse education, employment and nursing achievements. It will also provide biographical details about yourself and store your records of study days and conferences etc., which might be considered the portfolio part of the document.

However, a more important function of your profile is as a vehicle for the structured acquisition of and reflection upon learning, both from everyday nursing experiences and from your own formal learning outlined above.

Perhaps the most important benefit of keeping an up-to-date profile will be to help you gain some control in your professional growth. Sometimes it feels like you are missing so much of what is going on around you. You may feel too close to a situation to be able to gain a really detached view about it to solve a particular problem in practice. The PPP may simply help you become more aware of your strengths and weaknesses and which direction you want your career to take.

The UKCC (1995) states that your profile will:

- help you assess your current standards of practice;

- develop your analytical skills, skills that are fundamental to your professional practice;

- enable you to review and evaluate past experience and learning regularly, in order to plan and negotiate your continuing education and career moves;

- provide effective, up-to-date information to use in application forms and interviews when you apply for jobs or courses;

- provide evidence of what you have learned from experience.

## Getting started

There is no such thing as an official profile document produced by the UKCC. There are many PPPs available from several sources but they can be expensive. One advantage of buying a ready-made profile is that they often provide the reader with useful advice and exercises to help with reflection. I believe that a perfectly adequate profile can be made cheaply from a ring binder, some dividers and a simple A4 writing pad.

Once you have your profile assembled you can start to build up your own PPP which reflects you, your role and where you want to be. Your PPP is a living document, which grows and changes just as you and your nursing roles do. That means you must keep it updated when circumstances change or you gain new knowledge or insight into your role. Whether you buy a ready-made profile or create your own, there are certain pieces of information that you should include. This is because the UKCC may need to audit your PPP, subjecting it to scrutiny to ensure you are maintaining it with the correct type of information. There will be a section on factual and personal information such as:

- personal biographical details;

- professional qualifications;

- recordable qualifications;

- other general academic qualifications;

- employment details throughout your career;

- other activities that you think are important in your personal or professional development such as voluntary or community work, or informal caring.

Also included are self-awareness issues such as:

- strengths and weaknesses;

- occupational achievements;

- reflective notes on these issues;

- areas you may wish to improve on.

The PPP will help you become more systematic and ordered. From analysis of your strengths and weaknesses you will be able to develop an action plan for your progress. You may also be able to use your PPP to claim credit accumulation and transfer (CATS) points (Teasdale, 1995) enabling you to reduce the time spent in certain areas of study because of previously gained experience and learning.

You will need to chart the following:

- goals — short, medium and long-term;

- what you need to do and who can help you, for example, a clinical supervisor, manager, colleague or tutor;

- a clear set of aims and outcomes with review dates to help measure your progress;

- dates when you achieved your goals and what you learnt in the process;

- perhaps most important of all, how you have enhanced patient care by making the change.

Your profile should record all your study, including lectures, study days, visits, conferences and personal study time. If used correctly they will add up to form your mandatory study time of a minimum of five days' learning activities in three years (approximately 35 hours). It is not enough to simply record what you studied or enclose certificates of attendance. You must systematically reflect on the following:

- How did the study enhance patient care?

- Was it valuable?

- What will you do with the new knowledge?

- How will you share your new knowledge?

By being honest with yourself you will become clearer about other areas you need to study. The key is to become organised and disciplined in your professional documentation and make updating your PPP part of your life. Finally, the UKCC states that you need to keep a record of the study hours you have achieved and for ease of access, this would best be kept on a separate summary sheet.

# REFLECTIVE PRACTICE

Reflective practice has become very important in recent years and much has been written on the subject. All formal courses now contain sessions on reflective practice and much can be gained by those who include formal reflection in their practice.

However, a certain mystique has also arisen.

## Reflection and you

Reflection is not a new invention. Indeed, to be a nurse, midwife or health visitor you must constantly be reflecting upon your practice to remain safe and competent. Perhaps the best way to think about reflection is to divide it into two: simple reflection and deep reflection. Simple reflection involves using professional knowledge, attitudes and skills to react to the many challenges that we face in our daily practice. Deep reflection, which is perhaps more hidden, occurs when we reflect on a particular issue or incident.

Simple reflection:

- occurs at all stages of practice;

- supports planning, implementing and evaluating care;

- helps us make safe and timely decisions.

Deep reflection:

- allows us to consider the more hidden dimensions and issues relating to professional practice;

▸ helps us challenge the issues relating to how we practise;

▸ asks searching questions of the individual;

▸ supports deeper exploration of the self, increasing one's awareness of personal strengths and weaknesses.

Reflecting could be defined as thinking purposefully about clinical practice to gain new insight, ideas and understanding. Among the many issues currently surrounding reflection (Haddock and Bassett, 1997) the most prominent are:

▸ finding the time to formally reflect;

▸ how does one reflect in an effective way?

The first issue is particularly worrying for nurses when workloads are high and time precious. The benefits from structured reflection can be great, as it may shed light on alternative approaches to care. You do not necessarily need to write a large volume to record reflective insights for the PPP. Short notes will do, summarising clearly the key issues and possible ways forward. Part of a clinical supervision session could form the basis of a reflective passage for the profile. Reflection can be achieved by reading around the subject; your ability to reflect on issues develops gradually over time, along with your nursing skills. An evaluation of recent learning may also provide a valuable insight into practice.

As you develop your reflection skills you may wish to keep a reflective diary as an aid to your practice. There are no absolute rights or wrongs, just what suits you and is significant in helping your practice. Key issues of an event can crystallise in your mind on your journey home, for example, so that you can write them down by the time you get home. The reflective cycle as cited by Bynom (1998) offers a helpful model (see Table 1).

This is a simple and straightforward method of exploring an incident. It breaks up the key areas into discrete sections, enabling the practitioner to understand better the factors involved. This approach will clarify the theoretical background that you may need to examine as part of your further study (Dewing, 1990). It may help ensure that a bad situation does not happen again or show how you might repeat something very good in practice, which benefited your patient or client.

# CONCLUSION

This chapter has made clear the vital importance of keeping up to date for the nurse, midwife or health visitor. All practitioners are subject to the Code of Professional Conduct and all of its rules. We have explored what PREP means and have made clear that any form of learning acquired either formally or informally through personal study can meet your study time requirements. And finally we have examined some of the simple ways we can use reflection to enhance practice.

Hopefully practitioners will not see this requirement as being an onerous and tiresome chore, but instead take up the exciting and essential opportunity for learning to improve the care they provide for their patients and clients.

## References

Bynom, S. (1998) Reflection — a lost swab. *British Journal of Theatre Nursing*; 8: 5, 15-17.

Dewing, J. (1990) Reflective practice. *Senior Nurse*; 10: 10, 26-28.

Dimond, B. (1995) *Legal Aspects of Nursing*. London: Prentice Hall.

Haddock, J., Bassett, C. (1997) Nurses' perceptions of reflective practice. *Nursing Standard*; 11: 32, 39-41.

Power, K. (1997) The legal and ethical implications for nursing. *British Journal of Nursing*; 6: 9, 885-887.

Teasdale, K. (1995) Using a personal profile to claim CATS points. *Professional Nurse*; 11: 2,103-104.

UKCC (1995) *Implementation of the UKCC's Standards for Post-Registration and Practice (PREP)*. London: UKCC.

## Recommended reading

Basset, C. (ed) (in press) Clinical supervision: a guide to implementation. London: NT Books.

Cameron, B., Mitchell, A. (1993) Reflective peer journals — developing authentic nurses. *Journal of Advanced Nursing*; 18: 4, 290-297.

Dimond, B. (1992) *Accountability and the nurse*. London: South Bank University.

Schon, D. (1987) *Educating the reflective practitioner*. London: Josey Bass.

Young, A. (1994) Law and professional conduct in nursing. London: Scutari Press.

## Table I. Reflective cycle

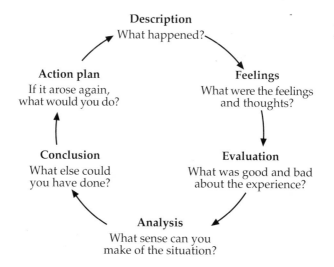

**Description**
What happened?

**Action plan**
If it arose again,
what would you do?

**Feelings**
What were the feelings
and thoughts?

**Conclusion**
What else could
you have done?

**Evaluation**
What was good and bad
about the experience?

**Analysis**
What sense can you
make of the situation?

# Clause 4:
# A knowledgeable doer

**Ray Field**

> '...acknowledge any limitations in your knowledge and competence and decline any duties or responsibilities unless able to perform them in a safe and skilled manner.'

This chapter deals with a question most nurses ask themselves and one which the public have the right to ask of all nurses — are you able to answer for your actions?

The suggestion that you might not know what you are doing and may be incompetent concerns most professionals. Though very few nurses are incompetent, Post-Registration Education and Practice (PREP) regulations require all practitioners to maintain their own competence, knowledge and skills in their particular area of practice in the context of continually changing health care (UKCC, 1997a). This chapter examines in a practical way the key elements of Clause 4 and how nurses might deal with some of the problems in practice arising from the requirement to 'acknowledge any limitations'.

It discusses how nurses can know if they have the necessary knowledge and skills to carry out a particular procedure or practice competently and what is involved if they have to decline any duties or responsibilities on the grounds that they do not regard themselves competent to carry them out.

It is rare in day-to-day practice for nurses to refuse to practice on the grounds that they do not know what they are doing. They are more likely to be concerned with how relevant and up-to-date their knowledge and skills are in relation to their current job and how they need to develop them in response to the advances in research, medicine and technology. As the baseline standard of competency required to be a registered nurse is raised to 'advanced' or 'higher' practitioner levels, nurses also need to assess their competence at this new specialist level.

We will also consider how the *Scope of Professional Practice* (UKCC, 1992) has increased the emphasis on individual nurses deciding their own levels of competence in their particular work situation. The UKCC clearly recognises that every nurse is accountable for their practice and the 'onus is on the individual practitioner to define the limits of their practice' (UKCC, 1997b).

This new freedom, while removing the need to collect certificates of competency for individual tasks, poses a fresh problem. Nurses must now decide for themselves if they are competent or not, although they are not completely on their own when making the decision. How can the Code and Scope help nurses decide? They are also affected by their contract of employment and by the law generally. So they need to consider the combined effect of the Code with Scope, as well as the more general legal position, including their contract of employment.

## ADEQUATE KNOWLEDGE AND COMPETENCE

We need to clarify what the Code means by adequate 'knowledge and competence' before nurses can assess whether they meet its requirements. They will need to be aware of what level and depth of knowledge is appropriate, along with practical experience needed, to provide skilled patient care in their chosen area of practice. Otherwise they are unlikely to know when they are out of their depth.

The *Shorter Oxford English Dictionary* definition of competency is: 'legally qualified, or sufficient in amount, quality, or degree' to function in a particular way. The Nurses, Midwives and Health Visitors Act (S1 1983 No. 837 The Nurses, Midwives and Health Visitors Rules Approval Order) provided the framework for judging who can be 'legally qualified' to practice as a competent practitioner. It identifies nine competencies as requirements for registration as a nurse at the end of a three year pre-registration educational programme. This programme will have assessed the students in theory and in practice and deemed them competent and safe. The four national boards of England, Wales, Scotland and Northern Ireland will have monitored practice standards to ensure they are similar across the UK, thus setting a minimum level of competency of newly qualified nurses. This standard-setting function of the national boards offers the public some reassurance that a registered nurse in Chester will be as competent as one in Cardiff, Dundee or Belfast.

The nine competencies revolve around the nurse's ability to:

- devise a plan of nursing care based on assessment of their patient's health/well being;

- implement and review its effectiveness;

- be able to work with medical and para-medical colleagues.

These basic care assessment and planning competencies were added to in 1989 under Rule 18a (2) with the original nine competencies expanded in detail for the new Project 2000 training. The term 'competency' was dropped in favour of 'outcomes' in the 1989 statutory amendment to the Act (UKCC. 1989), but despite the attempt to replace it, the word has remained in most curriculum and statutory documents. The expanded Rule 18a (2) specified several new 'competencies/outcomes' such as the need for the nurse to:

- use relevant literature and research to inform the practice of nursing;

- understand the requirements of legislation relevant to nursing practice;

- understand the ethics of health care and of the nursing profession and the responsibilities these impose on the nurse's professional practice.

The rule repeats the emphasis of Clause 4 that the nurse should refer to the appropriate person on matters not 'within his/her sphere of competence'.

The competencies define the new practitioner and are set at a minimum level of practice. In terms used by Benner (1985) students progress in their pre-registration training from being a 'novice', to 'advanced beginner' to 'competent' at the registered nurse level. Stakeholders in health care have questioned the adequacy of these skills and the relevance of the knowledge taught in Project 2000 programmes. They claim that the basic pre-registration nursing programmes are not based on 'real life' and are not equipping nurses with the knowledge and skills to deliver quality care (NHS Executive, 1998). This perceived 'theory-practice gap' and the adequacy of pre-registration training to produce nurses fit for practice is being reviewed by the UKCC Education Commission (UKCC, 1998a).

As pre-registration student nurses move from advanced beginner to competent, how do they then develop to become 'proficient' and 'expert' practitioners? The UKCC recommends that newly-qualified practitioners have a preceptorship period of support following registration to consolidate and develop enough experience to become proficient in nursing (UKCC, 1992).

The demand on nurses, not just to maintain their level of knowledge and competence, but to actually increase it, has been identified in the PREP requirements (UKCC, 1997), which state: 'all nurses, midwives and health visitors must demonstrate that they have maintained and developed their clinical competence.'

A UKCC survey (UKCC, 1998b) indicates that most nurses say they are meeting their PREP requirements. The survey of 12,000 registrants found that nearly three-quarters said they were fulfilling their PREP requirements fully, with a further quarter meeting them partly. Nurses are clearly beginning to consider how they might develop their knowledge and clinical competence.

The term 'competence' is used in the Code and in PREP documents without necessarily always being specifically defined. For our purposes we should regard the competent nurse as one whose knowledge and skills are adequate, sufficient and appropriate for their nursing activity. The nurse should be fairly self-sufficient and responsive to changing circumstances.

If nurses are not open to new knowledge and skills they can become out of date, and though superficially they may be safe and competent, their practice may not be up to current standards. They may have been competent once in a particular setting, at a particular time, but they need to keep pace with developments in clinical practice. Practitioners will remain 'capable' only if they have the necessary self-awareness and wisdom to learn from their own experience and that of others.

# How do you know you are competent?

Knowing they are 'personally accountable' for their practice and that they must provide evidence of having the necessary knowledge and skills for their level of current practice does not help nurses if they do not know how to assess their own competence. They may wish to assess if they are safe at a minimum level, or at a higher level equivalent to the practice of their specialist colleagues.

Competence levels may vary in a nurse from time to time, depending on the clinical circumstances and how confident they feel at the time. The anxiety of not knowing whether they had enough knowledge and skills for current practice was possibly one of the reasons why 27,000 nurses failed to re-register with the UKCC (News story, *Nursing Standard*, 1998).

In assessing their competence nurses should begin by gathering information from several sources and not just rely on their own opinion. The assessment is a judgement between what is required in clinical practice and the experience, knowledge, skills and attitudes they have acquired. They should start by measuring their own experiences against other sources of information derived from: supervision, policy documents, clinical guidelines, clinical audit, protocols and evidence-based data sources. The questions the nurse should ask are outlined below and the whole process can be documented in the personal professional profile.

# Am I qualified to do the job?

First, most nurses can be reassured by the fact that they are qualified and registered by the UKCC and are therefore regarded as competent according to Rule 18a (2). They already have been assessed in theory and practice and considered to have the necessary knowledge and skills to practice as competent practitioners.

Some practising nurses may be concerned that their knowledge is not up to date, while others may feel they are out of date because they have not practised for some time. If nurses have not practised for a minimum of 100 working days or 750 hours at any time in the previous five years, they will need to do a statutory return-to-practice course. This does not involve a return to complete novice levels of knowledge and practice, but entails a careful reassessment of how their knowledge applies to current practice.

# AM I COVERED LEGALLY?

The nurse will be bound by the terms of their contract of employment. The employee is expected to obey the reasonable demands of their employer and work with reasonable care and skill. Many employers incorporate the Code as a term of the contract. The employer thus assumes that the nurse will practice according to the principles of the Code and expects them to acknowledge any limitations in knowledge and practice. Having reasonable skill means that the nurse is working within appropriate professional standards and has the necessary underpinning knowledge and experience to perform their duties and responsibilities at the required level.

A nurse who claims to be a specialist practitioner will be expected to have the appropriate knowledge and skills to perform the claimed 'specialist' role. It is their responsibility to be aware of the professional standards expected at that level and to ensure that they have the necessary training and skills. The law does not prescribe what this might be but rather leaves it to the statutory bodies — the UKCC and national boards — to maintain standards through monitoring education practice.

The UKCC in turn places the onus on each individual to assess their own competence. Apart from registration as a nurse, midwife or health visitor there are no specialist registered qualifications. There is a long list of recorded qualifications which indicate that a practitioner has been through an approved programme of education in a particular area of practice, for example, intensive care or community psychiatric nursing. The UKCC cannot prevent practitioners from using different specialist titles. However, the nurse must be aware that if claims are made to specialist skills and knowledge, then they will be judged on the basis of that level of competence. Specialist nurses may be expected to demonstrate medical skills and knowledge if they carry out activities normally undertaken by doctors. The patient is entitled to no lesser standard of care from a nurse than from a doctor.

The employer is also responsible for ensuring that nurses have been trained for their task. They cannot prescribe in detail in a job description the knowledge and skills required to work as a clinical nurse specialist, but will expect the nurse to work within appropriate professional standards, defined referring to:

- the Code and Scope, and other relevant statutory body documents which set out the requirements for training as a specialist;

- the courts, who would be likely to refer to the UKCC documentation for guidance and consider what could be reasonably expected of a professional colleague who traditionally performs the activity;

- the employer, who will be concerned that the nurse is working within her contract of employment and has undertaken the work with reasonable care and skill.

There are occasions when nurses may be trained to carry out tasks that employers prevent them from doing. For example an emergency nurse practitioner may be trained to request X-rays, but the employer does not allow her to do so.

# IS MY KNOWLEDGE UP TO DATE?

Nurses who believe their knowledge may be outdated and need reassuring can use the following to make an assessment:

- **Job descriptions:** these should contain an outline of the knowledge and skills required to undertake the job, using sentences such as 'will have an understanding of…', and 'will be aware of…'

- **Competency statements:** good job descriptions also contain competency statements which attempt to describe the attributes necessary for effective practice. Though job descriptions tend to describe jobs and people in broad general terms and can be difficult to apply to an individual, they are a starting point. Some trusts have developed 'competency profiles' which outline general and specific requirements for a particular post or clinical speciality. Nurses can compare their knowledge to the requirements listed, for example, thinking about such issues as management, influencing/political, organisational, and communication skills. But such lists can be too steeped in the past and too narrow. Competence and capability should be about being able to respond to changing situations.

- **Evidence-based practice:** if nurses need to identify current knowledge in their chosen areas of practice, these are among the best sources:

- Research evidence: nurses need to critically appraise the most recent research evidence in the literature. Sometimes they will discover they are behind the times, or they may find little has changed.

- Clinical audit: these are clinically-led initiatives that have reviewed practice against agreed explicit standards.

- Clinical guidelines: treatment of specific conditions, such as wound care, may have changed based on research, audit and practice. Guidelines contain specific statements about appropriate and effective treatment for the specific condition.

▸ **Patients' reports:** evidence about patients' experience of care is a valuable source of information. Patient satisfaction surveys or complaints may indicate a gap in nurses' knowledge. For example, patients may want nurses to be more aware of their cultural preferences.

▸ **Experience:** through exposure to many clinical situations nurses will recognise recurrent patterns and responses. An experienced nurse will view the whole situation and work out priorities, while a less experienced nurse may be distracted by something unimportant. They will have been involved in clinical audit, research and collecting their own evidence for what makes good practice. Of course, unless it is rigorously reviewed, years of experience can amount only to accumulation of error, prejudice and a lack of openness to new developments in practice.

## ARE MY SKILLS RELEVANT?

By answering the questions above nurses can work out if their skills are underpinned by the most relevant, effective, up-to-date knowledge. Practitioners will also need to judge whether their skills are appropriate to their client group. The skills of a nurse who has worked in an acute general medical, psychiatric or children's setting may not apply to another specialist area, such as care of the elderly. Nurses will have to decide if those skills are transferable.

Nurses can use the following measures to assess their level of skill:

▸ **Clinical supervision:** this allows nurses to meet in a group or one to one with a professional colleague with whom they can discuss their clinical practice. Butterworth (1993) defines it as 'an exchange between practising professionals to enable the development of professional skills'. Discussions can include examples of practice gleaned from memorable incidents, difficulties and written records, such as patients' notes. The professional colleague can thus assess the nurse's skill, and identify whether extra learning support is needed.

- **Individual performance review:** nurses can use a management review of their performance as another source of useful information. It is an opportunity to get feedback on existing practice and to discuss perceived learning needs for future professional development. If the review is undertaken by the nurse's immediate manager, he or she may be well placed to provide resources to help nurses develop their skills.

- **Portfolios and profiles:** the speed of change in clinical practice often means that many skills cannot be learnt from textbooks or other information sources but must be based on actual practice. The portfolio, or profile, apart from being a formal requirement of PREP, is another source of feedback. The portfolio should not only record areas of deficiency but recognise achievements. However, an incompetent nurse can also reflect on her practice without any insight into her deficiencies. The reflection must be carried out within guidelines related to clinical research, audit and protocols as outlined above.

A portfolio can be used to record examples of practice to be discussed in clinical supervision and/or individual performance review. But it cannot demonstrate that skills have been acquired simply by recording attendance at courses and study days, which may reinforce a nurse's previous way of learning in the initial pre-registration training.

The UKCC refers to other learning routes, such as conferences, seminars, distance learning, visits to other areas of practice to observe care, personal research, including a literature search. But most nurses regard attendance at study days, lectures and seminars as the preferred way to maintain adequate knowledge and skills (UKCC, 1988).

# Have I got the resources?

Nurses have to decide if they have the personal resources and adequate support systems to undertake their professional practice. They need to address their own attitudes to cultural and ethical issues as part of their personal accountability for practice. A nurse may be knowledgeable, skilled and educated to an advanced level, yet not sufficiently take into account issues such as gender, age or ethnicity in their patients or areas of practice.

Sensitivity to particular patient groups, for example, teenagers, children with HIV or elderly people, will require a different range of skills and awareness. Moral or ethical issues related to nurses' area of care are an important part of up-to-date practice. Many cases referred to the UKCC relate to a practitioner's competence, rather than professional misconduct. In these cases the practitioner is not up to the standard and 'may demonstrate a poor attitude, lack of insight...' (UKCC, 1996).

A proficient practitioner can resolve moral dilemmas in their practice and has developed an ethical framework for decision making. Lack of support from other colleagues, including nurses, poses a frequent challenge. There may be too few nurses on duty, or not enough nurses trained to the required level. So-called 'support' staff may be unsupportive. In these circumstances nurses must decide if they are competent and have adequate resources to perform their duties in a safe and skilled manner. If the nurse feels limited in their practice or the environment affects their ability to perform safe and skilled practice, the Code clearly states they must 'decline any duties or responsibilities'.

## DECLINING ANY DUTIES OR RESPONSIBILITIES

Declining a duty is difficult and requires skill. After assessing the situation, it may be easier for the nurse to say: 'I won't do it', than 'I can't do it,' because the latter implies a lack of personal competence.

Declining a duty because of lack of staff and the need to maintain standards does not immediately reflect on the competence of the nurse. If it happens, it needs to be handled with care, to ensure the patient's best interest.

If a nurse believes they cannot deliver safe and skilled care, they will have to decide on what grounds — using the criteria of qualifications, knowledge, skills, experience or legal position — and explore alternative solutions.

For example, a nurse may refuse to accept a patient requiring continuous infusion from intensive care to a general medical ward, because none of the staff feels competent to accept responsibility for the patient's complex drips and drains. Pressure on bed allocation may mean a child being admitted to an adult ward or a patient who has just had orthopaedic surgery being admitted to a gynaecology ward. In both instances the staff may feel unable to provide the specialist level of care these patients need.

Similar situations arise in all areas of nursing, where patients with specialist needs are transferred to less intensive areas, such as nursing homes, group homes or the patient's own home. The situation is often more complex because the nurse in charge may be under pressure from a doctor or manager to get the patient out of the intensive area. The nurse's refusal to deal with what intensive care staff, doctors and managers consider a simple procedure can only add to the pressure to give in.

The nurse should explore all informal channels to solve the problem without resorting to the phrase: 'I cannot be accountable for… under the Code of Conduct.' This perpetuates the problem. Instead, the nurse should explore alternative solutions with colleagues and managers.

Management may have to review the mix of nurses available to deal with the situation. The nurse should communicate their concerns and rationale in a clear and professional manner. This will defuse the situation and prevent arguments from becoming too polarised and emotional. They should keep a written record of all decisions in case they later have to justify them. If a nurse declines a duty because they feel they have neither enough, nor suitably experienced, staff, they must explain their reasons to appropriate person or authority, verbally and in writing, as outlined in Clause 12 of the Code. It is often easier for the nurse or manager to blow the whistle on lack of resources, because the blame is usually reflected on someone else, or the health service generally.

It is harder when nurses' knowledge and competence are stretched by a procedure for which they should have the requisite specialist skills. They may be self-proclaimed specialists, or considered as such by their colleagues, yet regard themselves as having limited competence. Their colleagues or employer may point to the Scope as justification for allowing them to carry out specialist practice, if they feel competent.

Nurses need to resist the pressure to carry out a duty for which they feel inadequately prepared and articulate a rationale for not undertaking the duty. Their reasons should amount to more than 'I can't' or 'I won't' and should include a comparison of the nurse's self assessment of their skills and knowledge with that of the skills needed to carry out the task. The employer may claim that the skill is appropriate and has become custom and practice for all nurses. An appeal to the argument that they have not been trained to undertake the task will not, in itself, be sufficient without evidence of a personal skills review.

# CONCLUSION

The new freedom provided in such documents as The Scope of Professional Practice (UKCC, 1992) has helped nurses find ways of improving care to their patients and clients, without having to collect certificates task by task. The Scope has not replaced the Code, but has reinforced its principles, allowing nurses to exercise full professional accountability, yet providing flexibility for them to respond to change.

Scope reminds practitioners that the onus is on them to define the limits of their practice. The Code reminds practitioners that defining the limits of their own practice also means acknowledging limitations. This chapter has regarded the competent nurse as one whose knowledge and skills are adequate, sufficient and appropriate for their specific nursing activity. Yet the numerous situations where nurses may feel they lack the necessary knowledge, or where they feel pushed by colleagues, circumstances or their employer to 'have a go', has left some nurses questioning their own competence.

We have emphasised and hopefully reassured the practitioner that most registered nurses are competent and have a wide range of sources to use to gauge the adequacy of their practice. UKCC surveys show that most nurses both find the Code helpful and say they are undertaking education to meet their PREP requirements. To put it in perspective, while there are 637,000 practitioners on the register, only about 140 cases a year find their way to a full UKCC professional conduct hearing, and only some of these relate to issues of professional competence.

## References

Benner, P. (1984) *From Novice to Expert, excellence and power in clinical nursing practice.* Menlo Park, CA: Addison Wesley.

Butterworth, C.A. (1993) Clinical supervision: a position paper. Manchester: School of Nursing Studies, University of Manchester. Cited in: Smith, C. (1997) Professional competence. Can it be accurately measured or defined? *Nursing in Critical Care*, 12: 4, 186-190.

NHS Executive (1998) *Integrating Theory and Practice in Nursing. A report commissioned by the Chief Nursing Officer/Director of Nursing.* Leeds: NHS Executive.

Nursing Standard: Recruitment strategy threatened as 27,000 nurses fail to reregister (1998). *Nursing Standard;* 12: 47, 5.

UKCC (1992) *The Scope of Professional Practice.* London: UKCC.

UKCC (1996) *Issues arising from professional conduct complaints.* London: UKCC.

UKCC (1997a) *PREP and you.* London: UKCC.

UKCC (1997b) Scope in Practice. London, UKCC.

UKCC (1998a) UKCC Education Commission news. *Register;* 25, Autumn 1998, 5.

UKCC (1998b) UKCC PREP evaluation update. *Register,* 25, Autumn 1998, 5.

# Recommended Reading

Le May, A. (1999) Evidence-based practice. *NT Clinical Monographs No. 1.* London: NT Books.

# Clause 5: The centre of attention

**Jill Fardell**

> '...work in an open and cooperative manner with patients, clients and their families, foster their independence and recognise and respect their involvement in the planning and delivery of care.'

Everyone has the right to be respected and valued, to make choices and decisions about what happens to them, particularly when it seems that illness, impairment or injury has changed their lives. The pay-off for receiving health care can no longer be the patient's loss of self-esteem and personal identity. It is fundamental to the role of every health professional to enable clients to maintain a sense of control as it has a significant effect on the outcomes and quality of the care provided.

Clause 5 is, arguably, the most important in the Code because, in essence, it sets a framework for defining the nature of the nurse-client relationship. Enabling people to maintain or regain a sense of independence should be a key objective in planning a person's care and services, irrespective of the client group, or the circumstances in which these are provided. Clients are not simply a condition or set of symptoms, they are people with lives beyond their illness or impairment. Therefore, nurses and others involved in care or support need to ensure that the illness, impairment or injury is addressed within the context of the patient's life. At the heart of client involvement in care, service planning and delivery is the issue of power and the locus of control.

This chapter will explore how Clause 5 affects the relationship between nurses and their clients, and the nature of the care and services they provide.

## THE NURSE/CLIENT RELATIONSHIP

The relationship between the nurse and the client has an enormous bearing on the way care is provided, how well the client progresses and how well they cope at the time and afterwards. Most of our relationships develop over a period of time but this one is usually established very quickly, often in stressful circumstances and when the client is feeling very vulnerable.

Good relationships are built on trust and mutual respect for each other's values, knowledge, experience and beliefs. They need to be reviewed and renegotiated from time to time in a climate of tolerance and understanding.

Enabling clients to be independent and to contribute to their own care planning and delivery is a test of true professionalism. Many nurses have no problem with this at all. For them it seems a normal part of their work and their relationship with their clients. Others find it much more challenging.

We hear a great deal about how difficult it is to be a nurse in today's health service: long hours, insufficient staff, unsafe working conditions — the list seems endless. On the whole the public is concerned and sympathetic. People who receive good care recognise the personal skills and dedication of the nurses who provide it. But sadly not everyone's experience is a positive one, and it is often down to the attitudes and the communication skills of the professionals involved.

From the other side it sometimes seems as if the professionals have lost the plot and forgotten that clients are their raison d'être, and that without clients, knowledge and skills are purely academic and health professionals would not be needed at all.

# BEING A PATIENT/CLIENT

Most people will use the health service at some stage in their lives, either directly or vicariously through someone close to them. Therefore, it should not be too difficult for nurses to think about their own experiences of the health service, to try occasionally to put themselves in the client's shoes and see the world through their eyes.

Remember playing the game blind man's bluff as a child? You are placed in the centre of a ring, blindfolded, and whirled around by the other players until you lose all sense of direction and control. Then you have to run about to catch someone. You know the others are there somewhere, you can hear them but they keep moving about, to keep out of your way and confuse you further. Meanwhile you are stumbling about and have to depend on them to ensure you do not hurt yourself. Of course it is only a game but at the time you feel nervous, vulnerable, even a bit frightened, depending on who the other players are and how well you know them. Being a patient/client can feel just like that.

Most of us only access the health service when we are worried about our health or unable to manage our illness or injury ourselves. In an emergency others may make that decision without reference to us or anyone close to us. This puts us at an immediate disadvantage. When this happens we are vulnerable and have a sense that our power and ability to control events are diminished. Quite often we do not understand what is happening and therefore have little alternative but to accept what is on offer and play by the rules of the organisation.

These health-related episodes can turn our world, and the way we see it and ourselves, upside down. The situation may be quickly resolved or it may transform our lives and those of people close to us. For many people this represents the start of a journey, the duration and nature of which are uncertain. The balance of power is shifted away from us, albeit temporarily. The professionals are in control. They have the knowledge, they know the language, it is their territory, they know the rules and they choose to be there. It is largely up to the professionals to enable clients to regain some control over what happens to them.

So nurse and client begin this journey together from very different starting points and the balance of power lies with the professionals.

# POWER AND CONTROL – POSITIVE OR NEGATIVE?

The idea of personal power is abhorrent to many people, because it conjures up visions of exercising negative control over other people or their environment without their consent. Personal power is the inherent ability to control the things that influence our lives, to have the freedom to make informed choices, to have authority to act upon them and the ability to focus our energies to realise them. This is what most people want and strive to achieve from a very young age. It is the goal of every thinking person in a free society.

## The client

When we are ill or injured we often have neither the energy nor the authority to do any of these things. Yet maintaining an acceptable level of control over what is happening to us can have an enormous impact on recovery rates, on how well we respond to care and how well we cope (Rinehart, 1991). It should therefore be more cost-effective as well as personally satisfying for nurses to enable clients to regain and maintain independence and control over their lives right from the start.

## Family, loved ones and carers

Families and friends are also affected by their loved one's health problems and episodes of illness or injury, albeit in a different way, and this has to be acknowledged in care planning and service delivery. The needs of both parties are quite different but at the end of the day the professional's first duty is always to the client.

In the words of one family member: 'All I could do was stand by and watch. I have never felt so powerless in my life.'

Those who become 'family carers' of someone who is either born with or develops a condition requiring continuing support and care are separate entities with individual needs. They have the right to opt out of the caring role or to negotiate the nature and level of their involvement. It is vital that they have their own needs assessed and maintain a sense of control over their lives if they are to continue to fulfil this role effectively. Understanding this relationship and helping to address and resolve the tensions between the sometimes conflicting needs of both parties is crucial.

## The nurse

Nurses should also be clear about their own need to maintain power and control, to understand and manage the tensions between their personal needs and the needs of the client. These, in turn, are affected by the culture, rules and regulations of the organisation and the other professionals involved in the individual's care and services. For example, it can be quite a challenge to 'work in an open and cooperative manner with patients, clients and their families, to foster their independence', for someone who works in a controlling organisation or has to work with people who do not agree with this approach at all.

Is there a genuine move to foster a person's independence? Being admitted to hospital can be a particularly disempowering experience, because whatever the rhetoric, the system tends to foster dependence and many nurses and others believe in the 'do unto' rather than the 'do with' approach to care.

On admission you are usually asked to change into pyjamas or a gown. You are given an identity label and then you get into bed which immediately puts you in the position of a child being 'done to' by other people (Robinson, 1972). From there on it seems as if your only interest and value to others is your condition or symptoms. This can make you feel devalued and your sense of being able to control events or their outcomes rapidly diminishes (Lerner, 1986).

Similarly outpatient clinics and GP surgeries often seem to be run for the benefit of the professionals rather than the clients who could be forgiven for feeling they are an unnecessary interruption in an otherwise ordered world!

No matter how busy or difficult a day is, if people are treated with courtesy, kindness and consideration, they in turn will be patient and understanding when staffing levels are low or they are moved down the priority list because of a more pressing case.

User surveys consistently show that people want to be respected and understood by the professionals providing their care and services. They want to be given an accurate diagnosis and prognosis sensitively in a supportive environment, by someone who is knowledgeable about and has an interest in their condition. And they want to be involved in the planning and delivery of their care and services (Baker et al, 1997). The three key areas of dissatisfaction — all inextricably linked — are:

- professionals' attitudes and approaches;
- communication;
- information.

## INFORMATION AND POWER

'Without information we can't make rational choices. Without it we cannot give our informed consent… We need information to increase our expectations and understanding' (Beresford and Croft, 1993). If people are to be actively involved in the planning and delivery of their care and services, if they are to cope with the effect of their condition or injury on their lives, they need to be able to make informed choices based on accurate, timely information.

Surveys conducted by SCOPE in 1995 and the Stroke Association in 1996 showed that as many as 50% of the people they represent, including their family carers, have difficulty accessing services because of lack of information and advice on what is available. Young people who suffered a stroke were even more disadvantaged. People 'don't know what they don't know', and unless professionals see information as an important element of care, this deprivation will continue.

Having the right information and being able to understand its significance is also empowering and helps people to regain their self respect and control. It gives them the confidence to cope more effectively with what is happening to them and their loved ones. How and when that information is given will influence its effectiveness. For example, when people are given difficult news, or immediately after an accident, they may be too stunned to absorb much detail. Yet they do want some information to help them make sense of what is happening. It is important to get the balance right.

People with similar experiences in self-help groups and voluntary sector organisations can bring this experience to bear and help professionals develop new approaches in providing information and improving services as demonstrated in the following example.

# An example of good practice

At the Romford neuro-care clinic, the local Parkinson's Disease Society persuaded the neurologist and the clinic staff to collaborate in changing the way the clinic was run and in particular what happened to people when they were given their diagnosis. Together they identified key questions which the neurologist needed to ask as part of the process of giving and supporting the diagnosis, even down to writing a script which he used in the initial stages of the project!

The first clinic appointment is kept very short and the neurologist sees the client with the specialist nurse or the social worker. Before he gives the diagnosis, he asks the client, 'What do you think might be wrong with you?' This enables them to explore any misconceptions and allay their fears. Having then told the client he has Parkinson's disease, the doctor says, 'Tell me what you know about the disease,' again to enable the doctor to deal with any misconceptions about the disease itself.

The doctor then gives him a short, honest but constructive description of the disease, its treatment and management. The client is taken to a quiet room with the nurse or social worker who explores and, if necessary, clarifies what information he has absorbed, and rectifies any misunderstandings. The client is also given written information to take away which is produced by the Parkinson's Disease Society and explains about the disease, its treatment and the Society.

By the second appointment some weeks later, having had time to come to terms with the news and consider the implications for him and his family/partner and their lives, the client is ready to ask constructive questions. He will also have sufficient information to make informed choices and to participate in making decisions about his care and future.

This model has been highly successful and has since been adopted for people with other neurological diseases in that clinic, and in Parkinson's disease clinics in other parts of the UK. (Summary of a description by Pauline Smith, formerly Director of Welfare and Education, Parkinson's Disease Society.)

# SHARING KNOWLEDGE – RELINQUISHING POWER?

To explain what is happening, to teach people self-care and to answer their questions are as important a part of a person's recovery as doing a dressing or giving drugs. However, on a busy day, when there seem to be wall-to-wall clients all needing attention and staffing levels are low, it may seem more important to get the tasks done than to stop and take time to do these things. Finding ways of organising staffing levels and routine work may be necessary to ensure that these important aspects of care are achieved.

The way and to what level information is provided varies according to the person and circumstances. But the key elements are to find out what people know and where their information came from. It is important to listen to and respect their fears and misconceptions rather than trying to negate them, as this will not make them disappear and can block their ability to take on new information.

Establish what people want to know. It helps to have a menu of what is possible, to choose the level of information or skills needed at the time and negotiate how this can be built upon to enable clients to participate in their care.

Knowledge is power. It can increase our confidence and our perception of who we are and how others value us. Some professionals find it difficult and even quite threatening to share their professional knowledge. They often cloak what they do in mystique and professional jargon as a means of maintaining their power and control. This applies as much within and across professional groups as it does between professionals and their clients. They may fear that it will leave them open to criticism, to being challenged and perhaps to be found lacking (Rinehart, 1991).

Sharing knowledge shifts the balance of power in the relationship, enabling the client to regain independence and perhaps forcing the professional into a more facilitative role that they may find less satisfying. There is a hierarchy of knowledge in all areas of society which places some groups in superior positions to others. In the health service medical research-based knowledge tends to be on top, with experiential knowledge pretty low on the list. This has enabled the medical profession to dominate the health service for so long.

But knowledge is not finite, it changes when it is applied and may have greater or lesser relevance in different contexts. A range of knowledge and perspectives from all stakeholders — client, family and multidisciplinary professionals — should be brought to bear in planning and providing health care and services.

Synthesising the different sets of knowledge is like mixing a fruit cake. The client and family have the cake mix, with knowledge about themselves, their lives and their expectations. The professionals have the fruit of professional knowledge! The client can actually make a cake of sorts without the fruit, but the professionals' fruit is redundant without the vital cake ingredients. Any cook knows that if the two sets of ingredients are not combined skilfully, the fruit sinks to the bottom, resulting in neither one thing nor the other.

## LANGUAGE AND CONTROL

Some elements of care are quite complex and difficult to understand unless you have specialist knowledge and experience and professionals must cultivate meaningful dialogue with clients. The language we use to convey information to others, especially in stressful situations, should be clear and simple but not patronising or demeaning. A reading age of 11 is said to be appropriate.

The way we communicate conveys much more than the information itself. It conveys our attitudes to others, whether we respect and value them, how open we want to be with them and whether we feel comfortable with ourselves and the situation in hand. Professionals and their clients express themselves quite differently. Professionals use a more formal language while the average person in the street has a more anecdotal and interpersonal style. Both are legitimate and should be accorded equal respect (Harding and Oldman, 1996).

Poor communication skills are in the top three of service users' views of their care and services. Professionals often overestimate patients' knowledge of their medical problems. Professionals as patients often fare just as badly, probably due to similar assumptions.

Most nurses and doctors genuinely feel a strong sense of personal responsibility for the care and services they provide and may therefore be defensive if their actions or decisions are questioned. This kind of attitude can get in the way of constructive dialogue.

# PARTNERSHIPS IN CARE

It is surprising that including clients in the evaluation of care and services is not mentioned in the Code, yet this is surely central to good practice and quality care. Nurses can only improve their practice and identify their education needs if they have feedback from their clients and their families. They need evidence of the effectiveness of what they do in all aspects of the service they provide and the impact this has on the lives of the clients and the families.

To involve people in the planning, delivery and evaluation of their care and services if they so wish is no longer an optional extra. Morally and practically it is the only way to provide an effective, quality service. This has been recognised in all the White and Green Papers relating to organisational development in health and social services issued recently. Making it a reality poses quite a challenge. Some health professionals argue that clients are already involved in the planning and delivery of care. Others feel that in reality consulting them is simply a cynical exercise to rubber stamp decisions that have already been taken. However, the world is changing.

People now entering the professions, including medicine, seem to be more comfortable with the idea of collaborating openly with clients and it is being emphasised on their educational programmes.

One carer commented: 'I think many of the younger doctors are improving. There isn't the old attitude that there used to be. I've had much younger doctors who will listen and as one said "you know a lot more about epilepsy than I'm ever going to know". The GP would listen to what I had to say, but a lot of the older doctors thought they knew best.'

A client's comments on younger doctors: 'They're more up-to-date. There's new methods coming through all the time. Also, doctors now are more down to earth and friendly. They get people to talk more.' (Baker et al, 1997).

# THE FORCES OF CHANGE

Until now, the information highway has been exclusive to computer users. Soon it will be possible for anyone to interact with their television set and survey information sources on almost any topic. Voluntary sector organisations will be able to provide extensive information that a person might wish to access about their condition, the treatment options available and the track records of those providing them. Ultimately more people will have the information they need to make real choices about treatment and, armed with the latest research, will be able to challenge the way their conditions are being managed.

Change to a client-centred service is also fuelled by cases such as the recent child heart surgery scandal at Bristol Royal Infirmary, where many children died; and the disgraced Kent gynaecologist Rodney Ledward, found guilty of ten counts of serious professional misconduct. These cases shocked the public, shaking their faith not only in medical professionals but in the system that supported them. People are appalled that these doctors were able to practice for so long without anyone challenging them. It also begs many questions about whether other professionals colluded, albeit implicitly by doing nothing, in maintaining these doctors' power and simultaneously disempowering the patients and the parents of the babies involved. While such cases are thankfully relatively rare, they do emphasise the need to include service users in clinical governance — setting and monitoring standards of care and service at all levels (DoH, 1997).

This will require a significant shift in the current culture of the health service and some will find that a hard pill to swallow. But changes are occurring and across the UK groups are seeking ways of working more effectively with clients and family carers. The NHS Executive's Patient Partnership Initiative is helping to identify and promote examples of good practice. There is a representative in every regional office in the country and they are all particularly keen to hear about initiatives to improve collaboration between professionals and clients.

'Working openly and cooperatively...', as stated in Clause 5, is not exclusive to the nurse/client relationship and family members. It applies equally to all the professionals involved in providing care and services for clients and is an important part of the approach, with interprofessional and team collaboration stressed in Clause 6. Successful collaboration between professionals has to be based on mutual understanding of and respect for each other's knowledge, values and skills. The cost of poor collaboration is enormous.

There is a wealth of anecdotal evidence of poor communication between professionals, for example leading to 19 people going in to visit one person. The client has no idea who most of them are, nor why they are visiting and most of the professionals are unaware that the others are visiting either. One nurse described her experience: 'I felt on my own although other people were going in. I called a case conference. No one realised how many other people were involved and no one knew what other people were doing. Over the months people drifted away. We nurses hung on to the physical bits – bowels, catheters, because we could do something positive.'

# EDUCATION

Many professionals feel that their education has not adequately prepared them to work in partnership with clients and their families. Neither has it prepared them to cope with the often difficult emotional and social situations with which some of them are confronted (Baker et al, 1997).

In a recent education needs survey of health and social service professionals, detailing critical incidents, one nurse speaking about a young mother who died said: 'She was an incredibly sensible, brave girl. I couldn't cope with my own emotions. I was absolutely overwhelmed. I had to run away.'

Another nurse caring for an old lady with chronic leg ulcers who developed an incurable brain tumour said: 'It's very difficult going in to people you can't do anything for. All our training was task-oriented, we were told never to get involved.'

Nurses are well-educated professionals but what is missing in that education is the opportunity to be aware of their own needs in complex and often highly charged situations. Education must support nurses to develop awareness and understanding of the complexities of human behaviour, of human emotions, their own as well as those of other people. Enquiry-based education based on the reality of clients' needs is a good starting position. Reflective practice is also useful (see Clause 3).

# THE NEED TO CHANGE

An analysis of some of the work carried out over the past five to 10 years involving users and family carers consistently shows that the basis for quality care and partnerships are professionals' attitudes and approaches, information, and communication (Baker et al, 1997). The following points form a useful checklist of criteria for good practice in service delivery and nurses' education:

## Clients' wishes

- time and space to talk with professionals and care providers;

- professionals to be available and accessible, particularly in crisis situations;

- professionals to listen to them and really hear what they are saying;

- to be asked what they want and for professionals not to assume that their silence implies agreement or that their concerns are symptoms;

- to develop a relationship with them based on rapport and empathy;

- to be spoken 'to', not 'at', not 'around' nor 'above' them by other professionals;

- to use language that is easy to understand – and to avoid using jargon that is exclusive;

- to explore ways of overcoming communication difficulties rather than use them as a reason for excluding users from discussions on care and services.

## Attitudes and approaches

The users wanted professionals:

- to use an individual rather than a conveyor belt approach to treatment and service provision;

- to work with, not for, them;

- to respond to their emotional, psychological and social needs as well as their medical/physical needs;

- to be non-judgmental and not to make assumptions about them;

- to understand that they may be anxious, nervous, lack confidence, be at a disadvantage with professionals who hold considerable power over them;

▶ to accept that they, the clients, may be angry at the helplessness they feel or at not being listened to;

▶ to share difficult decisions with them, for example, about rationing of services and treatment options;

▶ work at the user's pace, to push or go softly-softly depending on the individual and the situation in hand, not just use a one-formula response.

## Information

The users wanted to be given:

▶ an accurate diagnosis and prognosis sensitively and in a supportive environment;

▶ information about their conditions and the treatment options.

## User involvement in care provision

Users wished to have:

▶ involvement from the start, as partners and at all stages from planning to evaluation of care and services;

▶ control, choice, a voice in decision-making;

▶ consultation for a purpose, not as an end in itself (many users saw consultation as a cynical exercise giving legitimacy to decisions that had already been made);

▶ support to enable them to participate effectively in decisions and service provision;

▶ involvement in the evaluation of professionals' work, based on user-derived indicators;

▶ professionals open to the experience and influence of users, not dismissing anecdotal evidence.

These are all perfectly reasonable points which have more to do with human decency, respect and consideration for others. Why then is it so difficult to achieve, and how long before we see the changes which clients want and need?

# Conclusion

Despite the fact that patient-centred services have been on the agenda for many years, little attention has been given to the cultural change which will be needed across the board to really achieve this approach in health and service provision. Obviously it is not top priority for nursing any more than it is for medicine, where it is placed in fifth position in the Code, and veiled in imprecise and anachronistic language. The very use of the word 'patient' interchanged with 'client' further illustrates the ambivalence of the profession. I would suggest that 'patient' implies a dependent, passive recipient of care, hardly consistent with someone who is involved in the planning and delivery of their care and services.

It is time the profession took a stand on this issue and it is certainly beneficial that the UKCC endorses the concept that nurses must work in partnership with clients in care planning and delivery. It will help nurses see its importance and relevance to the way they practice, particularly when faced with opposition from other professions and systems of work. Nurses can make a real difference and have a major role to play in empowering clients to be involved in their care and services, and will require a continued lead from their regulatory body.

The profession really must square up to the need for change, to take a firm position on clients' involvement in service provision, and give nurses at the cutting edge the lead and support through education and policy development which they need to undertake this complex role in today's health service.

## References

Baker, M., Fardell, J., Jones, R.H.V. (1997) *The Case for Action — Full Report*. London: Disability and Rehabilitation Education Foundation.

Department of Health (1997) *The New NHS: Modern, Dependable*. (Cm 3807). London: The Stationery Office.

Harding, T., Oldman, H. (1996) *Involving service users and carers in local services; guidelines for social services departments and others*. London: National Institute for Social Work.

Rinehart, N.W. (1991) *Client or Patient? Power and related concepts in health care*. St Louis: Ishiyaku EuroAmerica, Inc.

## Recommended reading

Department of Health (1998) *A first class service — quality in the new NHS*. London: The Stationery Office.

Vousden, M. (1999) The NT Directory of Health Care Information and Resources. London: NT Books.

# Clause 6: Working together

## Jane and John Eastland

> '...work in a collaborative and cooperative manner with health care professionals and others involved in providing care, and recognise and respect their particular contributions within the health care team.'

Interdisciplinary collaboration between health care professionals, including doctors and nurses, promotes positive consequences and outcomes in patient care (Makaram, 1995).

The term 'collaboration' originates from the Latin words *col*, meaning with or together, and *laborare*, meaning work. In terms of health care, it has been described as an 'attitude' (King et al, 1993). Roberts (1987) states: 'Collaboration implies sharing of information and also implies that each participant in the health care system respects the other skills and expertise.'

This chapter will focus on interdisciplinary collaboration and show that each discipline is interdependent. Such relationships have been described as 'visionary', in that they provide an optimal, seamless, holistic approach to patient/client care (Beattie et al, 1996; Denner, 1995).

Specialist nursing practice, in particular, opens up new avenues for the development of collaborative relationships that will continue to close the gap between patient care and service provider.

Though nursing is a unique discipline, nurses are part of an interdisciplinary team. Traditional interpersonal relationships between nursing and medicine have changed as a consequence of technological advances in health care, changes to nursing education and the move towards giving nursing professional status. Traditional values and practices within health care delivery are being challenged. Collaboration is no longer optional.

# WHAT IS COLLABORATION?

Bagg and Schmitt (1988) focus on collaboration as a predominantly nurse-physician objective, with both disciplines 'sharing responsibility for problem solving and decision making, to formulate and carry out plans for patient care'. In fact, the collaboration of a number of professions and services is vital to promote effective, high-quality, patient/client care:

- **Medical staff:** They traditionally play the central role in delivering health care services. The emphasis on 'curing' in the medical model is important. But the relationship between medicine and nursing is also crucial. The collaboration of both professions is pivotal to successful outcomes in patient care. The 'caring' element in nursing is fundamental and complementary to the medical model. Asked what he thought was the greatest leap in medical science in the 20th century, Dr Jonathan Miller argued that it was nursing, not technology (Neubauer, 1995).

- **Professions allied to medicine:** These include physiotherapists, occupational therapists, speech therapists and dietitians. Each speciality shares a common purpose in maximising the patient's or client's health and well-being. In a critical care unit for example, holism is achieved via an interdisciplinary approach to the assessment, planning, implementation and evaluation of care (Woodrow, 1997).

- **Laboratory/scientific staff:** These staff are continually relied upon but perhaps not always fully appreciated. One reason may be that they are not physically present. But in critical situations, laboratory staff add a further dimension to the health care team, improving the quality of specialist intervention for critically ill patients.

▶ **Pharmacists:** Not only does the pharmacy department supply the drugs the patients require, pharmacists and their assistants also provide information and advice about these therapies. They are also responsible for specialist services such as parenteral nutrition and cytotoxic drugs.

▶ **Hotel services:** What porters, receptionists and voluntary organisations do is not only important for hospital staff, but also for patients, families and friends. The 'humanising' of the hospital environment is often regarded as a unique quality of nursing (Neubauer, 1995), but nurses could not achieve this alone. Strict hygiene practices are essential when caring for all patients, and it is here that domestic staff play their part.

▶ **Family members/carers/parents:** Family members are increasingly involved in the caring role and should be seen as team members who need guidance and education from health professionals. Clients under hospital-at-home and early discharge schemes, sick children nursed at home, terminally-ill clients and chronically disabled people are among those who rely on carers not only for emotional support, but also to carry out practical tasks.

True collaboration is an ongoing, dynamic process and takes time to develop. It requires energy and commitment from all involved and must be built on a foundation of mutual respect and an understanding of the unique, complementary perspectives of each profession (Beattie et al, 1996; Makaram, 1995; Woodrow, 1997). Professionals should be viewed as interdependent, each relying on the other, sharing the same values and goals, and respecting each others' contributions (Vanclay, 1998).

Attitudes, relationships, mutual understanding of role function and respect are all key qualities (Denner, 1995; King et al, 1993). If values and beliefs within caring and curing are truly shared, collaboration is a natural progression — and is also associated with positive patient outcomes (Lorentzon, 1998).

Other benefits include: enhanced professional development; increased job satisfaction and a more co-ordinated and holistic approach to care delivery (Henneman, 1995; Makaram, 1995; Miccola and Spanier, 1993; Woodrow, 1997).

# NURSING PROFESSIONALISM

The increase in specialist nursing roles is contributing to the growth of collaborative working. To understand how nursing has become a unique discipline, sensitive to changes in society's expectation of practical and organisational care, we need to explore how the concept of 'professionalism' has evolved.

In the past, nursing's bid to achieve professional status was criticised as elitist and undesirable (Salvage, 1988). Davies (1996) argues that professionalism is steeped in 19th-century ideas of masculinity and competitiveness which conflict with the ideals of reflection and interdependence. The medical model of professionalism offers an 'old' framework.

Davies argues that elements of 'old' and 'new' professionalism co-exist in nursing and health care today. She challenges nursing to move towards 'new professionalism' ideals, which support reflective practice, interdependence and collective responsibility.

Within 'old' professionalism, mastery of knowledge is thought of as a personal possession, a struggle to control, in order to create order and reduce uncertainty (Davies, 1996). In contrast, reflective practice values and believes in nurturing experience and intuition (Behi and Nolan, 1995).

The negative aspects of professionalism within nursing lead to divisiveness and minimise the team approach (Salvage, 1985). Lessening the team approach is regarded as an 'old professional' ideal (Davies, 1996). Collective responsibility means viewing nursing and medicine as interdependent, sharing an equal power base as part of an interdisciplinary team. This philosophy of care is increasingly prevalent in many practice areas (Fagin, 1992; Ford et al, 1997; Henneman, 1995; Vanclay, 1998).

Although nurses have many so-called 'professional characteristics', they lack the crucial power base of the traditional professions of medicine and law. Parkin (1995) advocates 'functional deprofessionalisation', and argues for a return to the ideals of 're-humanising' care, based on informed consent and patient autonomy. Moving towards a shared vision will create more meaningful practitioner-patient relationships.

Nurses will always face a challenge when it comes to maintaining traditional professional ideologies in their practice. Indeed, technological advances have accelerated the overlap and merging of medical and nursing boundaries (Quinn and Thompson, 1995), a process that can only intensify in the future.

# HISTORICAL PERSPECTIVES

The expansion of specialist posts is driven by the desire to improve delivery of patient/client care and underpinned by the Scope of Professional Practice (UKCC, 1992), the foundation for current nurse practice developments.

Holism, greater interdisciplinary collaboration and continuity of care have been heralded as the way forward for nursing professionalism (Beattie et al, 1996; Denner, 1995). Evidence that this strategy works includes: improvements to patient outcomes through evidence-based practice; increased quality of care; satisfaction in professional role function; and improved therapeutic interdisciplinary relationships (Fagin, 1992; Henneman, 1995).

The debate is not new. The Briggs Report on nursing education and practice (1972) recommended greater collaboration between the traditional nursing and medical divide. A Department of Health working party published guidelines on the legal and ethical implications of role extension for practitioners and health authorities (DHSS, 1977). The UKCC's Code of Professional Conduct and Exercising Accountability (UKCC, 1989) documents developed the concept of 'role extension'.

The Scope sought to remove barriers which had prevented nurses from enhancing and expanding their practice (Quinn and Thompson, 1995). In doing so, it stated that 'extended roles' — based on 'official' extension of the nurse's role 'by certification' — were 'no longer suitable'. Instead an alternative, wider concept of 'expanded roles' has emerged, which highlights the need for nursing to move forward in response to political and economic change (Neubauer, 1995). 'Extended roles' were seen as limiting practice, whereas 'role expansion' promoted nurses as autonomous, independent practitioners (Castledine, 1993).

In defining 'role expansion', Wright (1995) states: 'Nursing is seen as valuable and therapeutic… taking on medical or technical tasks is not seen as status enhancing but expanding nursing activity to make care more personal, effective and holistic.'

Scope sets out six key principles to govern practice development, based on the existence of appropriate education, training and experience (Autar, 1996; Langstaff and Gray, 1997). The freedom outlined in Scope has allowed many new nursing specialism roles to emerge.

The increasing collaboration between nursing and the medical profession was acknowledged in a joint statement from the Royal College of Nursing and the Royal College of Physicians (1996). It highlighted the trend towards sharing skills in specialist areas such as gastrointestinal endoscopy, myocardial infarction and oncology. Both organisations felt that it was necessary to further explore standards of care, safeguarding efficacy for patients, by publishing guidelines for physicians and nurses.

# EXPANDING ROLES

Among the emerging roles is that of nurse practitioner, which originated in the USA and enabled primary health care to reach rural areas (Autar, 1996). Traditionally, nurse practitioners have developed in a more general capacity in areas of primary health care delivery.

Nurse specialists have emerged in areas of medical speciality or specific skilled techniques (Langstaff and Gray, 1997). According to the Future of Professional Practice policy statement (UKCC, 1994) a specialist nursing practitioner has to 'exercise higher levels of judgement and discretion in clinical care'. Miller (1995) views the specialist nurse in an intensive therapy unit (ITU) as an 'adjunct' — a person who can link the wealth of knowledge between specialisms. In this case, the link is between the ITU and the ward, ensuring patients receive continuity and quality care, while supporting ward staff.

Nurse specialists have been described, among other things, as: agent of change, skilled communicator, researcher, clinician and leader (Carver, 1998; Miller, 1995). And more specific to their specialist field are added: clinical expert, resource, consultant and advocate (Poole, 1996). They collaborate with physicians and other disciplines to deliver comprehensive, seamless quality care, while serving as a role model to other staff through their ability to research problems rigorously and apply research to their clinical practice (Langstaff and Gray, 1997; Miller, 1995).

At this point it may help to look at some concrete examples of how areas of specialist practice relate to education, training and accountability, and how overall greater levels of collaborative practice are achieved.

## Advanced neonatal nurse practitioner (ANNP)

The ANNP role first came about in the USA because of a shortage of neonatal doctors and a desire by neonatal nurses to exercise a greater degree of autonomy (Dillon and George, 1997). In the UK a similar situation arose, along with the need to reduce junior doctors' working hours from 80-plus a week. According to Zukowsky and Coburn (1990) ANNPs 'have taken further education and training which allows them increased responsibilities for the care of the high risk infant'.

Research examining their interaction with medical colleagues, patients and the organisation showed genuine benefits. Mutual respect and trust developed between ANNPs and their consultant colleagues, and high levels of job satisfaction were reported. Challenges included a sense of isolation from other nursing colleagues who viewed the ANNPs as elitist (Dillon and George, 1997).

The view of the nurse as 'doctor's handmaiden' has largely been eradicated from many progressive interdisciplinary relationships, but sometimes this criticism has been levelled at specialist nurses for taking on traditional medical/technical roles (Denner, 1995). It is further complicated where a lack of role definition exists, and can contribute to feelings of isolation (Holmes, 1994; Miller, 1995).

In an earlier study of attitudes to ANNPs, physicians, nurses and parents all described benefits from the role (Trotter and Danaher, 1994). Education for the ANNP is through the English National Board (A19) course.

## Nurse endoscopists

The growth of nurse endoscopists is a natural progression for experienced nurses working in the field of gastroenterology/hepatology and endoscopy nursing. A US study explored nurses' skills in performing upper and lower gastrointestinal endoscopy and, compared with medical colleagues, no statistical differences were found in the range of competencies required for flexible sigmoidoscopy (Froerer, 1998).

In the UK the growing demand for gastroenterology services has led to a number of nurse specialists working in either upper or lower gastrointestinal endoscopy specialisms. Training to practice as a nurse endoscopist requires the completion of the English National Board (A187) course, with practical and theoretical components of assessment by a gastroenterologist clinical adviser, who is a consultant.

In many aspects the nurse endoscopist's role and function is similar to other nurse specialists — participation in research, education of and collaboration with other interdisciplinary professionals and dissemination of information. More specific aspects of the role are the advanced assessment, diagnosis and treatment of patients, and patient education.

## Cardiac pain assessment nurses

The management of acute myocardial infarction (MI) has been revolutionised by thrombolytic therapy (Quinn, 1996). This shows benefits if the patient meets specific criteria and treatment is begun early (FTT, 1994) with maximum benefit when therapy starts within the first hour of symptom onset (Morris, 1993).

The responsibility for assessing patients with suspected MI and prescription of a thrombolytic drug has traditionally rested with medical staff, often resulting in unnecessary delays (Birkhead, 1992). In some centres assessing patients' suitability for thrombolysis has now developed into a specialist nursing role (Alderman,1996; Flisher, 1995), significantly reducing delays. In at least one centre, specialist nurses have also taken on responsibility for prescribing thrombolytic therapy according to strict protocols (Caunt, 1996).

## Other examples

Wood et al (1997) discuss how a multi-disciplinary approach was used to develop an enteral feeding protocol in an intensive care unit and Hurst (1996) describes how a collaborative style was used to promote a seamless approach to patient discharge planning.

# ACCOUNTABILITY

As well as being professionally accountable to the UKCC, specialist nurses have a contractual accountability to their employer and the law for their actions (UKCC, 1996).

All nurses are responsible for determining their own level of competence, irrespective of their chosen speciality. Nurses can 'transcend' the boundaries of practice provided adequate training and assessment has been undertaken (RCN and RCP, 1996). Any nurse who chooses to do so would have to provide the same standards of care expected of a doctor (Dimond, 1995).

The case of the theatre sister in Truro who was disciplined as a result of performing parts of an appendectomy operation fuelled debate in national and professional press. The sister in this case was acting in the capacity of surgeon's assistant which, following investigation, did not meet the criteria laid down in the National Association of Theatre Nurses (NATN) guidelines. Therefore the sister was disciplined (Campbell, 1995).

Although distressing for her, this case prompted real discussion regarding the boundaries of nursing and professional and public perceptions. There are a number of lessons. Nurses need to gain a firm understanding of their remit and boundaries of their role, together with the elements of accountability within that role when pursuing specialism in collaboration with medical colleagues.

Interdisciplinary protocols are viewed as an essential management tool (Tingle, 1995) and the NHS executive (1996) supports their use. If an incident of alleged neglect occurs in the course of practice, vicarious liability provides the nurse specialist with support. This means the employer can be sued instead of the employee personally, provided that the latter has been acting in the course of their employment and within the boundaries, protocols and policies agreed within their role (Elliott Pennels, 1998).

## FACING UP TO DIFFICULTIES

There is no doubt that barriers to collaboration between doctors and nurses do exist. Traditionally the blame has rested with the physicians, although the education and socialisation of nursing may also have unintentionally built barriers. This has been aggravated by nursing being promoted as an independent and unique discipline, with many nursing curricula failing to encompass the role of the nurse as part of a team. Critics argue that at the pre-registration stage of education 'seeds of distrust and disrespect' for medical colleagues are planted and the socialisation that accompanies this process results in physicians being viewed as the enemy (Henneman, 1995).

Past attitudes can help to clarify why and how nursing and medicine have chosen to move towards an equal power relationship.

Stein et al (1990) reflect on the 'doctor-nurse game' first described in 1967, and how relationships between nurses and doctors have evolved since then. Doctors were traditionally classed as superior to nurses, with all interactions carefully managed so as not to upset the hierarchy. Nurses at this time endeavoured to have initiative while remaining passive.

They were allowed to make recommendations to physicians, which then had to look as if they had been the physician's idea. Open disagreement between the players was to be avoided at all costs. Physicians who needed advice had to ask for it without appearing to. Rewards of the game included: an efficient doctor-nurse team; the physician being able to use the nurse as a valuable consultant; and self-esteem and professional satisfaction for the nurse. If either side failed to play the game, however, the relationship deteriorated.

Nowadays most nurses refuse to play the game because of changed expectations of the value and practice of nursing.

Traditional power struggles within nurse-doctor relationships contribute explicitly to the sense of detachment, competitiveness and lack of co-operation between professions (Walsh and Walsh, 1998). Breaking through preconceived notions of what nursing is, its position within the interdisciplinary team and its unique contribution to health care is a challenge for all nurses.

Education is the main vehicle for change. Nurse education has moved from hospital-based schools to universities. Graduate and diploma nursing courses have pushed nursing closer to true professionalisation. But reactions to this transition are not always supportive. Hay (1994) argues: 'Nursing has undergone a dangerous quasi-intellectualisation over the last few years. Clinical autonomy has become the goal, self-improvement the spur, and service to the patient the abandoned policy of yesterday.'

Recognising that change often attracts criticism, Neubauer (1995) suggests nurses drop the victim mentality and seize the opportunity to change traditional widespread perceptions of nursing by articulating its value and contribution to the interdisciplinary team.

A study by Walsh and Walsh (1998) evaluated the 'team climate' of a group of professionals for practice development accreditation. They identified several barriers to collaboration, including: a lack of shared vision, tribal loyalties and a need to invest in individual development. They concluded that team building was necessary before accreditation and collaboration could take place.

## COLLABORATIVE CASE NOTES

A collaborative approach to patient records was introduced in the 1980s when a 'care map' document was developed for inpatients as a variation of total quality management.

Duplication of data collection and transmission of records, and incomplete and contradictory records were among communication problems highlighted in a report by the Clinical Systems Group (1998), led by chief nursing officer for England, Yvonne Moores, and then chief medical officer, Sir Kenneth Calman. They found that record keeping was regarded by the nursing profession as a 'chore' instead of a 'skill' and that paper and computer records were often badly kept and contradicted each other. The report called for better training for medical and nursing students and expressed a desire for all professional bodies to work together to agree a common method of record-keeping and adopt a more collaborative approach to documentation.

Collaborative case notes should flow naturally from an interdisciplinary, holistic approach to the assessment, planning, implementation and evaluation of care (Finnegan, 1993). The introduction of collaborative care plans has benefited patients and clients, providing more holistic care and continuity. It has also improved communication between disciplines (Johnson, 1997; Morgan, 1997).

Ignatavicius and Hausman (1995) describe clinical care pathways as 'interdisciplinary plans of care that outline the optimal sequencing and timing of interventions for patients with a particular diagnosis, procedure or symptom'. Such care pathways allow flexibility and enable concise, streamlined, standardised documentation to be made available to all patients. This requires investment of time and commitment from all team members.

Clinical pathways can also be used as a risk management tool. Unco-ordinated, fragmented documentation may result in misunderstandings, complaints and litigation.

# RESOLVING CONFLICTS

For collaboration to advance, differences of opinion need to be resolved constructively (Walsh and Walsh, 1998). A round-table approach fosters open channels of communication and provides a forum for problem-solving discussions (Cooke, 1997).

A 'safe' environment is needed, where interactions between disciplines take place without fear of causing offence or breaching group confidentiality. In the experiences of Damien et al (1997) monthly round-table discussions provided a supportive and action-orientated structure for disciplines to understand each other's role. Benefits included an accelerated route to problem-solving and conflict resolution, and enhanced communication about how to improve care quality.

Clinical supervision can also be instrumental in reducing health workers' stress levels (Butterworth and Faugier, 1997). Coping with personal stress while working as part of a collaborative team is vital. One-to-one supervision requires investment in time and resources. An alternative is team or group supervision. Though evidence on this is sparse, one study conducted in a mental health setting found the following benefits:

- interdisciplinary support;
- improved skill development;
- improved team building;
- the impression of 'sharing' across disciplines.

The clinical supervision relationships were developed among members of the same discipline. But there did appear to be scope to move relationships across disciplines and into a team forum (Thomas and Reid, 1995).

Keeping collaborative relationships and practices alive and well requires commitment and a shared vision. Learning to work together, resolve problems and plan for ongoing developments through regular discussion forums is vital for continued success.

# CONCLUSION

Collaboration is a challenge to all disciplines within health care. Despite evidence of collaborative partnerships achieving successful outcomes, it is truly demanding. Within nursing, practitioners are accountable for their actions, and the choice not to work collaboratively could ultimately mean that patient/client care is not improved.

Nurses must remember they have a duty to collaborate under Clause 6. If asked the question: 'Do you work in a collaborative and cooperative manner with health care colleagues?', most nurses would answer 'yes'. And on a day-to-day basis this is probably true.

But the challenge comes with change, where new and uncertain practices threaten to upset the status quo. The emergence of specialist nurse roles has in many ways helped to bridge the gap between medicine and nursing, with patients receiving specialist interventions and care from a holistic perspective. Negative attitudes and in certain cases tribal conflicts within nursing, along with suspicion by medical colleagues, have been barriers to collaboration. Misconceptions and misunderstandings of interdisciplinary roles have further fuelled problems.

Time, energy, commitment and organisational support are vital if true collaboration is to be achieved, built on a foundation of mutual respect and understanding of the unique contribution each interdisciplinary member brings to the team.

For nursing to continue to develop as a profession, it must focus itself within the interdisciplinary team and promote its uniqueness through articulating the many facets of its role. As a profession, nursing needs to accept and support the variety of new roles and view the challenges of merging medicine and nursing as not status-enhancing but patient/client care-enhancing.

## References

Alderman, C. (1996) Heart to heart. *Nursing Standard*; 10: 34, 22-23.

Autar, R. (1996) The scope of professional practice in specialist practice. *British Journal of Nursing*; 5: 16, 984-990.

Bagg, J., Schmitt, M. (1988) Collaboration between nurses and physicians. *Image*; 20: 1, 145-149.

Beattie, J., Check, J., Gibson, T. (1996) The politics of collaboration as viewed through the lens of a collaborative nursing research project. *Journal of Advanced Nursing*; 24: 4, 682-687.

Behi, R., Nolan, M. (1995) Sources of knowledge in nursing. *British Journal of Nursing*; 4: 3, 141-159.

Birkhead, J. (1992) Time delays in provision of thrombolytic therapy in six district hospitals. *British Medical Journal*; 30: 5, 445-448.

Briggs, A. (1972) *Briggs report of the committee on nursing*. London: HMSO/DHSS.

Butterworth, T., Faugier, J. (1997) *Clinical supervision and mentorship in nursing*. London: Stanley Thorne Ltd.

Campbell, L. (1995) Chairman's message. *British Journal of Theatre Nursing*; 4: 12, 1.

Carver, J. (1998) The perceptions of registered nurses on role expansion. *Intensive and Critical Care Nursing*; 3: 1, 82-90.

Castledine, G. (1993) Nurses should welcome a wider scope of practice. *British Journal of Nursing*; 2: 13, 686-687.

Caunt, J. (1996) The Advanced Nurse Practitioner in CCU. *Care of the Critically Ill*; 12: 4, 136-139.

Clinical Systems Group (1998) *Improving clinical communications*. Wetherby: Clinical Systems Group.

Cooke, C. (1997) Reflections on the health care team: My experiences in a multidisciplinary program. *Pulse*; 277: 13, 1091.

Damien, F.J., Smith, M.F., Krauss, B.S. (1997) Conscious sedation roundtable: A collaborative practice model for problem solving in the emergency department. *Journal of Emergency Nursing*; 23: 2, 153-155.

Davies, C. (1996) A new vision of professionalism. *Nursing Times*; 92: 46, 54-56.

Denner, S. (1995) Extending professional practice: benefits and pitfalls. *Nursing Times*; 91: 14, 27-29.

Department of Health and Social Security (1977) *The extended role of the clinical nurse*. London: DHSS, HC(77)22.

Dillon, A., George, S. (1997) Advanced neonatal practitioners in the UK: Where are they and what do they do? *Journal of Advanced Nursing*; 25: 2, 257-264.

Dimond, B. (1995) *Legal aspects of nursing* (2nd ed). London: Prentice Hall.

Elliott Pennels, C.J. (1998) Specialist nurses. *Professional Nurse*; 13: 6, 382-383.

Fagin, C.M. (1992) Collaboration between nurses and physicians: No longer a choice. *Academic Medicine*; 67: 5, 295-303.

Fibrinolytic Therapy Trialists (FTT) Collaborative Group (1994) Indications for fibrinolytic therapy in suspected acute myocardial infarction: Collaborative overview of early mortality and major morbidity results from all randomised trials of more than 1000 patients. *Lancet*; 343: 8893, 311-322.

Finnegan, L. (1993) Collaborative care planning. *The British Journal of Health Care Computing & Information Management*; 10: 5, 104-111.

Flisher, D. (1995) Fast track: early thrombolysis. *British Journal of Nursing*; 4: 10, 562-565.

Ford, K., Middleton, J., Palmer, B., Farrington, A. (1997) Primary health care workers: training needs in mental health. *British Journal of Nursing*; 6: 21, 1244-1250.

Froerer, R. (1998) The nurse endoscopist: Reality or fiction? *Gastroenterology Nursing*; 21: 1, 14-20.

Hay, R. (1994) A nurse's place. *Nursing Standard*; 8: 27, 42-43.

Henneman, E.A. (1995) Nurse-physician collaboration: A post structuralist view. *Journal of Advanced Nursing*; 22: 2, 359-363.

Holmes, S. (1994) Development of the cardiac surgeon assistant. *British Journal of Nursing*; 3: 5, 204-210.

Hurst, S. (1996) Multidisciplinary discharge planning. *Professional Nurse*; 12: 2, 113-116.

Ignatavicius, D.D., Hausman, K.A. (1995) *Clinical pathways for collaborative practice*. Philadelphia: W B Saunders Co.

Johnson, S. (1997) *Pathways of Care*. Oxford: Blackwell Science.

King, L., Lee, J.L., Henneman, E. (1993) A collaborative practice model for critical care. *American Journal of Critical Care*; 2: 6, 444-449.

Langstaff, D., Gray, B. (1997) Flexible roles: A new model in nursing practice. *British Journal of Nursing*; 6: 11, 635-638.

Lorentzon, M. (1998) The way forward: Nursing research or collaborative health care research. *Journal of Advanced Nursing*; 27: 4, 675-676.

Makaram, S. (1995) Interpersonal co-operation. *Medical Education*; 29: Supp. 1, 65-69.

Miccola, M.A., Spanier, A.M. (1993) Critical care management in the 1990s: Making collaborative practice work. *Critical Care Clinics*; 9: 3, 443-453.

Miller, S. (1995) The clinical nurse specialist: A way forward? *Journal of Advanced Nursing*; 22: 3, 494-501.

Morgan, U. (1997) The introduction of collaborative care plans. *Professional Nurse*; 12: 8, 556-558.

Morris, D.C. (1993) Early treatment of myocardial infarction: The myths, the mystery and the magic. *Heart Disease and Stroke*; 2: 4, 308-312.

Neubauer, J. (1995) The value of nursing. *Journal of Nursing Management*; 3: 3, 301-305.

NHS Executive (1996) *Promoting clinical effectiveness*. Leeds: NHS Executive.

Parkin, P.A.C. (1995) Nursing the future: A re-examination of the professionalisation thesis in the light of some recent developments. *Journal of Advanced Nursing*; 21: 3, 561-567.

Poole, K. (1996) The evolving role of the clinical nurse specialist within the comprehensive breast cancer centre. *Journal of Clinical Nursing*; 5: 6, 341-349.

Quinn, T. (1996) Myocardial infarction: Knowledge for practice. *Nursing Times*; 92: 6, Supp. 1-4.

Quinn, T., Thompson, D.R. (1995) The changing role of the nurse. *Care of the Critically Ill*; 11: 2, 48-49.

Roberts, S.L. (1987) The role of collaborative nursing diagnosis in critical care. *Critical Care Nurse*; 7: 1, 81-86.

Royal College of Nursing and Royal College of Physicians (1996) Skill sharing, joint statement from the Royal College of Physicians of London and the RCN. *Journal of the Royal College of Physicians of London*; 30: 2, 57.

Salvage, J. (1985) *The politics of nursing*. London: Heinemann Medical.

Salvage, J. (1988) Professionalisation — or struggle for survival? A consideration of current proposals for the reform of nursing in the UK. *Journal of Advanced Nursing*; 13: 3, 515-519.

Salvage, J., Wright, S.G. (1995) *Nursing development units: A force for change*. London: RCN Publications.

Stein, L., Watts, D., Howell, T. (1990) The doctor-nurse game revisited. *New England Journal of Medicine*; 322: 8, 546-549.

Thomas, B., Reid, J. (1995) Multidisciplinary clinical supervision. *British Journal of Nursing*; 4: 15, 883-885.

Tingle, J. (1995) Clinical protocols and the law. *Nursing Times*; 91: 29, 27-28.

Trotter, C., Danaher, D. (1994) Neonatal nurse practitioners: A descriptive evaluation of an advanced practice role. *Neonatal Network*; 13: 1, 39 -47.

UKCC (1989) *Exercising Accountability*. London: UKCC.

UKCC (1992) *Scope of Professional Practice*. London: UKCC.

UKCC (1994) *The future of professional practice: Policy statement*. London: UKCC.

UKCC (1996) *Position statement on clinical supervision for Nursing and Health Visitors*. London: UKCC.

Vanclay, L. (1998) Team working in primary care. *Nursing Standard*; 12: 20, 37-38.

Walsh, M., Walsh, A. (1998) Practice development units: A study of teamwork. *Nursing Standard*; 12: 33, 35-38.

Wood, A., Hill, K., McKenna, E., Wilson, E. (1997) Developing a multidisciplinary protocol for entral feeding. *Nursing in Critical Care*; 2: 3, 126-128.

Woodrow, P. (1997) Nursing perspectives for intensive care. *Intensive and Critical Care Nursing*; 13: 2, 151-155.

Wright, S.G. (1995) The role of the nurse: Extended or expanded? *Nursing Standard*; 9: 33,25-29.

Zukowsky, K., Coburn, C. (1990) Neonatal nurse practitioners: Who are they? *Journal of Obstetric Gynecologic and Neonatal Nursing*; 20: 2, 128-132.

## Recommended reading

Allen, C.V. (1997) *Nursing process in collaborative practice: A problem-solving approach* (2nd ed). Connecticut: Appleton and Lange.

Wilson, J. (1997) *Integrated care management: The path to success*. London: Butterworth Heinemann.

# Clause 7: My patient – my person

**Patricia Black**

> '...recognise and respect the uniqueness and dignity of each patient and client, and respond to their need for care, irrespective of their ethnic origin, religious beliefs, personal attributes, the nature of their health problems or any other factor.'

Clause 7 describes the heart of good nursing practice — the respect for each patient's individuality and our care for them in a non-judgemental or selective way. The nursing process facilitates the planning of appropriate care and enables the nurse to respect the uniqueness and dignity of each client.

The feminist theorist Nel Noddings (1984) argues that the caring ethic has its roots in a 'feminine' approach, 'which is not to say, of course, that it cannot be shared by men, any more than we should care to say that traditional moral systems cannot be embraced by women. But an ethic of caring arises, I believe, out of our experience as women, just as the traditional logical approach to ethical problems arises more obviously from masculine experience'.

Responding to the patient's care needs is a complex, intricate and subjective process that requires an understanding of the patient's world (Noddings, 1984). By recognising and respecting each patient's individuality nurses indicate their desire to get to know and help the patient. Noddings distinguishes between situations where caring appears to come naturally and those when caring requires an effort from the nurse.

Virginia Henderson (1987) suggests that nursing is primarily an intimate and essential service and, in an age characterised by change and ambiguity, nurses must learn to develop their caring skills. In 1977 the Department of Health and Social Security (DHSS) suggested that whatever happened at the periphery of nurses' work, caring for the patient would always be their central task.

Studies since then have shown caring to be at the centre of nursing. In 1981, Ford asked 200 nurses to define caring and describe their own caring behaviour (Ford, 1981). Two categories of caring emerged:

▷ a genuine concern for the well-being of another;

▷ the giving of oneself.

In further research, Ray (1981) observed and identified caring in clinical settings, and systemised caring into four categories:

▷ psychological — cognitive and affective;

▷ practical — technical and social organisation;

▷ interactional — social and physical;

▷ philosophical — spiritual, ethical and cultural.

## How can nurses recognise and protect the dignity of patients?

The unthinking actions of health care professionals may inadvertently lead to patients feeling undignified or experiencing a loss of self-respect. Because a particular test, examination or procedure is always done in a certain way the practitioner may not stop to consider that it may be undignified or embarrassing for the patient.

For example, a teenage girl who has undergone colectomy with an ileostomy is likely to feel embarrassed and upset when the surgical ward round comes to her room to see how she is progressing. The team may comprise of young male house officers and older male consultants who expect her to expose her abdomen, ileostomy and buttocks for examination.

The nurse can help the patient maintain her dignity by asking her before the ward round if she wants all the doctors in her room, and by then explaining to the surplus doctors that their presence will not be required. The nurse can also make sure that the patient is wearing pants before the bed covers are pulled down.

The loss of dignity is a common topic for radio and television comedies, especially in the area of bodily functions that do not work. Jokes about enemas, sigmoidoscopies and stoma bags may be crude and seem funny, but for patients who have had to undergo these procedures, they can be upsetting and embarrassing and undermine their dignity and self respect.

As a society we are not used to revealing our most intimate bodily functions to a stranger who may be as young as our grand-daughter. The nurse can overcome this by treating the patient with dignity and distancing themselves appropriately. Girard (1988) recognises the need to establish precisely how much distance the patient is entitled to to feel respected. To help the patient overcome an invasion of privacy, nurses must never show contempt or distaste, and should treat every procedure seriously and as worthy of their professional skill and expertise.

Parent (1988) defines privacy as: 'the condition of not having undocumented personal knowledge about one possessed by others.' This might involve facts about a person known to his/her close circle of friends and relatives and a few professional associates, but which the patient/client would not want spread further. It could include details of sexual proclivity, excessive alcohol consumption or drug habit, marriage breakdown or mental health problems.

Documented information about an individual is that which is in the public domain, such as in newspapers or public records. Information collected and held on a general practitioner or hospital medical file is not in the public domain and unauthorised access is prevented. Health care professionals cannot ignore the need for privacy and their primary duty is to protect the rights of patients entrusted to their care.

# CROSS-CULTURAL CARE-GIVING

Although aspects of caring for ethnic-minority groups feature increasingly in the nursing curriculum, some nurses still find that caring for such patients challenges their own beliefs and values.

Burrows (1983) points out that in many areas the health service remains geared primarily to the needs of the indigenous white population, reflecting society's failure to acknowledge that Britain is a multi-racial society. Failure to include multicultural perspectives as an integral part of the curriculum in nurse education 'represents a form of institutionalised racism since it inevitably results in sub-standard care being given to those from minority groups whose needs are not adequately met'.

All UK residents are entitled to free health care at the time of need and point of delivery, as part of the NHS's underlying philosophy. But there is a long way to go before the *Health of the Nation* (Department of Health, 1993) requirements for professionals to meet the needs of the ethnic minorities, refugees and asylum seekers is achieved.

Nurses' ethnocentric beliefs about western health standards and biomedicine are a potential barrier to the therapeutic interaction between health care professionals and ethnic-minority patients (Bonaparte, 1979).

When a nurse is unable to interpret the way a patient from another culture is responding to their illness and health care, it can compound the problem. A patient who feels misunderstood is less likely to comply with care, and thus more likely to be labelled 'difficult'.

The term 'cultural relativism' describes the implicit principle underlying conceptual approaches to cross-cultural care-giving by health professionals. Baker (1997) suggests that cultural relativism is an outlook which believes people's behaviour should be judged only from the context of their own cultural system. It is seen as a buffer against parochialism, encouraging openness towards others and resulting in flexibility when cultural differences are encountered.

A dilemma incongruent with nursing culture and abhorrent to western women and women's groups is the excision of female genitalia. However, it is a cultural tradition in parts of Africa, where it is linked to female purity and family honour. Some immigrant communities are now beginning to import the practice into western European countries and nurses face dilemmas in making judgements in cross-cultural situations.

How do nurses react when they are approached with requests for help in a young girl's circumcision? Should the nurse provide a culturally congruent response or be ethnocentric? There are several issues to think about.

One possibility would be to impose a penal law against this custom. But not only would this penetrate the intimacy of families and impose the host country's way of thinking and living on foreigners, it may actually have an adverse effect.

At present, there is no legislation to outlaw the custom. But if under judicial guidance it is felt that circumcision is better under a sterile procedure, that is in a hospital, this may prevent the child being illegally removed back to the country of origin, where the operation would be done in less than favourable conditions.

In cross-cultural encounters, the nurse will interpret the patient through his or her prejudices, and the patient will interpret the encounter through his or her culture and tradition. Neither interpretation is definitive and both the nurse and patient may change their views after dialogue and experience. Cultural beliefs, values and customs are never stationary but are fluid, and a cross-cultural encounter may result in a better understanding of shared meaning.

While differences in health between social classes have been long recognised — with social classes A, B and C experiencing better health than D and E — it is now also accepted that there are differences in health within and between ethnic-minority groups.

Smaje (1995) suggests that people from ethnic minorities face the dual problems of racism and an increased likelihood of experiencing poverty and disadvantage, both of which affect their health. Often enforced migration, such as that of refugees and asylum seekers, will produce different health experiences — they may not seek out or trust health care workers for fear of being reported to the authorities. Nurses looking after refugees need to be aware of the conditions under which they may have fled and understand their specific problems.

In the past patients were usually cared for by nurses and doctors from their own area, who may have lived and practised in the same regions all their lives. Nowadays, nurses, doctors and patients may be from different cities, regions, countries, religions and cultures. Somehow they must meet the challenge of understanding each other first, before attempting to anticipate the needs of patients who come from different ethnic backgrounds. Although it is unrealistic to expect every nurse to be an expert on the cultural and religious needs of all ethnic minorities with whom they come into contact, they should be familiar with the basic tenets of the major cultures and religions of immigrant populations, especially communities prevalent in their locality.

Occasionally a nurse from one ethnic-minority may care for a patient with profound religious or political views that are an anathema to that nurse. It makes sense for this nurse not to have to care for this patient, as care may be compromised or treatment affected. The ward manager should be sensitive and aware if a nurse has a conflict of belief that will affect the care the patient receives. The issue should be discussed, and it may be better for the nurse to be allocated to other patients. Managers must react flexibly and view the circumstances of each case, but nurses should be encouraged to discuss possible conflicts and not just carry on giving poor substandard care, or ignoring the patient.

When some immigrant patients share their 'private lives' with health care staff — often the nurse — the patient may come to see the nurse as part of their extended family, and may want to offer gifts, or may feel it appropriate to ask favours. Among some Middle Eastern immigrants this can symbolise trust and a deeper level of relationship (Lipson and Meleis, 1989). But it can make nurses feel they have been put in a difficult position.

Culture and religion can affect what a patient may or may not eat while in hospital. Patients may leave food uneaten because they fear it contains ingredients forbidden to them. They may not be able to read, write or understand English, and therefore unable to order culturally acceptable food from the menu. A ward clerk or nurse may order what they believe to be appropriate, thinking they are helping. In fact, by imposing their often limited view and knowledge of the patient and jumping to conclusions, they may be causing harm.

Take the following case of a nurse who thought she was being sensitive to an Asian patient's cultural needs. The Hindu patient complained to his doctor that the food he had been given for the last ten days was inedible. All he had been offered were vegetable curries, and they were giving him terrible abdominal pain after his bowel surgery. The doctor spoke to the patient's named nurse and it transpired that she had automatically assumed that because the patient was a Hindu he was vegetarian and had ordered accordingly on his behalf. In fact the patient was a westernised non-orthodox Hindu and had always enjoyed a good western diet, including meat every day.

This illustrates very clearly how the practitioner must beware of making stereotypical assumptions based on background knowledge acquired about a certain aspect of a person's life, whether it be ethnicity, religion, age, sexual proclivity or health status.

# RELIGIOUS BELIEFS

Sampson (1982) suggests that nurses do not deliberately neglect the customs and spiritual beliefs of their patients. In general they are much too badly informed in this area to do anything deliberately.

Nurses should familiarise themselves with the basic outlooks of the major religions and the differences between religious sects. Religious artefacts should be treated with care and holy books should be accessible, especially in the case of baptism or death. A facility for quiet contemplation, meditation or prayer should be available on the ward or in an ancillary area.

Occasionally a Muslim patient may want their bed turned towards Mecca. This may not be feasible on a Nightingale ward or four-bedded unit, so a suitable side ward may be more convenient.

Religious beliefs which may not be paramount to the patient during their lifetime may suddenly come to have new meaning during serious illness or approaching death. An appropriate nursing model of care will allow a patient's spirituality to become apparent.

How nurses react and what they say to the patient and the family at the time of death will often be remembered many years later. Nurses should learn the names of the key books of each major religion, in case the family or relatives request it at a time of impending death.

Knowing what to do at the time of death and how to treat the body is essential. When undertaking last offices for a patient, the nurse must be aware of religious rites or observances. For example, if the deceased person is Jewish, the nurse must not touch the body at all, but should call the rabbi.

Difficulties can be created on a ward when a dying patient has family and friends wailing at the bedside, which may be culturally appropriate for them. In an open ward this can upset other patients and their visitors. Finding a more suitable environment may be a challenge for ward staff, managers and the organisational structure.

Islam can be found in nearly every country of the world and is a rich, dynamic religious tradition practised by a billion people, making it the second-largest world religion. Every nurse is likely at some stage to look after a Muslim patient. The foundation of belief and practice is the Qur'an, and patients may strictly adhere to this.

For Muslims, termination of pregnancy and organ donation are strong taboos, and in situations where the life of the patient may be at risk by not agreeing to surgical intervention, the nurse may experience cognitive dissonance and feel very uncomfortable caring for the patient and the family.

The Jehovah's Witnesses' belief in prohibiting the administration of blood or plasma to themselves, their children or next of kin can often cause dissonance with health care professionals. It can cause concern for staff when surgery is needed or when the patient is a child who needs regular transfusions, as in the case of leukaemia. If necessary, legal action may be required to make the child a ward of court, causing distress to the child, family and nurses involved in the care of the patient.

Some ethnic cultures combine their own medical systems with those of western medicine, and nurses need to be aware of their beliefs and approaches to illness and health care. The social and cultural aspects of medical pluralism that occur in groups of ethnic minorities cannot be studied in isolation from other aspects of that society, especially its religious, political, and economic organisation.

As well as the western biomedical system, alternative systems such as herbalism, homoeopathy, and spiritual healing may be recognised by ethnic-minority groups. Each can be termed as a medical sub-culture which has its own way of explaining and treating ill health. These sub-cultures, with their own healers, may be indigenous to a particular ethnic-minority group.

Nursing care should promote an environment in which these values, customs and spiritual beliefs are respected. Nurses should be aware that in some cases, where there is doubt or argument over whether the patient believes an action is morally right, he or she may choose to consult the appropriate religious authority to decide on a medical issue, rather than a physician.

In many immigrant and ethnic groups people interact by relationship rather than role. Often consent forms pose a problem. Asking some Middle

Eastern patients to sign a consent form implies that the nurse or doctor lacks trust in the patient's word.

# PEOPLE'S PERSONAL ATTRIBUTES

## Older people

In Britain old age is often regarded as a negative experience, with elderly people seen as unproductive and a burden (Carroll and Brue, 1993). Nurses who have only worked with elderly people during their careers often adopt a paternalistic approach to caring. A nurse or care team makes decisions for the patient, negating their independence and autonomy. Patients' requests may go unheeded because the practitioners consider that they know better.

Research examining student nurses' attitudes towards old people in hospital (Field, 1986) found that nurses frequently exhibited paternalistic attitudes towards their patients, and expressions of anxiety were often ignored.

Many nurses wrongly believe that accidents will result if elderly patients are allowed to make decisions on matters such as walking unaided, not being confined to a chair restrained by a table, not being kept in a bed with cot sides and not taking chemical-confining drugs. They fear litigation by patients' families and the risk of hospitals or homes incurring financial losses through compensation. This attitude leads to ritualistic routines and completely task-orientated days for ward or home care staff, who see feeding, dressing and toileting as a necessary nuisance.

To judge whether they are treating an elderly patient with respect, nurses should ask themselves the following:

- Am I being fair and impartial to this patient?
- Is the patient able to make some of their own choices safely?
- Am I doing this for the patient, or because we are busy and it is quicker for me to do it?
- Do I reject this person because I do not like or understand their behaviour?

## Ethnic-minority patients with mental illness

Racism in the mental health services can compound distress for the patient and their family. The Department of Health (1993) has recognised that institutionalised racism over the last 25 years has caused problems in service access and responses. According to the RCN (1996a) these include:

- Alternatives to hospital admission are less likely to be offered to all minority ethnic groups.

- Black and ethnic-minority people are more likely to be detained under the provisions of the Mental Health Act.

- Black and ethnic-minority people are more likely to be regarded as 'dangerous'.

- Black and ethnic-minority people are more likely to be detained in locked wards.

- There is a shortage of bilingual professionals and skilled trained interpreters with an understanding of racial, cultural and mental health issues.

## Refusal to eat

Occasionally the nurse may have to look after patients, including elderly people, who refuse to eat or drink. This is a way of telling staff that the patient is still in control. The patient may be objecting to being in an institution or not being allowed to decide where and when to eat. Reasons for refusing food and drink include: socio-cultural problems that have not been recognised by staff; delusions; staff attitudes or actions; medication side-effects; lack of dentures; or elimination of odours at meal times.

In young patients with anorexia, treatment may begin with removal of all privileges, which are only reinstated as food is eaten and weight gained. This can turn into a battle between staff and patient and again the nurse can experience cognitive dissonance. Because food is so important in sustaining life, tension occurs when a person's behaviour does not match their attitude or belief system. But eating or not can provide an opportunity for the person to express independence and control which they cannot exert in other areas of their lives.

What framework can nurses use when they experience dissonance because of a conflict between personal beliefs and professional behaviour, faced with an anorexic patient near death or a patient who is refusing life-saving surgery? The patient's illogical choice seems bewildering and irrevocable. But by continually listening to the patient and their reasoning the nurse may be able to adapt their beliefs to those of the patient, or the patient's misconceptions may be corrected so their behaviour may meet the nurse's beliefs.

## Suicide and self-mutilation

The unconditional acceptance of patients' unconventional behaviour can be extremely hard when suicide and self mutilation are involved. Self-harming is not considered as a suicidal intent. Self-mutilators are usually labelled as malingerers by medical staff, and Munchausen's syndrome is deemed to be a variation on a similar theme, in which there is no physical pathology but sufferers opt to undergo polysurgery, that is, self-mutilation by proxy.

Managers and clinical supervisors should provide nurses caring for these patients with adequate clinical preparation and guidance on attitude, enabling a proper discussion about their feelings on equity and entitlement of care.

Culturally institutionalised values, organisational management and a view that nurses should only care for the *deserving* sick may result in routine medication and seclusion for this group of patients. This in turn prevents nurses being able to intervene to help the patient gain some control over their self-mutilating activities.

## Gender dysphoria

Sometimes surgeons are reluctant to be involved in reassignment surgery for people with gender dysphoria as it is seen as mutilating a healthy body. But in some NHS hospitals surgery is now undertaken routinely. Nurses caring for these patients require a high degree of professionalism and must be comfortable with their own sexuality.

Support from senior, more experienced nurses will help junior colleagues. The nurses' views should be explored so that their feelings are not detrimental to the patient's care and recovery. By being open-minded and respecting the individual's personal attributes nurses may find caring for this group a rewarding experience.

# Patients in prison

Although prisons aim to provide medical services comparable to the rest of the NHS, the prison environment must necessarily be geared to order, control and discipline. Custody reduces the prisoner's ability to take charge and be responsible for their own health, therefore prison nursing staff play an important part in providing health care to this vulnerable group. Often the nurse may perceive the prisoner to have a genuine medical problem but the assigned officer may believe the prisoner is trying to manipulate the system, seeking to relieve boredom by a visit to the medical wing.

Prison nursing staff bring their knowledge, skills and attitudes to a unique and vulnerable population and can provide a positive interface between custody and health care. Nurses must be careful not to be judgemental. As far as the Code is concerned, these patients are entitled to equitable health care, while their crime and punishment is incidental.

# Violent patients

No organisation would condone abuse of its staff, yet daily we read and hear of violence and abuse, particularly in hospital accident and emergency departments. Nurses in A&E suffer more abuse and violence than teachers and the police force, often having to put up with racist taunts, unpleasant behaviour, sexual harassment and personal attack. Yet at all times the nurse is required to treat the patient as an individual and give them respect. Having to accept this can be frustrating.

The latest RCN guidance (1996b) makes it clear that any nurse with the appropriate competence must provide care and that unpleasant behaviour often arises from mental or physical illness or the stress of continuing pain or illness. Although in some cases care could be withdrawn, managers must be flexible in each case and, if necessary, transfer the patient to another suitable area or change the care. Staff working with people who behave in this anti-social way require the support and commitment of managers at grassroots level, and from the trust, in regularly monitoring and reviewing policies on violence.

## Health problems

How do nurses respect and respond to the care needs of a patient whom they believe to be responsible for their own state of ill health?

Nurses are increasingly likely to come into contact with people who have HIV-related health problems or AIDS. Some may feel that a patient has contracted the virus because of actions they find unacceptable. Nurses must not ostracise these patients or treat them differently from others. They cannot make a conscientious objection to nursing patients with AIDS — only to carrying out specific procedures that are either contrary to their moral beliefs and values or that they feel are harmful to the patient (Rumbold, 1993).

Social stereotypical and stigmatic attitudes towards homosexuality may interfere with care giving. Research has shown that nurses are less willing to look after homosexual patients than heterosexual patients with the same illness (Kelly et al, 1988). Issues of sexual orientation and health issues must be tackled so that lesbian, gay and bisexual people receive quality health care without prejudice.

Drug takers who become pregnant are invariably a source of concern for health professionals who may question the mother's ability to care for the baby if she is still taking drugs after the birth. Many children born to drug addict mothers are at risk from neglect and the effects of a chaotic lifestyle. However, the family situation should be assessed individually and not from the premise that drug use leads to poor child care.

Nurses cannot refuse to care for patients who are promiscuous, homosexual, drug users or prostitutes because they disapprove of their lifestyle. Imposing their own values and opinions on others, and judging some patients to be less worthy than others, shows lack of respect by nurses for patients as individuals.

## CONCLUSION

Clause 7 of the Code makes it clear that it is unacceptable and unprofessional to refuse to be involved in the care of patients because of their condition, behaviour, culture, religion or age, personal belief or lifestyle.

The International Council of Nurses on Regulation: Towards 21st Century Models (ICN, 1973) suggests that health is a vital social asset and health for all should be a global objective. Nurses must respond to changing health needs and priorities in their own areas, and develop care for each patient to its fullest potential.

Trusts, PCGs and other health care organisations should ensure that nurses fulfil their role to purchasers and patients in the light of socio-political, economic and environmental changes. Managers are responsible for reappraising practice as health care needs change, to ensure nurses adopt a dynamic approach to their role and achieve their full potential in offering a service to the public.

While adhering to the principle of universality, nurses should be ready to adapt to local demographics, culture and population make-up and to be sensitive to cultural differences within that population. In recognising and respecting each patient's uniqueness and dignity, nurses should not seek to impose their own beliefs and values on patients or colleagues, and should not be easily swayed by emotive argument.

Instead they should examine their own beliefs and values, how they arrived at them. Nurses must be non-judgemental, non-selective and responsive to the rich diversity of human existence in their delivery of professional health care.

## References

Baker, C. (1997) Cultural Relativism and Cultural Diversity: Implications for Nursing Practice. *Advances in Nursing Science*: 20: 1, 3-11.

Bonaparte, B. (1979) Ego defensiveness, open-closed mindedness, and nurses' attitude toward culturally different patients. *Nursing Research*, 28: 3,166-172.

Burrows, A. (1983) Patient centred nursing care in a multi-racial society: relevance of ethnographic perspectives in nursing curricula. *Journal of Advanced Nursing*; 8: 6, 477-485.

Carroll, M., Brue, L.J. (1993) *A nurse's guide to caring for older people.* London: Macmillan.

Department of Health and Social Security (1977) *The Expanded Role of the Nurse.* H (77) 22.

Department of Health (1993) *Ethnicity and Health: Health of the Nation Guide for the NHS*. London: Department of Health.

Field, P. (1986) *Attitudes Revisited: an examination of student nurses' attitudes towards old people in hospital*. London: Royal College of Nursing.

Ford, M B. (1981) Nurse Professionals and the Caring Process. Dissertation for EdD, University of Northern Colorado. In: Burnard, P., Morrison, P. (1997) *Caring and Communicating*. Basingstoke: Macmillan Press.

Girard, M. (1988) Technical Expertise as an Ethical Form: Towards an Ethic of Distance. *Journal of Medical Ethics*; 14: 1, 25-30.

Henderson, V. (1987) The Concept of Nursing. *Journal of Advanced Nursing*; 3: 2, 113-30.

ICN (1973) International Council for Nurses (ICN) *Code for Nurses*. Geneva: ICN.

Kelly, J.A., St Lawrence, J.S., Hood, H.V., Smith, S., Cook, D.J., (1988) Nurses' Attitudes towards AIDS. *Journal of Continuing Education in Nursing*; 19: 2, 78-83.

Lipson, J., Meleis, A. (1989) Methodological Issues in Research with Immigrants. *Medical Anthropology*; 12: 1, 103-115.

Noddings, N. (1984) *Caring: A Feminine Approach to Ethics and Moral Education*. Berkeley and Los Angeles: University of California Press.

Parent, W.A. (1988) Privacy, Morality and the Law. In: Callahan, J.C. *Ethical Issues in Professional Life*. London, New York: Oxford University Press.

Ray, M.A. (1981) *A philosophical analysis of caring within nursing*. In: Leininger, M. M. (ed) Caring: an essential human need. New Jersey: Chas. B. Slack.

Rumbold, G. (1993) *Ethics in Nursing Practice*. London: Baillière Tindall.

RCN, (1996a) Race, Ethnicity and Mental Health. *Issues in Nursing and Health*; No. 31. London: RCN.

RCN (1996b) *Refusal to Nurse: Guidance for Nurses*. London: RCN.

Sampson, C. (1982) *The Neglected Ethic: Religious and cultural factors in the care of patients*. London: McGraw-Hill Book Co.

Smaje, C. (1995) *Health, Race and Ethnicity: Making sense of the Evidence*. London: King's Fund.

## Recommended reading

Hunt, G. (1995) *Ethical Issues in Nursing.* London and New York: Routledge.

Leininger, M. (1979) *Transcultural Nursing.* New York: Masoon Publications.

Sampson, C. (1982) *The Neglected Ethic; Religious and Cultural Factors in the Care of Patients.* London: McGraw-Hill Book Co (UK) Ltd. (Note: a revised, updated version of this text will be published by NT Books in 2000.)

# Clause 8: A matter of conscience

**Malcolm Khan and Michelle Robson**

> '...report to an appropriate person or authority, at the earliest possible time, any conscientious objection which may be relevant to your professional practice.'

Clause 8 is the starting point for any discussion of conscientious objection, what it means and when it may be invoked by a nurse, midwife or health visitor as a reason for not participating in a patient's medical treatment.

It does not specify situations in which conscientious objection may be correctly invoked. This is understandable, since the Code is intended to focus on the broad parameters within which the relevant health carers must function, and if it was too prescriptive that could be very restrictive. As the Scottish National Board for Nursing, Midwifery and Health Visiting observed in 1985: 'Moral dilemmas cannot be solved by issuing rules to be followed.'

The UKCC Guidelines for Professional Practice (1996) do add some flesh to the bare bones of Clause 8, as follows:

▶ Conscientious objection is directly linked to a health carer's 'personal morality or religious beliefs'. However, it will be our contention that there may be other occasions when conscientious objection may be raised.

▶ Two specific areas in which conscientious objection can be raised are in the areas of abortion (The Abortion Act, 1967) and 'technological procedures to achieve conception and pregnancy' (The Human Fertilisation and Embryology Act, 1990). (In this chapter, these two areas will be subsequently referred to as the statutory grounds for conscientious objection.)

▶ In an emergency, care should be provided by the health carer even though there may be grounds for raising a conscientious objection.

▶ It is not acceptable to refuse to be involved in a patient's care simply because of the latter's condition or behaviour, for example violent or aggressive conduct on the part of the patient, even if directed towards the health carer.

▶ Health carers should seriously consider, in the light of their personal and religious beliefs, whether certain areas of health work are suitable to them.

▶ Procedurally, if health carers have a conscientious objection to a particular treatment procedure, then they should inform their managers as soon as possible to enable alternative arrangements to be made.

# STATUTORY GROUNDS FOR CONSCIENTIOUS OBJECTION

We will now consider the two statutory grounds referred to above.

## Abortion

The Abortion Act 1967, Section 4, states the following:

> *(1) Subject to Subsection (2) of this section, no person shall be under any duty, whether by contract or by any statutory or other legal requirement, to participate in any treatment authorised by this Act to which he has a conscientious objection;*

*provided that in any legal proceedings the burden of proof of conscientious objection shall rest on the person claiming to rely on it.*

*(2) Nothing in Subsection (1) of this section shall affect any duty to participate in treatment which is necessary to save the life or to prevent grave permanent injury to the physical or mental health of a pregnant woman.*

The interpretation of the above section has only once come before the courts (Janaway v Salford Health Authority, 1989). The issue before the court was who could rely on the conscientious objection clause and what was the correct interpretation of the words 'to participate in any treatment'. The conscientious objector was a secretary who had been asked to type a letter of referral for an abortion patient. She had refused on the grounds that it was contrary to her Roman Catholic faith and had attempted to rely on the conscientious objection clause contained within the Abortion Act 1967. The House of Lords held that the word 'participate' should be given its ordinary meaning, and as such it meant taking part in the treatment administered in the hospital or other approved place. The Lords decided that typing a letter was not assisting in the abortion but simply carrying out the obligations of her employment. Consequently the secretary could not rely on Section 4.

Therefore, since the word 'participate' is to be given its ordinary meaning, most nurses will participate in treatment and be afforded the protection of Section 4, although ultimate responsibility for the termination will lie with the doctor. In a 1981 case between the Royal College of Nursing and the Department of Health and Social Security, the RCN became increasingly concerned that their members might be acting outside the confines of the Abortion Act by administering the drug prostaglandin, which stimulates contractions in the uterus leading to the expulsion of the foetus.

Although the doctor would first have to insert the catheter into the woman's uterus before the drug could be administered, the College argued that as the nurse or nurses actually administered the drug then it was their act which terminated the pregnancy. Therefore they were outside the scope of Section 1 (1) of the Abortion Act which afforded a person protection only where the termination was carried out by a registered medical practitioner. The House of Lords held, however, that Section 1(1) was to be given a wide meaning and it referred to the whole process of treatment for which the doctor had responsibility throughout. In other words, as long as the registered medical practitioner is in control of the abortion process then, even though they may not physically be present at all times during the procedure, Section 1(1) is being observed. As Michael Davies put it (Davies, 1998): 'In essence, the practitioner or that person's substitute should be available throughout the abortion process.' Consequently, a nurse who assists with any part of the abortion enjoys the same statutory protection as the doctor who initiates the abortion procedure. A nurse should not be asked to administer a prostaglandin infusion if they have a conscientious objection to it.

But it is not so clear whether the statutory protection extends to any other nursing duties connected with the procedure. For example, could the nurse refuse to dispense an abortifacient drug such as mifepristone? Almost certainly the answer is 'yes'. What about such matters as care and counselling, both before and after the procedure? It would seem evident that these are simply obligations of the nurse's employment and the rationale in the Janaway case — that is, no conscientious objection — will apply.

Finally, does the nurse ever have a duty to inform a patient that they may have a right to an abortion if, for example, they saw a patient in a distressed state? This situation is unlikely to arise since the question should really be addressed to the doctor. It was a point of discussion in Mackay v Essex Area Heath Authority (1982), where it was said that in certain circumstances a doctor was under such a duty.

Section 4, however, does not give a nurse *carte blanche* to refuse to participate in all treatments under the Abortion Act. It does not permit the nurse to refuse to take part in life-saving treatment or procedures necessary to prevent grave permanent injury to the physical or mental health of the woman. A few of these terms require clarification. 'Grave' does not necessarily mean an immediate threat; Subsection 2 of the clause only refers to that treatment which is necessary. Perhaps, therefore, it could be argued that a nurse may not opt out of abortions performed under Section 1(1)(b) of the Act — abortions carried out where it is necessary to prevent grave permanent injury to the physical or mental health of the woman — though it would seem that parliament did intend the exception to be confined to emergency cases. 'Grave permanent injury' is not defined within the scope of the Act; therefore, it is perhaps a matter of individual medical discretion as to whether this ground is present. Subsection 2 of the clause also covers the mental health of the pregnant woman.

The British Medical Association recognises that a termination may properly be advised on account of 'reactive depression', which is a pathological state of hopeless despair. According to the World Health Organisation, health includes 'the state of complete mental, physical and social well being, and not merely an absence of disease or infirmity'. Hence where the risk of continuing the pregnancy might mean the woman concerned would suffer psychological harm, then this may constitute emergency treatment within the meaning of Subsection 2. The psychological harm need not be immediate, only a risk to the patient. Nurses may realise they have to set aside their conscientious objections to assist in a life-threatening situation, where the patient's physical health is at risk, for example preventing a patient from continuing to haemorrhage. But it is unlikely that they would have envisaged being required to treat a patient at risk of a mental breakdown.

Clearly the emergency exception is very widely drawn and gynaecologists will undoubtedly act on their own initiative. Therefore, one nurse may be prevented from relying on conscientious objection because the gynaecologist believes that an abortion is necessary to preserve the mental state of the patient, whereas another nurse in the same situation is allowed to rely on the clause because a gynaecologist takes the opposite view. Certainly conscientious objection is not written in stone and whether a nurse can rely on it will, to a large extent, depend on the subjective views of others.

Additionally nurses themselves bear the burden of proving they have a conscientious objection. The Tenth Report from the Social Services Committee, Session 1989-90, recommended that a conscientious objection may be on religious, ethical or other grounds and that the government delete the provision that the burden of proof shall rest upon the person claiming it. The government's response stated (1990) that Section 4 4(1) is 'in effect a restatement of the general legal principle that it is for the person who asserts something to prove it. It is uncertain what the effect in law would be if the proviso were repealed. In the government's view it is undesirable to create any uncertainty in this difficult area of practice'.

In practice the nurse should have little difficulty in satisfying the burden of proof as most conscientious objections are likely to be on the grounds of religion. However, would the nurse have to show that they were a practising member of a religious faith and what the tenets of that faith were? Should a lapsed Roman Catholic have the same rights as someone who is fervently devout? Probably the answer is 'yes' as the Abortion Act envisages that the nurse was acting in good faith in a similar vein to the doctor performing an abortion on emergency grounds under Section 1(4).

Could an overly sensitive nurse invoke the conscientious objection clause? Would they ever have to produce a psychiatric report or, if they knew they felt this way, should they have ever taken the job anyway (provided the employers were not at fault for a misleading job description)?

Employers are not allowed to mention any abortion duties in job advertisements, but they can refer to them in the job description. Nurses are therefore likely to have been made aware of future employment duties. So, if they fail to mention their beliefs at the job interview and later, to their employer's surprise, voice a conscientious objection, should they be treated less seriously than a nurse who made their intentions known at interview? Probably not, as interview questions should be confined to professional intentions and not the candidate's personal beliefs. Anything less would surely amount to discrimination.

An article in the Daily Mail (Cole, 1998) indicated that an increasing number of young doctors are refusing, on moral grounds, to carry out abortions. The author was commenting in advance on a since-published report from the Abortion Law Reform Association (1999).

# Human Fertilisation and Embryology Act 1990, Section 38

This section of the Act says:

> *(1) No person who has a conscientious objection to participating in any activity governed by this Act shall be under any duty, however arising, to do so.*

> *(2) In any legal proceedings the burden of proof of conscientious objection shall rest on the person claiming to rely on it.*

The Human Fertilisation and Embryology Act 1990 Code of Practice adds:

> *1.15 Anyone who can show a conscientious objection to any of the activities governed by the Act is not obliged to participate in them.*

> *1.16 Prospective employees should be provided with a full job description of all the activities carried out at the centre. Interviewers should raise the issue of conscientious objection during the recruitment process and explain the right of staff to object.*

These provisions mirror Section 4 of the Abortion Act, but they do not contain an exception for the right to object in cases of emergency treatment, probably because in practice such a situation is unlikely to arise. Abortion is expressly included within the activities governed by the 1990 Act and therefore there does appear to be a conflict between Section 4 of the Abortion Act and Section 38 of the Human Fertilisation and Embryology Act.

The distinction between a valid conscientious objection and simple prejudice threatens to become blurred in the 1990 Act perhaps more than in any other area. Again the word 'participate' causes difficulties. If a nurse objects to participating in treatment must they object to all forms of treatment or just certain aspects? There does not seem to be anything manifestly wrong in nurses stating that they have no objection to assisting in those fertility processes where the embryo is created *in vivo* (inside the body), but do object to techniques such as *in vitro* fertilisation (IVF), where the embryo is created *in vitro* (in a test tube). In the latter case the objection relates to the nature of the procedure. But could a nurse object on the grounds of who is receiving the treatment? Where is the distinction between a religious belief that children should be born into a heterosexual couple's household and a moral belief that treatment should be denied to gay or single parents?

It could be argued that the Act itself is discriminatory as Section 13(5) states that no woman shall be given treatment 'unless account has been taken of the welfare of any child who may be born as a result of the treatment (including the need of that child for a father)…'. Permitting a nurse to object to treating certain people is simply a recognition of that fact.

In his series of television programmes on infertility, Professor Lord Winston described the strong resistance encountered from his staff to treating an infertile woman who was HIV positive. (The programme, *Making Babies*, was shown on BBC1 in 1997.)

This raises the issue of whether conscientious objection should only ever extend to the nature of the treatment and not to those who are receiving it. Otherwise where would the limits be drawn? The UKCC states in its Guidelines for Professional Practice (1996): 'Refusing to be involved in the care of patients because of their condition or behaviour is unacceptable. The UKCC expects all registered practitioners to be non-judgemental when providing care.'

# COMMON LAW GROUNDS FOR CONSCIENTIOUS OBJECTION

Whereas earlier examples clearly related to religious and ethical objections, there are common law grounds in some situations where it is in the nurse's own interest not to participate in particular procedures. These common law situations are not covered by statute and are arguably not true conscientious objection situations. However, we believe the phrase 'conscientious objection' should not be restrictive and should encompass all those situations where it is in the interest of the nurse not to participate in treatment.

## Criminal acts

Nurses can legally refuse to participate in a treatment procedure which they know or have reason is criminal in law. So a nurse asked to administer a lethal injection to a patient would be guilty of a criminal offence if they carried out the procedure. The rule applies even if what they are being asked to do is at the explicit request of the patient, for example, in a case of active voluntary euthanasia. Assuming no nurse would want to be found guilty of a criminal act, they should refuse to carry this out.

This is, in many respects, easier to state than apply in practice. Since the nurse is not likely to be a lawyer how will they know if the requested/ordered procedure is indeed criminal/illegal? And what about the pressure and threats to which they may be subjected to carry out the orders? In some respects these problems may be more illusory than real since the type of acts under consideration here are probably ones which nurses will know are criminal. And if the nurse knows, or has reasonable grounds to believe, that the request or order is criminal or illegal, then legally (and morally) they ought to refuse to participate.

A nurse would arguably have reasonable grounds for refusing to participate if the following factors were taken into account:

- that nurse's overall training and experience;
- the nature of the treatment to be administered;
- the fact that a similarly qualified nurse faced with a similar set of circumstances would have refused to participate.

How the nurse reacts will depend on whether they know, or have reasonable grounds to know, that a request is 'criminal'. If they know for sure, they can be more adamant in their refusal, but must still ensure their objections are clearly raised with appropriate superior personnel and properly documented. Nurses who are not certain should first query the order and, if not satisfied, follow the two steps outlined earlier.

## Negligent acts

If a nurse is asked or ordered to carry out what they know or have reasonable grounds to believe is a negligent procedure — one which will cause injury to the patient — they may have both a legal and a moral duty not to participate. For example, if on consulting a patient's chart, the nurse notes that the patient is scheduled to receive 1.5mg of a particular medication by injection, but knows or has reasonable grounds for believing that the dosage should be 0.15mg, it could be argued that the nurse would be acting negligently if they administered the higher dose unquestioningly. The nurse could be sued personally or the employers made vicariously liable for the nurse's negligent actions.

Even lawyers may not agree on the existence of legal negligence in any given situation. So the nurse would have to be very sure of the facts before refusing to participate on these grounds. It may well be that the higher dosage is on a trial basis and the medical team needs to see the patient's reaction(s) to the new treatment, in which case the nurse's refusal to participate would undoubtedly be legally and morally wrong. Invoking these grounds of refusal is fraught with problems. But if the nurse is sure of the facts then that, allied with the conditions already mentioned for reasonable knowledge of criminal acts, should enable them to act in the appropriate manner.

## Safety

An objection cannot be raised on the grounds that to be involved in the patient's treatment procedure might harm the nurse, either through infection or because the patient is of a violent disposition. However, it will be legal in the circumstances above to ask the employer for proper safeguards, training and/or information (see also Clause 13). If that is not forthcoming, in theory the employee could take legal action against the employers on the grounds that they have failed in their duty of care to their employees. But it is a non-starter to argue that the employer's deficiencies legally and morally justify non-participation in the patient's treatment and that this is an illustration of conscientious objection. In fact the nurse's refusal here would be a breach of contract.

Clause 7 of the Code explicitly states that practitioners must 'recognise and respect the uniqueness and dignity of each patient and client, and respond to their need for care, irrespective of their ethnic origin, religious beliefs, personal attributes, the nature of their health problems or any other factor'.

This approach has recently borne out by the case of the nurse who was refused compensation after being threatened by a knife-wielding patient (see Daily Mail, 30 October 1998, p17). The reason given by the magistrate was that 'to a certain extent the risk goes with the parish'.

## A clash of professional views

If nurses genuinely believe the best interests of a patient are not being served by a particular procedure, for example they think that counselling rather than medication, or the present medication rather than a new drug would be better for the patient, then they are not legally entitled to refuse to participate on the grounds of conscience. In these circumstances they will have to accept that their professional judgement is subservient to that of, for example, the consultant, unless the treatment is criminal. The nurse may query a procedure in the appropriate manner and to the appropriate person, but a refusal to participate would be seen as a breach of contract.

## Withdrawing medical treatment

The 1967 Abortion Act and the 1990 Human Fertilisation and Embryology Act, which make specific provision for conscientious objection, both relate to the beginning of life. Yet it is apparent that it is the other end of the spectrum, the end of life, which poses almost as many dilemmas for the medical profession. This was recognised by Lord Goff in Airedale NHS Trust v Bland (1993), who said: 'It is not to be forgotten, moreover, that doctors who for conscientious reasons would feel unable to discontinue life support in such circumstances can presumably, like those who have a conscientious objection to abortion, abstain from involvement in such work.'

Doctors may find it difficult to reconcile this statement with their duty under the Hippocratic Oath. However, the courts have held that in certain circumstances it will be in the patient's best interests to withdraw medical treatment and that this will be within the Oath. Clearly this statement applies equally to the nursing staff caring for such a patient. But should health carers be allowed to opt out on a case-by-case basis?

On a purely practical level a health carer withdrawing from treatment on conscientious grounds does not pose problems, as another carer can undoubtedly be found. But should it be that simple? Should a health carer arguing conscientious objection on the grounds that he or she is particularly sensitive to nursing a patient in a persistent vegetative state be able to use the conscientious objection argument? Such carers should be given sympathy in these circumstances, but distress on its own is not really grounds for conscientious objection.

## Refusing medical treatment

Where the patient is conscious and has expressly refused treatment, then the issue takes on an entirely different complexion. The principle of self-determination should always be upheld and this was recognised by the Law Commission in their report on mental incapacity (1995).

The Commission ruled out conscientious objection to refusal of treatment stating that 'if the principle of self-determination means anything, the patient's refusal must be respected'. The recent decision of St George's Healthcare NHS Trust v S (1998) lends further support to this view. Hence the nurse who has a conscientious objection to caring for the woman refusing an emergency Caesarean section or the patient who refuses any life-saving treatment must be prepared to show tolerance and should never be permitted to compromise on a patient's health care.

## WHAT TO DO IF YOU HAVE AN OBJECTION

Subject to any specific requirement(s) laid down at the health carer's workplace by the employers and subject to the broad tone of paragraph 48 of the 1996 UKCC Guidelines, we recommend the following procedural steps:

- Raise and discuss your concerns with your colleagues.

▷ If you are still not satisfied with the situation, then voice your concerns with either your immediate supervisor and/or the person responsible for the particular instruction you are concerned about.

▷ If, despite 'clarification', there is still concern on your part then you should make a formal, written objection supported by appropriate documentation to the relevant senior personnel, such as the senior nurse or medical officer concerned.

These above steps should all be taken quickly, since the patient's care may be adversely affected by needless time-wasting.

# References

Abortion Law Reform Association. (1999) *Education on Termination of Pregnancy*. London: Abortion Law Reform Association.

Airedale NHS Trust v Bland [1993] AC 789, p874.

Cole, T. Why shouldn't doctors make moral judgements! *Daily Mail*, 16 November 1998.

Davies, M. (1998) *Textbook on Medical Law* (2nd ed) London: Blackstone Press Ltd.

Government response (1990) *Abortion Act 1967 Conscience Clause: Government response to the tenth report from the Social Sciences Committee session 1989-90*. London: HMSO.

Janaway v Salford Health Authority [1989] AC 537.

Kennedy, I., Grubb, A. (1998) *Principles of Medical Law*. Oxford: Oxford University Press.

Law Commission. (1995) *Mental Incapacity*. No 231, February. London: The Stationery Office.

Mackay v Essex Area Heath Authority [1982] QB 1168, 1180.

McHale, J., Fox, M., Murphy, J. (1997) *Health Care Law (Text and Materials)*. London: Sweet and Maxwell.

Morgan, D., Lee, R.G. (1991) *Blackstone's Guide to the Human Fertilisation and Embryology Act 1990*. London: Blackstone Press Ltd.

Royal College of Nursing of the UK v DHSS [1981] AC 800.

St George's Healthcare NHS Trust v S [1998] 3 WLR 936.

Scottish National Board for Nursing, Midwifery and Health Visiting (1985) *Guidance Paper: Questioning of or objecting to participation in medical procedures.* Edinburgh: Scottish National Board for Nursing.

UKCC (1996) *Guidelines for Professional Practice.* London: UKCC.

Young, A.P. (1994) *Law and Professional Conduct in Nursing* (2nd Ed) London: Scutari Press.

## Further Reading

Wilson, L. (1999) *Living wills.* NT Clinical Monographs no 7. London: NT Books.

# Clause 9: Honouring professional contact

**Chris Green**

> '...avoid any abuse of your privileged relationship with patients and clients and of the privileged access allowed to their person, property, residence or workplace.'

Clause 9 emphasises the privileged nature of the nurse-patient relationship and requires nurses not to abuse it. A 'privilege' is a special status, or freedom, allowed to some people but not to others. Patients allow nurses to do intimate and potentially dangerous things to their bodies, which most people would not be allowed to do. The privileges exercised by nurses each day are arguably greater than those given to doctors or policemen.

Privilege can also mean an honour. A person granted a privilege should not treat it casually but is expected to live up to the honour and prove that they are worthy of it.

The proper purpose of a nurse's privileged access to a patient's body is the well-being of the patient. If the nurse uses this privilege for sexual gratification, any personal gain or to inflict humiliation on a patient, then they are abusing that privilege.

# THE NURSE'S PRIVILEGED RELATIONSHIP WITH PATIENTS

The nature of the nurse's privileged relationship with patients takes a number of forms, which we shall examine here:

- **Access to the person:** Most patients allow nurses to carry out physical examinations and treatments that would otherwise be considered an outrageous invasion of privacy. If the patient is unconscious, confused or otherwise mentally impaired, the same procedures may be carried out without the patient's permission and even if they are resisting. Some nursing procedures are painful and some are potentially dangerous. Nevertheless, patients and their relatives rarely question whether the nurse is acting properly. Nurses also make decisions about powerful medicines. If a doctor prescribes major tranquillisers to be taken 'as required', it is commonly the nurse, not the patient, who decides whether and when the medicine is taken.

- **Intimate knowledge:** Patients and relatives usually answer nurses' questions and do not challenge their right to ask them. Nurses also have access to notes about the patient made by others and acquire knowledge of the patient's bodily functions, and personal and social history, including intimate and family relationships. They see patients at their most private moments, in pain, anxious or afraid. Sometimes the patient's behaviour may be uninhibited due to medication, confusion or mental illness. Counselling is now seen as part of the nursing role, especially psychiatric nurses. Within the counselling relationship, the patient is often encouraged to talk freely about the most intimate aspects of their thoughts and feelings. This may include details of fantasies or exploring the deepest sources of guilt and shame.

- **Access to the patient's property:** Hospital nurses usually take custody of any valuables which the patient has on admission and are trusted to keep them safe. In an emergency admission, nurses often needs to go through the patient's property without the patient being able to oversee the process, and may turn up private possessions. In nursing homes, staff may have custody of items such as pension books. They may cash the pension on behalf of the patient and may be trusted to use a patient's money to pay for goods and services.

Nurses caring for psychiatric patients and those with learning disabilities also have extensive access to their patients' money and other property. Money is often held for and spent on behalf of the patient, or given out in small quantities like pocket money to a child. If the patient is sectioned under the Mental Health Act, the nurse may exercise further powers. Potentially dangerous items like alcohol or pornography may be confiscated. Sectioned patients often face personal and room searches. In places such as special hospitals, where the patient may be sectioned for many years, a room search is essentially a search of the patient's home.

It is crucial that policies and practices are in place to check and safeguard patients' property in every care environment.

▶ **Access to the patient's residence and workplace:** Many nurses see patients at home and may be granted a degree of freedom few other guests would have. Community nurses sometimes let themselves in and out and move freely from room to room to find items they need. Occupational health nurses see patients in the workplace, as do other community nurses, for example as part of a rehabilitation programme. They can influence the patient's colleagues and affect his or her career.

▶ **Authority over patients:** Nurses have legal authority over sectioned mental patients. They also have effective authority over patients who are confused or otherwise mentally incapacitated, even if they have not been sectioned. Nurses commonly have authority over children 'in loco parentis'. All patients in hospital or nursing homes are subject to the authority of nurses to some degree and, unlike if they were on holiday, they are often not free to leave.

▶ **Influence on patients:** Patients are influenced by nurses because of their perceived expertise on health matters. That influence is also shaped by more subtle psychological factors. The patient's dependence on the nurse for basic needs can have a powerful psychological effect. Whether out of gratitude or out of fear — real or imagined — that the care may be reduced or withdrawn, patients may be eager to please the nurse and afraid to give offence.

Nurses have their strongest influence over patients when they act as counsellors. Already in an emotionally vulnerable state, the patient may become even more vulnerable in the course of counselling because of the self exposure involved. Counselling can affect major decisions on issues such as marriage, divorce, religion or career/employment. Even if nurses set out to be non-directive, their influence can be profound.

▶ **Lack of suspicion:** Nurses have a position of great esteem in society and patients generally do not suspect them of wrongdoing. They will trust them where they would not trust others. When patients have made allegations, historically the nurse's word has usually been believed against the patient's, especially when the patient has been mentally unwell or is a child.

# ABUSE OF THE PRIVILEGED RELATIONSHIP

The justification for the privileged position of nurses is that it enables them, in accordance with the Code, to 'safeguard and promote the interests of individual patients and clients' and to 'serve the interests of society'. Exploiting the privileges for any other purpose is an abuse and therefore a professional misconduct. The most serious kinds of professional misconduct occur when nurses use their privileged access to the patient as a vehicle for aggression, financial gain or sexual gratification. There are also more subtle ways in which the privileged relationship can be abused.

## Physical and verbal abuse

UKCC statistics consistently show that physical and verbal abuse of patients and clients is by far the most common type of case considered by the Professional Conduct Committee. Of cases considered between April 1997 and March 1998, 34.51% came into this category (UKCC, 1998).

The types of behaviour covered by the description vary. Clearly physical abuse includes deliberate assault for the sole purpose of inflicting a hurt or humiliation on the patient. It also covers rough or insensitive handling of patients while carrying out legitimate nursing tasks. These include carrying out tasks without consent, and use of excessive force to restrain patients (even when restraint of some kind is justified by the circumstances). Physical abuse can take more subtle forms such as inappropriate use of mechanical restraints, for example geriatric chairs, or of seclusion, sedative medication or non-consensual feeding techniques, for example holding the patient's nose. Verbal abuse clearly includes deliberate insults and expressions of hatred, but also involves more subtle kinds of disrespect, taunting and belittling of patients.

Abuse can take place in any nursing context and against any kind of patient. However, some patients are more at risk than others. Most cases reported involve dependent elderly patients, long-stay psychiatric or learning disabled patients, especially those held in secure institutions under sections of the Mental Health Act.

It is hard to estimate how common patient abuse is. Incidents reported to the UKCC are likely to represent the tip of the iceberg. One survey reporting on the abuse of elderly patients in nursing homes in the USA in 1989 showed 20% of staff reporting having witnessed physical abuse and 5% admitting to physically abusing patients themselves (Pillemer and Moore, 1989).

## Why are patients abused?

When entering the profession most nurses do not even remotely envisage the possibility that they might ever subject their most vulnerable patients to cruelty or inhumanity. This distressing subject should therefore be considered with some humility, for it is a pitfall which many of us may have only narrowly avoided. How does this patient abuse come about?

One reason is clearly opportunity. Nurses, like other people, sometimes lose their tempers and in a very few cases may be pathologically violent people. The nature of the job is such that a nurse can sometimes be violent for a long time before the violence is detected. The opportunities are greatest if the patient has difficulty articulating complaints and is not likely to be believed if they do complain. This obviously applies to many dependent, elderly patients because of associated confusion and dementia, and also to many psychiatric patients, especially if they have a history of criminal convictions.

Opportunities for abuse are greater in long-stay institutions with a low staff turnover. There is much less apparent independent scrutiny than in acute settings or the community. Notably the largest category of cases reported to the UKCC relates to nursing homes (UKCC, 1994).

Abuse can arise because abusive attitudes become institutionalised. A patient may come to be seen as perverse and undeserving. Nurses may come to the view that a patient needs to be treated roughly 'for their own good'. It can be hard for an individual nurse to set their judgement against that of the entire institution. When a case of abuse is reported to the UKCC, the report often comes from a new member of staff (UKCC, 1994), as they can perceive a situation with fresh, independent eyes.

Finally, patient abuse can be caused by staff stress and, in particular, the condition known as 'burnout'. A survey of the research into institutional abuse of the elderly (Pillemer and Bachman-Prehn, 1991) concludes that burnout among staff is the strongest predictor of abuse. Studies of psychiatric nursing suggest that the incidence of stress and burnout is exceptionally high among staff in the special hospitals, Broadmoor, Rampton, Ashworth and Carstairs (Gournay and Carson, 1997). These are also the institutions which have given rise to the most disturbing reports of patient abuse (Blom-Cooper, 1992).

## CASE STUDY: STRESS AND BURNOUT

Peter has worked on a ward in a special hospital for eight years. The patients have all been convicted of serious criminal offences — sexual, violent or both. Most of the patients are passive, inarticulate and highly dependent on nursing staff, only a few are ever violent and their outbursts are usually weak and ineffective. Self-harm and attempted suicide are more common than violence. However, during the years in which Peter has been working on the ward there have been some very serious violent incidents. Two of his friends have been injured and are permanently disabled.

Peter always used to be a good listener and very patient. Whenever one of the patients was discontented he would try to get to the bottom of the matter and often succeeded. For the last six months, however, he has been feeling terribly tired. Whenever a patient makes any emotional demands on him he feels helpless and panicky. Rather than try to get to the bottom of the matter he wants to escape. When a patient becomes agitated he does not try to talk to the patient any more. He will usually resort quickly to prn ('as required') medication, and will use control and restraint techniques and/or seclusion sooner rather than later. He has come to treat the patients as a management problem rather than as individual men in need, and has ceased to take any pride in his work.

Burnout is characterised by emotional exhaustion. The nurse is unable to cope with emotional demands and perceives these as a threat. Nurses most vulnerable to burnout are often those who have been most committed and taken the most trouble in the past. Like many nurses, Peter is trying to contain the problem by distancing himself from the patients, treating his job as a series of tasks rather than as the care of people. Often it is when the patient seems most sad and pathetic that the nurse might become angry, callous or actually violent, shocking himself and others. All carers, including informal carers in families, are vulnerable to this. It probably plays a major part in the abuse of the elderly and handicapped by family members.

It is easy to see how a culture of abuse can sometimes grow up in the special hospitals. The actual dangers to nurses are real and frightening, although most patients at any one time are not dangerous. But physical restraint of patients is frequently required, however skilfully the ward is managed. If nurses cannot preserve their motivation against the effects of this kind of stress, then all expressions of patient need can come to be seen as a threat to order.

To their credit the special hospitals have now recognised these hazards and a real effort been made to tackle them. One of the best safeguards against the destructive effect of stress and burnout is clinical supervision, as recommended by the UKCC (1996). This is now widely practised in the special hospitals and Peter will probably be having regular sessions with a trusted supervisor. This might enable him to discuss his problems constructively. One possible outcome is that he may be able to move to a rehabilitation ward where the hazards are less and he can see more positive results from his work.

Unfortunately, clinical supervision is rarely available in many areas of practice, for example long-term care of elderly people, especially in nursing homes. Nurses admitting to symptoms of burnout may risk being seen as lacking moral fibre and consequently, many nurses change jobs and suffer career disadvantage. An alternative is to seek help from occupational health departments, unions and professional organisations or local health services.

## Theft, fraud and financial exploitation

Between April 1997 and March 1998, 1.54% of complaints to the UKCC Professional Conduct Committee related to theft from patients and 2.86% to 'other dishonesty' (UKCC, 1998). More nurses are reported to the UKCC for non-work related dishonesty than for dishonesty involving patients, indicating that if they decide to commit crimes of dishonesty, because of financial hardship or for any other reason, they prefer not to commit them against patients. Financial exploitation of patients does not necessarily simply mean crimes of dishonesty. Any material advantage which results from the nurse's access to patients can be a breach of Clause 9.

Borrowing from a current patient should be avoided. Most patients would not otherwise lend money to a stranger, so it is likely to be a clear case of the nurse taking advantage of her position. Carrying out a trade with a patient, for example buying or selling second-hand goods, is less clearly exploitation. Nevertheless it could be construed as such and is generally unwise. Also it will often be specifically forbidden by employers. If the patient is mentally frail, then their financial affairs may be in the hands of the Court of Protection or subject to a power of attorney. If so trading directly with the patient may be a criminal offence. But if the nurse uses the procedures of the Court of Protection to carry out a trade, this may possibly be acceptable where other forms of trading are not. The Court of Protection receiver has a legal duty to act in the patient's interest, so the nurse will not be exploiting the patient. However, any trade is open to misinterpretation.

Borrowing from or trading with former patients is less clear cut. There is nothing innately unethical about forming a friendship or a business relationship with a former patient, though caution is necessary. Psychiatric nurses should be aware that they are sometimes perceived by former patients as very powerful so the relationship cannot be equal. In many cases a former patient will feel a debt of gratitude and nurses should avoid any suggestion that they are cashing in on this. Also any arrangement which might create any awkwardness if the former patient wishes to approach the service again should be avoided. The subject of gifts, favours and hospitality is considered in Clause 15 (see pp 191-203).

Nurses who have custody of patient funds need to understand their legal and ethical duties. Patient funds must be kept separate from other money, and there must be a clear delineation between those goods and services appropriately paid for with patients' cash, and those which should be paid for by the institution.

# CASE STUDY: BUSINESS FAILURE

Sheila is the matron and owner of a small nursing home in her village, which she has always thought of as a service to the local community rather than a business. She keeps fees as low as possible, rather lower than the market price. She has custody of the pension books of several patients and cashes these by arrangement with the local post office, keeping the cash in a safe. Also she is the social security 'nominee' of some patients and receives benefits on their behalf. For convenience these are paid into her business account.

Recently the business has had financial problems, which she counters in a variety of ways. She explains her problems to patients. As a temporary measure, she asks some patients to pay extra for some of the items they use, for example incontinence pads. Despite these measures, the business continues to lose money. The account is heavily overdrawn and she petitions for her own bankruptcy.

Sheila's bankruptcy is a misfortune for her in more ways than one. The payment of funds received as nominee into an overdrawn account will legally be construed as theft. Such funds should always be kept in a separate account, which should never be overdrawn. Her persuasion of patients to help her out is subject, in law, to a 'presumption of undue influence'. She will be presumed to have put improper pressure on patients unless she can positively prove otherwise. So together with her bankruptcy she will face criminal charges and professional conduct proceedings. Clearly, Sheila's lack of business sophistication has played a part in her fall from grace. The UKCC advises that all people responsible for management of patient funds should receive suitable financial training (UKCC, 1994).

## Sexual abuse

Allegations of sexual abuse represent a small proportion of complaints to the UKCC — 3.52% of Professional Conduct Committee cases between April 1997 and March 1998 (UKCC, 1998). However, there is good reason to suppose that a large amount of abuse goes unreported. In 1992, a BBC Public Eye documentary suggested sexual abuse of patients by community psychiatric nurses was common (Diverse Productions, 1992).

In the context of Clause 9, a nurse is guilty of sexual abuse if they take advantage of their position as a nurse to obtain any sexual gratification from a patient. This covers not only clear cases of assault but also where a nurse provides care with an unnecessary degree of intimate contact or exposure, asks a patient unnecessary questions about sex, indulges in conversation with an unnecessary sexual content, or behaves flirtatiously, seductively or provocatively. If the patient is currently cared for by the nurse then any sexual content to the relationship, including a positive or encouraging response to advances made by the patient, will be considered an abuse of the nurse's position.

However there are several grey areas. Nurses may have difficulty understanding their duty when considering a relationship with a former patient or one from another part of the service. The UKCC Preliminary Proceedings Committee takes the following matters into account when considering misconduct (UKCC, 1996):

- the relative power imbalance in the relationship;
- whether or not there has been any degree of coercion;
- the vulnerability of the patient involved;
- the context in which the relationship started;
- any restrictions imposed by mental health legislation.

# CASE STUDY: THE UKCC CRITERIA FOR SEXUAL RELATIONSHIPS

Roger is a nurse employed on a ward at a psychiatric hospital. His new girlfriend is Jenny. She tells him that she has had mental health problems and is receiving antidepressant treatment and counselling as an outpatient of the same hospital. He feels no uneasiness about this. He has had some mental health problems himself in the past and they understand each other well.

This seems a very innocent relationship. Nevertheless, Roger will commit a criminal offence if he has sexual intercourse with Jenny without first marrying her. Under section 128 of the Mental Health Act 1959, any male member of staff in a psychiatric hospital or nursing home who has sexual intercourse with a female patient of the same institution commits an offence. This applies to male members of staff, but female nurses in a similar position may still face a professional conduct investigation.

In the event of anyone questioning the propriety of this relationship, the UKCC will take into account 'restrictions imposed by mental health legislation' and may therefore decide that there is a case to answer. Considering the other UKCC criteria, in Roger's case there was no coercion and the relationship started outside work. He clearly believes that there is no power imbalance in the relationship and that he is not exploiting Jenny's vulnerability. However, he should be prepared for the possibility that others will take a different view. How this affects Jenny's future access to the service may also be questioned, especially if it is ever proposed that she be admitted to a ward as an in-patient.

To avoid an unpleasant investigation, Roger should be cautious. He should discuss his position with a supervisor to try to resolve the practical, ethical and legal problems. This is likely to be very uncomfortable, but is the best course of action.

Various other ambiguous situations come to mind. For example, if a former patient asks a hospital nurse to go out with him, may she accept? Should she wait until there has been a decent interval since the discharge of the patient, if so how long? Can a practice nurse form a relationship with a patient who is on the list of the GP she works for? There are no definite answers to these questions. Generally, the situation should be considered in the light of the UKCC criteria, and psychiatric nurses need to be much more cautious than general nurses. If there is any doubt, or it is possible that the situation could be misconstrued or there is any possibility that the patient's access to the service could be affected, then the nurse should discuss the matter with the managers. Further UKCC guidelines are expected in autumn 1999 on the whole of Clause 9, with the intention of redefining prevention, detection, breaches and management of breaches.

## What are the reasons for sexual abuse?

The popular image of the sexual abuser is as a cold and calculating person who considers only his own gratification and has little or no regard for the well-being of the person he abuses. This is the opposite of our conception of the good nurse. However there are many conscientious, otherwise good nurses who have had improper sexual contact with patients and it is worth considering how this may come about.

There are few subjects about which we can speak with less confidence or clarity than sex. Both nurses and patients have sexual needs which are likely to trouble and preoccupy them, often to the point of obsession. Sometimes sexual needs will come to the fore at a time when they can least well be understood or managed. The following three situations are quite commonly encountered in practice:

- Often the nurse will perceive themselves to be in love with the patient. To someone in love, the emotion is often given an absolute value and takes precedence over all other considerations. 'Love' is of course undefined and undefinable. It cannot be said that this nurse is any less truly 'in love' than any other person who uses the words. Like any other person, the nurse may later look back with embarrassment, shame and disbelief.

- The nurse may have a 'rescue fantasy' (Gallop, 1997) where they believe that through a sexual relationship the patient can be rescued from suffering and mental ill health.

- Finally, sexual abuse often takes place in the context of a serious mental breakdown and contributes to it. Like anger, sexual desire and frustration can break out in an uncontrolled way when the nurse is seriously depressed, especially if there is associated alcohol or drug use. As with physical abuse, the sexual abuse may be followed by overwhelming shame and attempted or actual suicide.

In the situations outlined above clearly the nurse is very vulnerable. This makes it all the more important to offer nurses clear and effective guidance. Historically it has not been provided and there is still some reluctance to discuss the matter in the depth required.

# CASE STUDY: 'MANIPULATIVE PSYCHOPATHY'

Andrew's diagnosis is 'dissocial personality disorder'. More informally, he is known to the local police and psychiatric services as a 'manipulative psychopath'. He is receiving help for his alcohol problems at a counselling service where he encounters Stella, a young nurse. He is very charming to her. She becomes convinced that other staff in the service are prejudiced against him and that she is the only nurse who understands his needs. They form a sexual relationship outside work which lasts for a month during which she is blissfully happy. However, he lapses back into alcohol use and becomes rough, unreasonable and demanding. Their relationship breaks up and he attempts suicide by overdosing on his antidepressants. When he recovers he makes a formal complaint against Stella.

We are inclined to sympathise with Stella and may view her as Andrew's victim. Objectively, however, she is strong while he is weak and vulnerable. She is a member of a respected profession while he is a social outcast with alcohol problems. One of the diagnostic criteria for 'dissocial personality disorder' is 'incapacity to form enduring relationships, though having no difficulty establishing them' (WHO, 1992). In so far as he fits this description, we may describe Andrew as sexually inadequate. His attempted suicide should be taken seriously as people with his diagnosis have a very high suicide rate. His alcohol treatment is now disrupted and his future access to the service compromised. While we are right (in my view) to sympathise with her, Stella has committed an act of sexual abuse against a vulnerable patient.

## Abuse of the counselling relationship

The word 'counselling' covers a number of activities. The discussion here will focus on 'talking therapies' rather than on counselling for teaching social skills, gathering or imparting information or giving practical advice.

Counselling in this sense is a recent addition to the duties of the nurse. It has quickly come to be seen as a central activity in nursing, especially in psychiatric nursing (Barker, 1999). At present, abuse of a counselling relationship rarely features in UKCC professional conduct hearings except where there is an allegation of sexual abuse. However, concern about the potential for harm in counselling is growing.

It is likely that there will be a large increase in court cases about counselling, as there already have been in the USA. In professional conduct hearings the case has to be proved against the nurse 'beyond reasonable doubt' and this will always be hard to do where counselling is concerned. Nevertheless it is of great importance that nurses engaged in counselling reflect on the ethics of their practice.

The counselling relationship between the nurse and client is an extremely privileged one. Clients are encouraged to talk freely about things which otherwise are their most closely guarded secrets, matters which cause the greatest guilt and shame. This can hardly take place unless the client comes to view the nurse as a friend. In practice, the nurse is often viewed as not only a friend but a lifeline and can acquire great influence and authority. This privilege should be used only for the benefit of the client. However, apart from the intuition of the nurse, there is little or no way of knowing what will benefit the client. Counselling depends on psychological processes and on verbal and non-verbal communication of a kind which cannot be measured, described with any precision or independently validated. Nurses, whose practice is supposed to be evidence-based, have no evidence base to refer to. They are left with their intuition.

The result is an ethical minefield. The nurse is exploring dangerous territory without a map. They may lead the conversation in a particular direction as a result of mere guesswork, curiosity or, indeed, voyeurism. Inevitably they are influenced by their own convictions. For example, they may have a religious belief in the sanctity of marriage or a feminist belief that women need to free themselves from the influence of men. Inevitably, too, they will be influenced by their own emotional needs.

Prominent among these may be the 'rescue fantasy', the emotional need to believe that through their own personal qualities or wisdom they can rescue the client. But as already indicated, this can lead to sexual abuse of the client. More commonly, it may result in counselling aimed at obtaining gratifying feedback from the client rather than promoting the client's well-being. There is a serious risk that the nurse can use the privileges of counselling to promote a hidden agenda, be it personal or political.

These hazards are recognised in counselling literature, and safeguards exist to reduce the risks. Clinical supervision, recommended in some form for all nurses (UKCC, 1996), has a particular function and content in counselling. However with the great increase in counselling in recent years, counsellors are not always supervised with much rigour, nor is the supervisor always appropriately qualified or experienced.

The potential for harm is eloquently explored by novelist Fay Weldon in her novel *Affliction* (Weldon, 1993). Weldon writes of marriages being destroyed as a result of counselling. Still more disturbing are the cases where counselled clients have 'recovered' memories of childhood sexual abuse by a parent — memories now believed to be false in many cases. This has given rise to much negligence litigation in the USA (Orr, 1996).

These comments about a controversial and relatively new activity of the nursing profession are intended to promote discussion rather than to provide clear guidance. Counselling is a career opportunity enthusiastically pursued by many nurses. But are they aware of the ethical and professional pitfalls?

## Insensitive and unprofessional behaviour

As well as requiring nurses to refrain from various kinds of criminal and seriously irresponsible behaviour, Clause 9 expects them to act sensitively and professionally. Acts of insensitivity, while they are relatively unlikely to result in professional conduct proceedings or legal action, are very damaging to the nurse/patient relationship.

In the course of their work, nurses will witness the consequences of diseased bodily functions and will learn of embarrassing personal habits and of past and present foolish, immoral or criminal behaviour. Their natural response may be to show distaste, disgust, mirth or moral outrage, but Clause 9 requires them to suppress these feelings and to respond, instead, in a professional manner.

Any behaviour by the nurse which demonstrates a casual, unprofessional approach to the privileges of nursing may breach Clause 9. Examples include the nurse who makes free with a patient's home and possessions, or gives way to curiosity and snoops around, or the nurse who responds to a request for advice with inappropriate humour.

# CONCLUSION

Breaches of Clause 9 consist largely of assaults on and exploitation of vulnerable patients. These are among the most serious forms of misconduct and the nurse who is found guilty of such unprofessional behaviour is unlikely to receive much sympathy from colleagues. Nevertheless, offences such as cruel treatment of elderly patients are more frequent than one might expect, and are a cause for serious concern. Often the culprit turns out to have an otherwise excellent record as a caring nurse. These offences must not be seen as the actions of wicked psychopaths who have somehow strayed into nursing but as pitfalls which might confront many nurses in the course of their careers.

A management style of openness and honesty will demonstrate that abuse or unprofessional behaviour to patients will not be tolerated. By addressing all complaints and developing appropriate protocols, staff are assured they can speak freely on the patient's behalf without fear of reprisal and will have management support. The nurse will be acting within the remit of the Code by refusing to condone poor practice and by acting accordingly.

Other important safeguards should be available to nurses. First, they should all have clinical supervision as recommended by the UKCC. This should be a source of support and not a punitive process. Where it reveals that a nurse is experiencing problems, the outcome should be appropriate help, not condemnation or panic. Nurses whose work includes counselling should receive supervision for this purpose from an experienced counsellor with appropriate qualifications.

Second, all nurses and supervisors should be aware of the symptoms of burnout and their significance. The nurses most likely to experience these symptoms are often those who have previously approached their work with the greatest commitment. Those who have to change direction in their careers as a result of burnout should be able to do so without disadvantage.

Finally, the fact that nurses may develop sexual feelings for patients should not be a taboo subject. Thorough discussion of this matter should take place in both pre- and post-registration nurse education programmes with the aim of understanding the tangle of emotions which might lead to this form of misconduct.

# References

Barker, P. (1999) *Talking Cures: a guide to the psychotherapies for the health care professionals*. London: NT Books.

Blom-Cooper, L. (1992) *Report of the committee of inquiry into complaints about Ashworth hospital*. London: The Stationery Office.

Diverse Productions (1992) *Public Eye: Sex in the forbidden zone*. BBC2, 13 November, 8pm.

Gallop, R. (1997) *Abuse of power in the nurse/client relationship: definition, research and organisational response*. Paper given at UKCC and RCN collaborative conference, patient-practitioner relations, 27 May 1997. Shortened version in *Nursing Standard*; (1998) 12: 37, 43-47.

Gournay, K., Carson J. (1997) *Stress in mental health professionals and its implications for staff working with forensic populations: review, critique and suggestions for future research*. (A review carried out for Department of Health, currently unpublished.)

Orr, M. (1996) False memory suits against therapists. *Counselling News*; March, 14-15.

Pillemer, K., Bachman-Prehn, R. (1991) Helping and hurting: predictors of maltreatment of patients in nursing homes. *Research in Ageing*; 13: 74-95.

Pillemer, K., Moore, D.W. (1989) Abuse of patients in nursing homes: findings from a survey of staff. *The Gerontologist*; 29: 3, 314-20.

UKCC (1994) *Professional conduct — occasional report on the standard of nursing in nursing homes*. London: UKCC.

UKCC (1996) *Professional conduct — issues arising from professional conduct complaints*. London: UKCC.

UKCC (1996) *Position statement on clinical supervision for nursing and health visiting*. London: UKCC.

UKCC (1998) *Statistical analysis of the UKCC's professional register, 1 April 1997 to 31 March 1998*. London: UKCC.

Weldon, F. (1993) *Affliction*. London: HarperCollins.

WHO (1992) *International Classification of Disease, 10th edition* (ICD-10). Geneva: World Health Organisation.

## Recommended reading

Bond, M., Holland, S. (1998) *Skills of clinical supervision for nurses: a practical guide for supervisees, clinical supervisors and managers*. Buckingham: OUP.

Eastman, M. (Ed)/Age Concern (1994) *Old age abuse: a new perspective* (2nd ed). London: Chapman and Hall.

Jenkins, P. (1997) *Counselling, psychotherapy and the law*. London: Sage Publications.

Maslack, C. (1982) *Burnout: the cost of caring*. London: Prentice Hall.

Millon, P. (1998) *Remembering trauma: a psychotherapist's guide to memory and illusion*. Chichester: John Wiley and Son.

Rutter, P. *Sex in the Forbidden Zone*. London: Mandala.

# Clause 10: Silent witness

## Mandy Pullen

> '…protect all confidential information concerning patients and clients obtained in the course of professional practice and make disclosures only with consent, where required by the order of a court or where you can justify disclosure in the wider public interest.'

Search for a definition of confidentiality in almost any dictionary and you will find the word 'trust'. As health professionals, patients come to us with their problems, dreams, troubles and secrets in the belief that we are worthy of their confidence. There is an implicit understanding that confidentiality is assured in the nurse-patient relationship. However, nurses are not silenced like priests after a confessional, and patients should not be led to believe this is so if they volunteer information.

Tschudin (1992) believes the following two questions should be explored to give a clear understanding of confidentiality:

- What is meant by confidentiality?

- What is confidential material?

By understanding the nature of confidentiality, data classed as confidential information becomes apparent. Confidentiality is the right to privacy of records, which are the confidential material.

# THE DATA PROTECTION ACT

The purpose of the Data Protection Act (1984) is to improve practices among computer users and raise public confidence in computing. The act sets out a list of eight data protection principles as the foundation for processing personal information on a computer.

Six specify that personal data:

- shall be obtained and processed fairly and lawfully;

- shall be held only for one or more specified and lawful purposes;

- shall not be used or disclosed in any manner incompatible with that purpose;

- shall be adequate, relevant and not excessive in relation to that purpose;

- shall be accurate and, where necessary, kept up to date;

- shall not be kept for any longer than is necessary.

The other two state that:

- a person should be entitled — at reasonable intervals and without undue delay or expense — to be informed if anyone holds personal data of which they are the subject, and to have access to any such data. Where appropriate they may have such data corrected or erased;

- appropriate security measures shall be taken against unauthorised access to, or alteration, disclosure or destruction of personal data, and against its accidental loss or destruction.

The Act only applies to information processed by a computer, and if it relates to living people. However, the Guidelines for Professional Practice (UKCC, 1996) state that a patient's death does not give a nurse the right to break confidentiality. Barber (1992) states that to allay fears and anxieties, the patient should be told at the beginning of any assessment that information is collected to assist in the provision and administration of health care.

Controlling access to patient information is an important area of computer systems. Passwords should not be disclosed to anyone and screens should always be situated so that they can only be viewed by the authorised person. Nurses should log out of the computer system at all times when they are not using it, and information printed from the computer should be treated as confidential.

Each hospital should have a procedure to check authenticity of records on a computer where there is no written signature, and the person writing up the record must be clearly identified.

Hospitals have an open-door policy and computer equipment can easily be stolen, along with confidential information. Computers need to be installed in a secure area and anyone on the ward without identification should be challenged. Computers that need repairing should not be removed from the premises without correct authorisation.

# DISCLOSURE OF INFORMATION

Disclosure of information occurs:

- with the patient or client's consent;
- without the patient or client's consent when the disclosure is required by law or by order of a court;
- without the patient or client's consent when the disclosure is considered to be necessary in the public interest.

The Guidelines for Professional Practice (UKCC, 1996) define the public interest as meaning 'the interests of an individual or group of individuals or of society as a whole'. Drug trafficking, child abuse or serious crime are instances when disclosure is deemed in the public interest.

## Exceptions to confidentiality

The following are examples where rules of confidentiality can be broken:

- The Abortion Act 1967;
- The NHS Act 1977 (notification of births and deaths);
- The Police and Criminal Evidence Act 1984;
- The Road Traffic Act 1988, Section 172;
- The Prevention of Terrorism Act 1989;

▷ The Public Health Control of Disease Act and the Public Health
(Infectious Diseases) Regulations 1988;

▷ The NHS Act 1974 Venereal Disease Regulations.

Nurses exercise both autonomy and legal responsibility and should know where the legal boundaries lie. A nurse can be sued through a civil court by an aggrieved patient alleging that confidentiality was broken. However, there is no statutory right to confidentiality.

Vicarious liability means legal responsibility shifts from the individual, often to the hospital or employer. However, this does not apply in the case of broken confidentiality and, if the patient sues successfully, a compensation award can be made against the individual nurse. If the patient believes there is going to be a breach of confidentiality they can ask a court for an injunction to prevent disclosure.

Wherever information is deliberately released the decision must be justified and reasons documented and discussed with a senior member of staff. A nurse can contact the UKCC to help make the correct decision. When information is discussed with other members of the multidisciplinary team, nurses must state that their personal accountability is first to the patient.

## Non-disclosure of information

Many nurses obey an unwritten rule that nurses must only tell patients the same story as the doctor. If the doctor chooses to deliberately lie to the patient, the nurse is forced to collude with this deception. This can lead to problems since nurses are legally and professionally accountable for their actions, including deliberately withholding information from patients or even lying to them.

However, nurses' assertiveness and professionalism generally ensure that patients receive information about their treatment, and Wells (1988) believes this also includes prognosis and diagnosis.

Faulder (1985) refers to the growing body of evidence that shows patients want to know the truth. Giving patients information helps to empower them and their family. Part of the nurse's role is to help people adapt and cope with the effects of disease. Therefore nurses should be involved in the disclosure of information which improves the relationship between team members and patients.

Fiesta (1988) states that no law exists requiring nurses to disclose information not given by the physician, but equally there is no law requiring the nurse to withhold this type of information. The issue then becomes one of ethical analysis rather than legal duty. It may be best addressed by discussing the situation with the doctor and other team members, away from the patient.

Before giving their consent to treatment, the patient should be given information which they can understand themselves. This is normally the medical profession's duty. The physician or surgeon performing the act will tell the patient the risks, benefits and complications. According to Fiesta (1988) the informed consent law also allows doctors the privilege of therapeutic non-disclosure, that is, to keep information from the patient that they think might harm them.

The UKCC, in Standards for Records and Record Keeping (1993), also argues that the health professional most directly involved in the patient's care has the right to withhold information which is thought to cause harm to the physical or mental health of the patient or will identify a third person.

Nurses must be able to justify their actions and keep the patient as their central focus while upholding the professional status of nursing. Technological advances have moved many nurses into specialisation where part of their role involves giving the patient and their family or carers full written and verbal information about their treatment and condition. Patients must be given a choice about how much information they receive and who to share it with. Denying the patient this choice takes away their rights and lessens their dignity and independence.

Many nurses are now performing techniques previously only undertaken by doctors. This helps to bridge the gap between doctors and nurses within the multidisciplinary team and create more effective communication. With extended roles comes extended responsibility.

## Family members

Nurses may need to consult relevant people close to the patient and to respect any previous instructions the patient may have given.

But in its Guidelines for Professional Practice (UKCC, 1996), the UKCC states that nobody has the right to give consent on behalf of another adult. If the patient is an adult, consent from relatives is not enough. The principles governing consent should also be applied to patients who are mentally incapacitated. This may be a temporary or a long-term situation such as the taking of sedative drugs or mental illness, coma or unconsciousness.

Disclosure of information to family members can be a very difficult area for nurses. Bosna (1998) helps to clarify this by stating that if the patient is competent, they must specifically give authorisation for their spouse to read the medical records. If the patient has chosen someone else to be their legal guardian and becomes incompetent to make a decision, then the spouse cannot have access to the records or make medical decisions on the patient's behalf.

Families have their own individual as well as group needs in sharing information about people with a life-threatening illness. Family members need to receive truthful information that is given in layman's terms. Fitch (1994) believes that 'resolving the issue of disclosing patient information to families demands that health care professionals engage in sensitive communication and achieve a delicate balance between the patient's right to confidentiality and meeting the family members' needs for information'. Nurses must remember that the patient is the focus of their responsibility and their decision is paramount, even when pressure is exerted by family and friends.

# OTHER AREAS OF CONFIDENTIALITY

A number of other areas in nursing where issues of patient confidentiality arise are examined below:

## Ownership of records

Organisations that employ the professional staff who make records are the legal owners of those records. However, this does not give anyone in the organisation the legal right to access information in the records. As a result of the Data Protection Act (1984), patients have the right to see their records on computer. And the Access to Health Records Act (1990) gives patients and clients access to manual health records about themselves made after 1 November 1991 (UKCC, 1993). But it is best if patients have a member of the multidisciplinary team with them so that information can be interpreted. Fiesta (1988) believes this procedure also provides monitoring to prevent patients from altering or removing portions of their records.

Anyone writing in the medical or nursing notes has a legal duty to use legible handwriting and to avoid medical jargon and abbreviations.

With many members of the multidisciplinary team involved in one person's care, shared records left in the patient's custody can be an advantage, since this removes any difficulties over access. Although these records are not their property, the patient does have access to the written notes. This type of record-keeping enables nurses to communicate effectively with other health care professionals and maintains continuity of care.

Patient-held records have the potential to increase the trust between carers and patients as well as cutting down on the loss of records and the risk of breaking confidentiality. The UKCC (1996) suggests that nurses worried about the security of notes should keep a second record for their own use.

Some employees have access to patient records but are not directly involved in the patient's care. Their employment contract must contain a clause emphasising the principles of confidentiality and action that may be taken if it is broken.

Patients' right to privacy should include the right for their information not to be overheard by other patients and relatives. This begs the question of nurses handing over information at the end of the bed or the doctor discussing patient care on the ward round. Confidentiality also extends beyond the workplace, and nurses should be cautious of casual chat about patients. One example was a midwife who delivered the baby of a famous person, and then told her husband, who in turn told a colleague who knew the patient's husband. The patient complained of being the subject of gossip by her professional carer.

Keeping patient records at the end of the bed is subject to much debate since many issues, such as charting bowel movements, are private to the patient. Bosna (1998) states that divulging what is on the patient's chart without their permission violates privacy. If a relative or friend is seen to be reading notes at the end of the bed and wishes to have information clarified, the patient's consent should be sought first.

## Research issues

With increasing opportunities for study for diplomas, degrees, National Board courses and PREP, nurses are encouraged to look at reflective practice and use research to change practice. A commitment to research raises several ethical issues, and must be taken seriously as an integral part of professional responsibility.

In both quantitative and qualitative research methods, Couchman and Dawson (1990) outline the following ethical responsibilities where patients are involved:

- not to be harmed;

- informed consent;

- voluntary participation;

- confidentiality;

- anonymity;

- dignity and self respect.

Patients have the right to withdraw from the research at any point and to have their own data, including recordings, destroyed (Ayer, 1994). Information obtained about participants during an investigation is confidential. If confidentiality cannot be guaranteed the participant has the right to be informed before agreeing to take part in the research.

The UKCC Guidelines for Professional Practice (1996) state it is the responsibility of the person providing training of nurses to ensure that students understand the need for confidentiality. Nurses have a duty to keep their knowledge updated and if they are unsure of an answer they should seek to find the correct answer or plan of action to be taken.

Disease management packages are a structured systematic care approach to specific diseases, which bring together research evidence, cost-effective interventions and interprofessional interagency working. Nurses need to understand the element of confidentiality in disease management.

For example, sponsors of some disease management packages are unlikely to be altruistic and companies may request information on product use or patient numbers. Nurses need to know that NHS data is confidential, and explicit patient consent should be obtained before any information is passed on. When this information is required for clinical audit, it must be presented in an anonymous form to protect patient confidentiality.

## Police enquiries

Just as under English law the public does not have to answer police questions, so a nurse on a ward is not obliged to answer police questions about a patient. However, to remain silent may not be in the person's best interest (Criminal Justice Act, 1994). There are exceptions, for example the Prevention of Terrorism Act (1989), and if people withhold information relating to acts of terrorism they can be prosecuted.

If the police require access to the patient's records the patient does not need to be told but the hospital administrator must be informed (McHale et al, 1998). To obtain such access the police must first obtain a warrant under the Police and Criminal Evidence Act (1984). A judge must also grant a warrant for police to enter a general practitioner's surgery to gain access to confidential information held there.

## HIV and hepatitis

It is obvious that nurses should not discuss details of patients outside the hospital environment, and patient records should always be filed correctly. The smallest number of people should share the information that a patient is HIV-positive or has a hepatitis infection. If staff are using universal precautions, there is no need for the patient's status to be known.

The General Medical Council (1995) has informed doctors that disclosure is justifiable if there is risk to an individual person, for example if a patient is diagnosed as being HIV-positive and refuses to tell their sexual partner of their diagnosis. McHale (1998) suggests the position is unclear but that a court would be prepared to hold the breach of confidence as being in the public interest.

It is also questionable as to whether a GP has the right to know if their patient has tested positive for HIV.

## Children and confidentiality

A nurse should think long and hard before disclosing a child's medical information without their consent (McHale, 1998). In the House of Lords it was proposed that: 'A child is able to consent to medical treatment where they have sufficient maturity to do so.'

Where the child is very young, disclosure of information to a third party may be an integral part of the child's care and the Data Protection Act (1984) allows the data user to give information to the child's parents. Difficulties may arise when a child uses a school nurse as a confidante, or when a practice nurse is approached by young people seeking contraceptive advice. If children are regarded as being mature, they are allowed to see their own records but this does not give the parents the right to see them.

## CONCLUSION

Although the British Medical Association produced a draft bill on confidentiality in 1995, it failed in the House of Lords, leaving the situation still confusing. Nurses need to follow their Code of Professional Conduct and remain updated on the legal issues connected with confidentiality, disclosure of information and consent within their own working environment.

The law calls for careful monitoring of confidentiality and information should be handled with great care. Patient privacy should be at the forefront of our minds at all times. The patient is the primary consideration and complete trust must form the basis of a professional relationship.

## References

Ayer, S. (1994) A Proper Process of Scrutiny. Developing a college research base. *Professional Nurse*; 9: 9, 595-599.

Barber, B. (1992) Security screening. *Nursing Times*; 88: 49, 50-52.

Bosna, M. (1998) Legal Questions. *Nursing*; February, 30.

Couchman, W., Dawson, J. (1990) *Nursing and Health-Care Research*. London: Scutari Press.

Data Protection Act (1984) London: HMSO. In: *Data Protection Act Handbook* (1988) Birmingham: Information Management Centre.

Fitch, I. (1994) How Much Should I Say To Whom? *Journal of Palliative Care*; 10: 3, 90-100.

Fiesta, J. (1988) Nurses' duty to disclose. *Nursing Management*; 19: 30, 30-32.

Faulder, C. (1985) *Whose Body is it?* London: Virago.

General Medical Council (1995) *HIV and AIDS: The Ethical Considerations*. London: GMC.

McHale, J. (1998) *Law and Nursing*. London: Butterworth Heinemann.

Tschudin, V. (1992) *Ethics in Nursing*. Oxford: Butterworth Heinemann.

UKCC (1993) *Standards for Records and Record Keeping*. London: UKCC.

UKCC (1996) *Guidelines for Professional Practice*. London: UKCC.

Wells, R. (1988) Ethics and Information. *Senior Nurse* 8: 6, 8-10.

## Recommended reading

Woodrow, P. (1996) Exploring confidentiality in nursing practice. *Nursing Standard*; 10, 32, 38-42.

# Clauses 11 & 12:
# Safe and sound

**Ron Steed**

> '…report to an appropriate person or authority, having regard to the physical, psychological and social effects on patients and clients, any circumstances in the environment of care which could jeopardise standards of practice.' (Clause 11)
>
> '…report to an appropriate person or authority any circumstances in which safe and appropriate care for patients and clients cannot be provided.' (Clause 12)

At first glance, Clauses 11 and 12 seem to be saying the same thing. But closer scrutiny reveals that they cover separate yet related topics. The distinction between the two may be blurred but the intention behind both is clear: safety for the patient.

Clause 11 concerns circumstances that may diminish or impair the standards of care that influence the client's well-being. This means that, although care may be provided, because of circumstance A, B or C, that care will not be of the highest standards. Clause 12 goes beyond this and identifies the absolute — where, because of circumstance D, E or F, safe and appropriate care for the client cannot be provided.

Both clauses help move the practitioner towards professionalism but do not offer practical guidance to meet what is clearly an ideal.

Although the UKCC distinguishes between them, there is no official interpretation of the two clauses. Both clauses clearly indicate that the practitioner should be an advocate and 'report to an appropriate person or authority' those situations that lead to lowered standards of care or inability to provide safe and appropriate care.

But neither elaborates on what can be done if the 'appropriate person or authority' fails to respond or act in the appropriate way. The UKCC indicates that its duty is primarily to the public, rather than to the staff it seeks to regulate. There are times when reporting to the proper authority may lead to unfair treatment or dismissal of the practitioner for carrying out the very role the UKCC demands. Yet the UKCC offers no protection for doing so.

Mandie Lavin, director of professional conduct at the UKCC, recently spelt this out in a letter to *Nursing Times* (1998): 'Ultimately, it is the UKCC's role to protect the public. Protecting the interests of individual nurses, midwives and health visitors is properly the role of a range of professional membership organisations and trade unions.'

The lack of any clearer guidance suggests there is a Pontius Pilate attitude of: 'I find nothing wrong in requiring you to carry out these vaguely defined actions yet I leave it to others to decide whether they will protect you from my requirements.' Although the UKCC may fully support practitioners who raise concerns in an appropriate manner, there still remains the problem of defining who the person to raise them with is, and which manner is appropriate. For example, is it appropriate to inform the local or national media of your concerns — in essence whistleblowing — if you had previously voiced concerns through your employer's hierarchy but did not get an appropriate response?

The UKCC may impose the advocacy role on the practitioner, but it fails to provide a clear definition of what advocacy means or offer ways to support the practitioner when they attempt to fulfil that role.

The Code of Professional Conduct is an ideal — and striving for such an ideal is supposed to single out the professionals — a group of people with a select body of knowledge. The Concise Oxford Dictionary definition of an ideal is a perfect type or conception, an actual thing as a standard for imitation.

The UKCC Code contains idealistic values that are Utopian in nature. They are vague, unspecific and often unachievable. Surely the point of an ideal is to be able to actually achieve it? Continually striving for something unachievable inevitably leads to confusion, fear and dilemmas. Vague clauses mean the practitioner will not be able to live up to the ideal because of circumstances outside their control, and so will become demoralised and disheartened.

## ACCOUNTABILITY AND RESPONSIBILITY

Both clauses frequently deal with areas that the nurse has responsibility for but may not always have accountability to influence. Nurses need to grasp the distinction between accountability and responsibility, which is also important for interpreting Clause 14 and several other clauses in the Code.

Hancock (1997) has helped clarify the difference:

> *Accountability and responsibility are often mistakenly interchanged. Responsibility implies answerability, it entails the ability of the individual to 'choose one course of action or intervention over another as the correct choice in a given set of circumstances. Accountability... entails both personal and professional responsibility' (Holden, 1991b) and as such presents a sense of overriding concern for the whole process of decision making (Claus and Bailey, 1997). Thus it seems that accountability requires responsibility. Conversely, responsibility does not assume accountability, and in fact one may be held responsible, yet not accountable for a given action.*

Pearson and Vaughn (1986) have also made the distinction plain:

> *While the two ideas are inextricably linked, there is a clear difference between them. Accountability implies that a situation has been assessed, a plan has been made and carried out, and the results evaluated. Responsibility refers to the task of 'charge'. Thus nurses can be offered the charge or responsibility for carrying out a particular action. In agreeing to accept the responsibility for that action, they become accountable for fulfilling it.*

# EXAMPLES OF CLAUSES 11 AND 12

Some practical examples may help clarify the problems associated with lack of guidance on the difference between the two clauses. Examples of the 'circumstances in the environment of care which could jeopardise standards of practice' described in Clause 11 include:

- trailing electrical leads (tripping hazard);

- fixed-height beds and examination couches (biomechanically poor postures for the practitioner and difficult for some patients to get on and off safely);

- the noisy patient at night or the excessively noisy ward with its cacophony of sounds (disturbing the other patients);

- a patient with threatening behaviour either towards another patient or the practitioner;

- fellow ward practitioners without recent manual handling training (who may be using unsafe and frequently condemned methods to move patients);

- community practitioners concerned about hygiene or crowded conditions of the patient's home.

Examples of Clause 12 circumstances that prevent 'safe and appropriate care' are:

- providing care to accident and emergency patients on trolleys in the corridor;

- staff shortages leading to lack of staff and/or inappropriate skill mix on a busy ward;

- a male practitioner assigned to a female Muslim patient;

- a psychiatric patient cared for on a general ward;

- a 30-stone patient and no hoist available, or a hoist capable of only lifting 24 stone;

- discharging a patient home knowing that no appropriate equipment or services are available there;

- unsafe or unhygienic conditions in the patient's home;

▶ a physically frail patient who wishes to return home despite lack of independence, and with insufficient family and social support.

# ADVOCACY ISSUES

An advocate is described in the dictionary as a person who supports or speaks in favour; a person who pleads for another; a professional pleader in a court of justice or a barrister.

One associates an advocate with sufficient knowledge, power and authority to influence the circumstances surrounding the patient. The first — knowledge — is probably the easiest for a nurse to tackle. As for the other two — power and authority — the Code does not define how they can be achieved.

Even though the very nature of the word suggests an advocate must have power and authority to influence change, most practitioners are powerless to do so, even if they want to.

Who would willingly discharge a physically dependent patient with no independence and lack of family and social support to their home? Probably no one, yet how many nurses have the power and influence to alter this situation? Again, probably none. Few practitioners control the community services budget necessary to provide appropriate home care services and equipment, yet all are pressured to provide beds for other incoming patients, for whom they must also act as advocate.

Willard (1996) noted: 'There is very little evidence to suggest that patients want or have requested nurses to represent their views. This raises the very interesting question: by what authority does the nurse assume the obligation of representing the patient's interests?'

Clause 4 of the UKCC Code expressly enjoins practitioners to: 'decline any duties or responsibilities unless able to perform them in a safe and skilled manner'. Is this the 'get-out clause' found in many legal contracts? Should it be cited whenever the practitioner recognises he/she will not be able to achieve the ideals set out in Clauses 11 and 12?

## Problems of being an advocate

The role of advocate and client should be entered into freely by both parties, with either party able to terminate the arrangement at any time.

Chadwick and Tadd (1992) identified the following difficulties associated with being an advocate, which we will deal with point by point:

- an assumption that someone suffering ill health automatically requires an advocate;

- patients do not get to choose the practitioner who will act as their advocate;

- conflict when a practitioner has to act in the interests of two different patients;

- other groups acting as patient advocate may conflict with the practitioner's advocacy role;

- patients at times need protection from the practitioner;

- practitioners must also act for their employer (whistleblowing).

## An automatic requirement?

To assume someone suffering ill health automatically requires an advocate implies that the patient's rights may not otherwise be respected. It also suggests that ill health results in reduced decision-making abilities and that if presented with accurate information, the patient would be unable to adequately understand or process it to reach a reasoned conclusion. Some patients clearly need advocates: a toddler with no parent or guardian present; the unconscious patient; a patient with senile dementia. But at what point does a person who would normally be considered capable of making reasoned decisions lose this capability in the health care setting? And every patient's situation is different, as the next examples show.

## Patients do not choose

On admission to the ward or unit a practitioner is assigned as the primary nursing care provider for that patient for four out of six days while on duty. The patient is not generally given a choice of assigned nurse, or asked if they object to being cared for by a particular practitioner. An example when this could cause problems is the male nurse assigned to a female Muslim patient. This approach assumes the patient is in the sick role, incapable of making informed decisions.

## Conflict of interests

A conflict can arise if a practitioner has to act for more than one patient. Many nurses can act for up to eight at a time, and more if they are in charge of a ward. Suppose at 4am, when two staff members are caring for 30 patients, a confused patient, for the third time that night, loudly requests a bed pan, having forgotten she has a urinary catheter in place? The practitioner may be dealing with another loud, disoriented patient at the time. Whose advocate should they be — the patient wanting a bed-pan, the other patient causing a disturbance, or all the other patients, whose rest is being broken yet again?

## Conflict with other professionals

It could be argued that medical staff, intimately involved with the patient's care, should be the patient's primary advocate. They are, after all, involved in planning the treatment programmes and are informed about the medical implications. Traditionally they also have more power and influence than the nurse — some of the very attributes needed to fulfil the role of advocate.

On the other hand, perhaps this is precisely the reason patients need a nurse advocate. Those who are too medically focused may not be fully aware of conflicting needs in other areas of patients' lives.

For example, a physiotherapist may advise a patient with slow, unstable gait to always walk with assistance. What does a nurse do if that patient is desperate to visit the toilet in the middle of the night? Help the patient walk there slowly, even though they may not make it in time, thus increasing psychological distress? Or push the patient on a wheelchair and then help them walk back to bed afterwards (thus countering the rehabilitation programme but promoting the patient's psychological well being)?

## Protection from the practitioner

There seems to be an assumption that the practitioner-advocate will always act in the patient's best interest. But what if the opposite happens? Who will intervene if the advocate's behaviour is detrimental to or even unsafe for the patient?

One of the most notable cases concerns Beverly Allitt, who received 13 life sentences in 1993, including four for murder, for attacking children in her care. Other instances, in which practitioners were struck off by the UKCC for various reasons, include, to name but a few:

- Else Matthews, a nursing home sister, for telling staff not to feed elderly patients 'because they were on their last legs anyway' (*Nursing Times*, 1998a);

- Rosamund Mosely for having a sexual relationship with a 16-year-old pupil at the special needs school where she worked (*Nursing Times*, 1998b).

# Whistleblowing

Practitioners must follow the terms of reference set by their employer and act to promote the employer's best interest so long as it does not endanger the patient. But at what point does the practitioner's role of advocate override the responsibilities of being an employee? Certainly exposing to the newspapers sensitive issues not resolved to the employee's satisfaction may be detrimental to the employer. Decreased corporate image and standing within the community, leading to decreased revenue, may result from whistleblowing.

A model for whistleblowing was seen in 1990-91. Graham Pink, charge nurse on an elderly care ward, reported to proper authorities at Stepping Hill Hospital, Stockport (his employer) that there was a shortage of night duty staff. When his concerns were not addressed appropriately, Mr Pink maintained his advocacy role and campaigned publicly for more night duty staff by going to his local newspaper. This led the Stockport Health Authority to find him guilty of gross misconduct, including breaking patient confidentially, and to sack him in 1991. Mr Pink subsequently won a wrongful dismissal case against his former employer and his name is now synonymous with whistleblowing.

Tabone (1997) addressed the issue squarely: 'As an RN who has faced the fear of losing my job over practice standards and ethical issues, I can tell you: give up the fear. When you act from fear you become a target. If you stand genuinely on standards, if you are truly protecting the patient, if you are ethical you will prevail. This is not the easy road, but it is the only road. You have only one obligation. When you took your license you obliged yourself to the patient. Your license does not guarantee you a job. However, I can guarantee you without a license you will not have a job.'

The Graham Pink whistleblowing incident highlights the further issue raised by the UKCC that 'ultimately, it is the UKCC's role to protect the public' (Lavin, 1998). People in proper authority at Stepping Hill Hospital would have been the ward or directorate senior nurse, as well as the health authority's chief nursing officer, both of whom would be registered with the UKCC.

If Mr Pink reported through proper procedures (the hierarchy) that safe and appropriate care for the patients could not be provided due to staff shortages, what action has the UKCC taken against the senior nurse for the ward, and the chief nurse for the health authority where Mr. Pink worked, for failing to act in the patients' best interests by not providing sufficient staff?

The author is not advocating that there should now, so many years later, be further action against these two nurses, but uses this as an to demonstrate how the Code is too vague to assist even the UKCC.

# CONCLUSION

This chapter does not claim to offer all the answers to the broad topical problems associated with Clauses 11 and 12, but aims to stimulate discussion around developing a more concise guide for practitioners to help them to view the Code as an achievable ideal.

The Code accepts that the practitioner has responsibility and accountability but does not provide guidance on how the practitioner can achieve the power and influence necessary to fulfil the role of an accountable professional. It clearly imposes an obligation on all its members to become advocates without clearly defining what that entails, the restrictions placed on the role, and when it should be terminated.

The UKCC should not impose such an open-ended and vague obligation on practitioners, but should instead endeavour to provide greater guidance on how to achieve the ideals outlined in Clauses 11 and 12.

# References

Chadwick, R., Tadd, W. (1992) *Ethics in Nursing Practice*. Basingstoke: Macmillan.

Claus, R.E., Bailey, J.T. (1977) *Power and Influence in Health Care*. St Louis: Mosby.

Hancock, H.C. (1997) Professional responsibility: the implications for nursing practice within the realms of cardiothoracics. *Journal of Advanced Nursing*; 25: 5, 1054–1060.

Holden, R.J. (1991) Responsibility and autonomous nursing practice. *Journal of Advanced Nursing*; 16: 4, 118–123.

Lavin, M. (1998) UKCC's first duty is to protect public. Letter. *Nursing Times*; 94: 21, 20.

Nursing Times (1998b) Nurse struck off for sex with boy. *Nursing Times*; 94: 12, 9.

Nursing Times (1998a) Sister removed from register for telling staff not to feed residents. *Nursing Times*; 94: 32, 10.

Pearson, A., Vaughn, B. (1986) *Nursing Models for Practice*. London: Heinemann.

Tabone, S. (1997) Your practice or your job? *Texas Nursing*; 71: 4, 8-14

Willard, C. (1996) The nurse's role as patient advocate. *Journal of Advanced Nursing*; 24: 1, 60–66.

# Recommended reading

Pyne, R. Accountability in principle and practice. *British Journal of Nursing*; 1: 6, 301-305.

UKCC (1996) *Guidelines for Professional Practice*. London: UKCC.

# Clause 13: Mindful of colleagues

## Graham Johnson and Diane Haddock

> '...report to an appropriate person or authority where it appears that the health and safety of colleagues is at risk, as such circumstances may compromise standards of practice and care.'

This chapter considers the implications for nurses, midwives and health visitors of health and safety legislation and examines the health and safety measures required in the workplace. It focuses on helping nurses use appropriate reporting mechanisms in line with local, professional and legislative requirements, designed to identify health and safety issues that have a direct professional affect in accordance with Clause 13.

It shows how the occupational health nurse can be consulted as the 'appropriate person' referred to in Clause 13 and act as a mediator when the health and safety of colleagues is at risk.

## THE OCCUPATIONAL HEALTH NURSE

The occupational health nurse's role has been defined by the Royal College of Nursing Society of Occupational Health Nursing and the UKCC as a specialist branch of community health nursing. These nurses appear on the professional register and hold a post-registration qualification in occupational health nursing recorded with the UKCC, which may be a certificate, diploma or degree in occupational health nursing studies.

Occupational health nurses are employed in a range of workplaces, for example the NHS, retail or industry, and their practice is governed by the UKCC Code. They act as the employer's adviser and the employee's advocate. They act as the employer's advisor and the employee's advocate. The latter is an important consideration when conflict arises in the workplace and the employee seeks support from the occupational health nurse.

Central to the government's strategy outlined in *Our Healthier Nation* (Department of Health, 1998) is the creation of a healthier workplace with healthier workers, and occupational health nurses are in the vanguard for putting this policy into practice. The European Community has given the current health and safety legislation a higher profile and put occupational health at the forefront of proactive health care. Nurses will probably have had contact with the occupational health service at some point in their career, for example during pre- and post-employment health surveillance, for workplace immunisations, when reporting an accident or seeking the professional support of the occupational health nurse as a counsellor.

# NHS HEALTH AT WORK

The NHS is the UK's largest employer with over a million employees, providing a unique opportunity to educate staff and patients in disease prevention. As nurses we have a duty both towards our clients and our fellow colleagues to protect and maintain their health and well-being. This can be achieved by adhering to the highest level of nursing care and following the principles of relevant health and safety legislation together with the guidelines set out in the Code.

Back injuries and occupational stress are major causes of workplace sickness absence in the NHS and occupational health nurses are paramount in educating and managing staff who experience workplace ill health. A part of this education involves preventing workplace injuries by developing training programmes so nurses adopt safe working practices. This will help create a safety culture within the organisation.

## Risk assessment

The first step to creating a safe working environment is to carry out a risk assessment. Evaluating risk means identifying any potential hazards — sources of danger — that must be removed.

## Reporting arrangements

Practitioners must be alert to breaches in health and safety and report incidents and near misses that might compromise the safety of patients and staff.

Clause 13 refers to 'reporting to an appropriate person or authority'. But what does 'reporting' involve, and who are the appropriate people? The occupational health nurse may play a role here, though junior staff are most likely in the first instance to express their concerns to their ward sister or line manager.

Reports about nursing care are usually written in the patient's case notes or care plan and will normally include a series of statements and outcomes which identify the patient's state of health, their treatment regime and other relevant factors.

A variety of reporting arrangements may be appropriate for a nurse wanting to report the type of incident outlined in the Code. Verbal reports may be appropriate to start with. They should normally be followed by a written statement of events, detailing the time, date and location of the incident, the people involved, names of witnesses to the event and the name of the person/s to whom the incident was reported, together with the author's name. They should always be signed and preferably typed.

Sometimes a legal model needs to be followed, such as when reporting a workplace accident which results in an employee being absent from work. In this case, nurses should follow the Reporting of Injuries, Diseases and Dangerous Occurrences Regulations 1995 (RIDDOR) (HSC, 1995).

Typical of the type of incident that should be reported under the RIDDOR regulations is when an employee sustains a needle-stick injury resulting in exposure to blood infected with hepatitis B.

Employers are obliged to report incidents to the appropriate authority — in this case the Health and Safety Executive (HSE). They would be expected to give details of the circumstances of the injury and name and place of work of the injured person. The HSE would probably investigate the incident to determine if it was the result of careless disposal of used sharps.

If a nurse was found to have placed the health and safety of colleagues at risk by failing to dispose of the sharp in an appropriate receptacle, they could be prosecuted under the Health and Safety at Work Act (1974) (section 2).

## THE PROBLEM WITH ALCOHOL

The UKCC document Complaints about Professional Conduct (1998) outlines the procedures when complaining about the conduct of a professional colleague. The most common examples of unfitness to practice on health grounds considered by the UKCC are alcohol and drug dependency, untreated mental illness and serious personality disorders.

## CASE STUDY: A GUIDING HAND

The following incident demonstrates how a registered nurse impaired by poor health acted inappropriately while caring for a patient, resulting in a complaint by the relative. It was brought to the attention of an 'appropriate person'.

Margaret was employed as an F-grade registered nurse on a busy surgical ward. The morning had been as normal, with new admissions and discharges throughout the day. During visiting time, a patient's daughter asked the nurse if she could shed light on why her mother's medication had been changed by the doctor.

In a rather abrupt and off-hand manner, Margaret replied that she knew nothing about it, as the doctor had not had the courtesy to discuss it with her, and in any case she was due to go off duty so the best thing they could do was ask another nurse. This attitude severely upset the patient's daughter, who then reported it to the senior nurse ward manager and asked her to investigate the complaint in accordance with the trust's complaints policy.

The following morning Margaret was interviewed by the ward manager and asked to explain her alleged attitude. The nurse replied that, as far as she could recall, she had not spoken out of turn and perhaps the relative had misinterpreted her comments. However a review of Margaret's personnel records showed that this was not the first occasion that such a situation had arisen. The ward manager advised Margaret to consider her actions and provide an explanation for her behaviour.

At this point Margaret broke down in tears. When she had composed herself, she explained that she did have a financial problem which was affecting her ability to cope with day-to-day work and her domestic situation. It was further compounded by Margaret's belief that she was dependent on alcohol.

The senior nurse ward manager — the 'appropriate person' in this scenario — sought advice from the general manager of the surgical directorate on what to do next. In accordance with the disciplinary policy, he was also identified as 'an appropriate person' to discuss the incident with.

The human resources manager responsible for the directorate also became involved, and recommended that Margaret be suspended from duty on full pay until she agreed to see an occupational health nurse within the trust. The occupational health nurse then saw Margaret, and advised her of the trust's alcohol policy, designed to support people through their alcohol problem and provide access, where appropriate, to internal or external agencies for help.

Margaret allowed the occupational health nurse to carry out a series of blood tests for gamma glutamyl transpeptidase (GGT) and liver function tests and agreed to return to the occupational health department to discuss the results.

She was interviewed four days later. By then, her attendance record had been reviewed and it was clearly typical of a person with alcohol dependency. Margaret had been off sick for short periods several times, particularly on Mondays, with various diagnoses, including diarrhoea and vomiting, flu symptoms, bad back and abdominal upset. The ward manager had discussed these absences on Margaret's return to work but as there had been no suspicion of an alcohol problem, no further action had been taken.

The blood results indicated a raised GGT and there were concerns over Margaret's liver function test. She was referred for professional assistance from the regional alcohol treatment service.

Her condition improved after treatment from this service, supported by the occupational health nurse, ward manager and other colleagues, including her family. The occupational health nurse agreed that Margaret was now at a stage to attend an internal disciplinary hearing where the allegations and subsequent findings of the investigation would be discussed with her. Appropriate action in accordance with the trust's disciplinary procedure would be considered there — in this case, a formal warning.

This case raises important issues about how nurses' competency and ability to practice may be compromised by the effect of drugs and alcohol. The ward manager and personnel manager acted correctly to maintain patient safety. The nurse was suspended from duty until appropriate assistance could be accessed through the occupational health service, which then referred her to an appropriate external agency for ongoing treatment and management. By successfully managing this problem at local level, this nurse may have been prevented from committing a more serious professional mistake that could have resulted in disciplinary action by the UKCC.

## STRESS IN THE WORKPLACE

Occupational stress exacts a heavy toll both on individual employees and the NHS's organisational and financial effectiveness, which is affected by absenteeism. Studies by Rees and Cooper (1990) concluded that occupational stress appeared at all levels of the workforce. Compared with white collar and professional workers in industry, health workers reported significantly greater pressure at work, with higher levels of physical and mental ill health, lower job satisfaction and less control over their working environment. Staff in many hospital departments exhibited signs of stress, but particularly in accident and emergency departments and mental health establishments.

The HSE's *Good Health is Good Business* campaign (1994) aimed to reduce the number of people who suffer ill health caused or aggravated by work. It estimated that 2.2 million employees nationally suffer ill health caused by their working environment. First on the list of causes were musculoskeletal problems, followed by stress/depression, thought to affect 100,000 workers.

## CASE STUDY: AN ACCIDENT WAITING TO HAPPEN

In a busy accident and emergency department, the waiting room was full of patients needing attention in the minor injuries area. Nursing numbers were 30% down on agreed levels and staff were showing early signs of stress towards their colleagues and in some cases, to clients.

Mr Roberts had arrived at A&E three hours earlier, and had been interviewed by the triage nurse, Jenny. She had determined that his condition was of medium priority and told him to take a seat in the waiting area. She advised him that the current waiting period was likely to be more than two-and-a-half hours. He waited patiently, though he seemed agitated and made threatening eye contact with any nursing staff who happened to pass by.

Unfortunately, the delay was suddenly increased when patients from a major road traffic accident were admitted and those people in the waiting area were told they might have to wait at least another hour. At this point, Mr Roberts marched across to Jenny. He berated her and attacked her physically, bruising her right arm. Security staff restrained him and he was later arrested and removed from the department by the police.

While there is no specific legislation dealing with stress at work, employers need to be aware of general health and safety obligations. Section 2 (1) of the Health and Safety Act (1974) states that it is the duty of every employer to ensure, so far as is reasonably practicable, the mental and physical health, safety and welfare of all employees.

Section 3 of the Management of Health and Safety at Work Regulations (1992) requires every employer to make a suitable and sufficient assessment of the risks to the health and safety of their employees to which they are exposed while at work, and base their control measures on such assessments. Employers are therefore encouraged to take stress into account when assessing possible health hazards, watching out for potential problems and being ready to act if harm seems likely.

After the attack Jenny was assessed by the A&E physician. She was told to go home and to see the occupational health department's physiotherapist the next day.

An occupational health nurse investigated the incident with other senior members of the A&E department. After receiving the accident report form, she requested information on agreed staffing levels, together with levels on the day of the accident. The department should have had five registered nurses, three health care assistants and a senior nurse manager on duty. But only three registered nurses and one health care assistant had been on duty on the day of the attack, because of sickness and other circumstances.

The investigation revealed that nursing staff in the department were regularly expected to cope with extreme pressures of work and cover for absent staff. Concern about this state of affairs had been raised many times with the department's clinical director and general manager, to little avail.

In this case, low staffing levels meant working in conditions that were unsatisfactory, heightening the risk of nurses being exposed to verbal and physical abuse.

When staff are making a formal complaint about the lack of adequate resources, it is important that they gather and retain documentary evidence.

## MANUAL HANDLING

One in four nurses has taken time off with a back injury sustained at work (Disabled Living Foundation, 1994). In some cases such injuries have ended a nurse's career. Despite the availability of appropriate knowledge and resources, the safety of colleagues and clients is still being placed at risk, with manual handling injuries accounting for 60% of all health care accidents, at a cost to the NHS in excess of £50m a year (Monkhouse and Williams, 1992).

## CASE STUDY: PAIN IN THE BACK

When Mrs Jones came to a busy medical admissions ward, in adherence with policy, a nurse completed a Waterlow score and individual patient assessment which highlighted her poor mobility. She needed a series of investigations and it was obvious she would need full assistance with her mobilisation. The porter arrived to take her to the radiology department, and sought assistance from two nurses, Christine and Penny. Mrs Jones was resting on her bed. Christine realised that they would require the hoist to manoeuvre Mrs Jones from the bed into the porter's chair. As she was about to collect the hoist, Penny stated that Mrs Jones would only need a quick lift into the chair.

Christine pointed out that there had been several manual handling accidents before because mechanical aids had not been used. But Penny was adamant that it was not necessary to use the hoist on this occasion. Reluctantly, Christine helped Penny to lift Mrs Jones into the chair. Mrs Jones, who weighed 85kgs, had recently suffered a cerebrovascular accident and had a left-sided weakness. She was unable to assist and fell to the floor, causing trauma to herself and both the nurses. Penny and Christine then faced having to manoeuvre Mrs Jones from the floor using an appropriate handling aid. They summoned the doctor to assess Mrs Jones's injuries and also reported the incident on the appropriate accident form. Fortunately Mrs Jones turned out to be unharmed, but her treatment was delayed as she had not been able to attend her X-ray.

The occupational health department received the accident form. The two nurses who had sustained injuries required physiotherapy and extended sick leave. The occupational health nurse adviser contacted the manual handling coordinator to discuss whether training had been given to the nurses and if mechanical aids were available.

This was one of the cases where, despite resources being available, nurses tried to take the quicker option. But it can have long-term implications and ultimately compromises safe standards of care. It is in breach of the Manual Handling Operations Regulations (MHOR) (1992), the Health and Safety At Work Act (1974) and Clause 13 of the UKCC Code of Professional Conduct.

Both nurses had received manual handling training and mechanical aids were available, so management had fulfilled its obligations to the employees.

The Health and Safety Requirements Regulation 5 of the MHOR (1992) states that each employee while at work shall make full and proper use of any system of work provided for their use by their employer. This should be implemented in conjunction with Regulation 4(1) b (ii) which involves considering the task, load working environment and individual's capability.

Duties are already placed on the employee in section 7 of the Health and Safety at Work Act (1974), where they must:

▷ take reasonable care for their own health and safety and that of others (colleagues and clients) who may be affected by their activities;

▷ cooperate with their employers to enable them to comply with health and safety duties.

Should Christine have reported Penny for continuing to carry out manual handling tasks in an obviously compromised unsafe manner, considering an awareness of her duty to safeguard and promote the interests of individual patients and to be mindful when the health and safety of colleagues is at risk? Should she have declined to agree to this action and refused to condone unsafe practice? The answer is, in each case, yes.

In this instance, both nurses could face litigation.

It is worth putting this health care scenario in perspective. If this was replicated in the construction industry, few employees would be prepared to lift an unsteady, unstable load of 85 kgs without mechanical assistance!

# THE JENKINSON REPORT

Sometimes nurses can be confronted with colleagues whose actions endanger patients in their care. The reasons may not be obvious at the time — it may not be clear whether this is deliberate cruelty, ineptitude, incompetence or mental illness.

And their actions can, wittingly or unwittingly, place the health and safety of colleagues at risk, both in terms of physical risk and stress.

Registered nurse Amanda Jenkinson was jailed in 1996 after being found guilty of causing grievous bodily harm to an elderly patient at Bassetlaw Hospital. She had tampered with a ventilator in the intensive therapy unit. It later transpired that Ms Jenkinson had been suspended and dismissed in the past for allegedly failing to disclose a previous history of mental illness to employers.

The independent inquiry following the trial of Ms Jenkinson raised issues which relate to Clause 13 (North Nottinghamshire Health Authority, 1997). The inquiry report said that when other nurses in the ward became aware of circumstances placing the patient who died at risk, they raised this with the 'appropriate authority', in this case the senior nurse on duty, who in turn reported his concerns to the clinical director. This demonstrated a positive and constructive 'whistle blowing policy'.

However, in general the report found that staff concerns could have been reported earlier. It identified a 'marked and noticeable reluctance' by health care professionals to pass on information to others who have a 'proper and legitimate interest' and felt this should be addressed throughout the health service. Professional bodies, including the UKCC, had to recognise there was no absolute duty of confidentiality. 'We must balance that statement by a view that health care professionals are reluctant to break the duty of confidentiality in relation to any patient and particularly in relation to their fellow professionals.

'There is difficulty in thinking the unthinkable, namely that a fellow professional may be either maliciously or because of illness committing an act which places fellow professionals or patients in jeopardy or which endangers the public at large.' (NNHA, 1997.)

Nurses need to be confident that they can report their worries to an appropriate person without fear of reprisal, and in the knowledge that this information will remain confidential and be thoroughly investigated by independent advisers. Those who blew the whistle in the Jenkinson case clearly did the right thing.

# CONCLUSION

As the Code points out, each registered nurse, midwife and health visitor is accountable for their own practice and if the health and safety of colleagues is at risk, either as a result of manual handling or of stress, they have a duty to report it to an appropriate person or authority. The occupational health nurse plays a vital role as a mediator when the health and safety of staff is at risk and can act as an advocate for the individual in these circumstances.

## References

Department of Health. *Our Healthier Nation* (1997). London: The Stationery Office.

Disabled Living Foundation (1994) *Handling people, equipment advice and information*. London: Disabled Living Foundation.

Health and Safety Commission (1974) *Health and Safety at Work Act* (1974). London: The Stationery Office.

Health and Safety Commission (1992) *Management of Health and Safety at Work Regulations*. London: HMSO.

Health and Safety Commission (1992) *Manual Handling Operations Regulations*. London: HMSO.

Health and Safety Commission (1995) *A Guide to RIDDOR*. London: HMSO.

Health and Safety Executive (1994) *Good Health is Good Business*. London: HMSO.

Monkhouse, A., Williams, C. (1992) Staff back injuries — The cost. *Health Service Journal* Managing Risk Supplement; 102: 5285, 4.

North Nottinghamshire Health Authority (1997) Report of the independent inquiry into the major employment and ethical issues arising from the trial of Amanda Jenkinson. London: The Stationery Office.

Rees, D.W. and Cooper, C.L. (1990) Occupational Stress in Health Service Employees. *Health Service Management Research*; 3:3, 163.

UKCC (March 1998) *Complaints about Professional Conduct*. London: UKCC.

## Recommended reading

Croner (1992) *Health and Safety in Practice — Risk Assessment*. Surrey: Croner Publications.

Heywood Jones, I. (1990) *The Nurse's Code*. London: Macmillan.

Mackay, L. (1989) *Nursing a Problem*. Buckinghamshire: Open University Press.

# Clause 14: Helping hands

**Carolyn Mills**

> '...assist professional colleagues, in the context of your own knowledge, experience and sphere of responsibility, to develop their professional competence.'

To understand Clause 14, we need to examine more deeply the meaning of several concepts — the bricks through which theories are constructed (Hardy, 1974) — and frame them in the context of our day-to-day practice. The framework developed by Johns is useful for this (1993, 1994, 1995).

In a participative study of primary and associate nurses at Burford Community Hospital, Oxfordshire, Johns (1994) identified four learning domains that are core to becoming effective in work, and linked them to Carper's (1978) four ways of knowing. These learning domains are:

- becoming patient-centred, which relates to knowing yourself as a practitioner in the context of care;

- becoming therapeutic with patients, which relates to understanding what therapeutic work is and encompasses decision-making, involvement with patients/clients and responding with appropriate and skilled action;

- giving and receiving feedback;

- coping with ways that sustain therapeutic work.

These learning domains are a useful framework from which nurses can put into context the explicit and implicit concepts within Clause 14. These concepts include:

- explicit: knowledge, experience, responsibility, team working, and competence.

- implicit: authority, accountability, delegation, managing team work, autonomy, power, giving and receiving feedback, role modelling and leadership.

Nurses need to ask themselves how their understanding of these concepts influences their practice and whether an increased understanding would have made them behave differently in the past.

# EXPLICIT CONCEPTS

First, we will outline in more detail the concepts explicit in Clause 14.

## Knowledge

Clause 14 talks about assisting professional colleagues in 'the context of your own knowledge and experience'. Knowledge does not just relate to facts, but also to experience and understanding. Avant and Walker (1995) define it as the sum and range of what can be learnt; the *Concise Oxford Dictionary* defines it as familiarity gained by experience of a person, thing or fact; and theoretical or practical understanding of a subject.

In the nursing context, some view knowledge as a product. Others recognise the impact of experience and add a further dimension by associating it with action and decision-making (Benner, 1984; Schon, 1983).

Nursing knowledge can be subdivided into: practice knowledge, clinical experience, tacit knowledge (which is embedded and incorporates both theoretical and experiential knowledge) and intuition. Intuition has been described as 'understanding without rationale' (Benner and Tanner, 1987) and is linked to expert human judgement.

The ways of knowing linked to the four learning domains referred to earlier are:

- knowing self;

- knowing therapeutic work;
- knowing responsibility;
- knowing others.

These specific aspects of knowledge are linked to each learning domain:

- To know self requires self knowledge gained through personal reflection and knowledge of authority and accountability.

- To be therapeutic with patients and families requires knowledge about the patient and their family/significant others, holistic practice knowledge, skilled know-how and knowledge about interpersonal relationships.

- Knowing responsibility requires specific knowledge, again related to interpersonal relationships and accountability and authority.

- Knowing others requires knowledge about organisational approaches/systems and interpersonal relationships.

## Responsibility

The concepts of responsibility and accountability are so closely related that they need to be considered in parallel, even though the former is explicit and the latter implicit in Clause 14. Being accountable is defined in lay language as being obliged to give a reckoning or explanation for one's actions.

From a professional perspective it is related to the law. A practitioner has four areas of accountability: to the public via criminal law, to the patient via civil law, to the employer via a contract of employment and the profession via the UKCC. I also believe that any practitioner has accountability to self, although this is more of an ethical issue than a legal one. The accountability of health care professionals is determined by what care can reasonably be expected from an appropriately qualified practitioner.

Accountability suggests that you have decided to carry out an action; that you are able to justify that action in relation to what you have done, why, and the outcomes; and that the actions you have taken are based on knowledge. You also have personal responsibility for those actions. We are all accountable for the actions that we take, regardless of the level of experience that we have. Inexperience is no defence.

Accountability is implicit in Clause 14 when it says 'assist professional colleagues in the context of your own knowledge and experience'.

All practitioners have a responsibility to ensure that they and anyone they delegate to are in positions they are competent to be in. We cannot be accountable for another's actions but we are liable if we place ourselves or others in a position or role, or if we or they undertake a task, without being competent to do it.

Responsibility is defined as having a legal or moral obligation to take care of something or to carry out a duty, having to account for one's actions. Responsibility in relation to practitioners implies that you are carrying out an action, and the result will be to complete it safely. However, you can also be held accountable for that action.

Clause 14 talks about 'your sphere of responsibility', meaning the field of action or influence that a person has. Every nurse has a minimum sphere of responsibility set out by the Code and other UKCC publications. Additional responsibilities relate to the roles we work in. For example both D and G grade nurses have the same responsibilities in relation to their professional conduct, but different employment responsibilities. A G grade nurse's sphere of responsibility is greater overall than that of a D grade nurse.

Take this simple example of statutory training on manual handling and fire. All nurses have a personal responsibility to ensure that they attend regular statutory training sessions. As a ward manager you would have further responsibilities to make sure your staff are aware of the training dates, times and so on, that they are able to have time off to attend, that you have a record of who has attended such training and that you follow up those who have not attended.

All nurses need to be clear about their sphere of responsibility and who they have a responsibility to. However, this may not always be as straightforward as it seems. With many new roles in nursing, the sphere is being developed beyond the 'normal' nursing role. In fact many of these roles may not be specifically for nurses but open to other health care professionals.

In some cases the traditional boundaries between professional groups are becoming blurred. Practitioners must ensure their roles are developed within a structured framework that clarifies educational and legal accountability issues. The following case studies illustrate some of the issues.

# CASE STUDY: RESPONSIBILITY

It was a particularly busy shift on the ward and several nurses were off sick with flu. A doctor wrote out a prescription for an antibiotic and asked Jane to give it to the patient. On looking at the drug chart Jane was concerned that the prescribed dose appeared to be rather high. Initially she made this judgement on specific knowledge that she had gained about drug dosage and administration through training and her past clinical experience.

Aware of her responsibility to the patient and others, and her accountability, she checked the dosage in the *British National Formulary*. This indicated that it was a higher than normal dose. She went back to the doctor who explained it was because the patient had meningitis and to treat that, the dose was always higher. Still not sure, Jane phoned drug information, where somebody confirmed that even if the patient had meningitis the dose appeared to be higher than that recommended. Up to this point Jane had checked out her knowledge to reassure herself that she was right.

Where did her sphere of responsibility lie if she believed the dose was not correct and might put the patient in danger?

In this situation, Jane had a responsibility to the patient and her colleague. To discharge these responsibilities while being aware of her own accountability, she needed to explain to the doctor that she was unhappy to give the drug herself, and give her reasons for this. If the doctor accepted her reasons and revisited the prescription in the light of her knowledge then the situation would be safely resolved.

If this had not happened, however, Jane would have needed to try other mechanisms to get the doctor to review the prescription, for example contacting someone in a position senior to him. At the end of the day, if the doctor chose to give the drug Jane could be sure that she had tried to assist a professional colleague, in the context of her own knowledge, experience and sphere of responsibility to develop their professional competence. She acted competently, she sought appropriate help, used her initiative. She recognised that she would be accountable for any actions that she took, but also that she had a responsibility to the patient and their family, her peers and other health care team members.

If Jane had just been thinking about her accountability she could have simply refused to give the drug and told the doctor that he had to give it himself, but she would not have been working within the UKCC Code in relation to her responsibilities.

# CASE STUDY: TEAM WORKING

Paul was working a shift on a busy surgical ward. Many patients were coming back from theatre that afternoon and the ward was short of qualified nursing staff. Paul had responsibility for two bays of six patients and was working with two health care assistants (HCAs).

He decided that the best way to manage the workload was to delegate some of the post-operative patient observations to the HCAs, who are trained at NVQ level three and able to perform post-operative observations. Where did Paul's sphere of responsibility lie?

To ensure that he assisted the HCAs to develop their professional competence in the context of his own knowledge, experience and sphere of responsibility, Paul needed to be clear in his mind that he was delegating tasks the HCAs were trained for. The nurse has a responsibility as the delegating senior member of the team to check this out with the HCAs and not make assumptions about their knowledge and skills.

Paul also had a responsibility to ensure that he shared his knowledge about the patient or proposed task with the HCA. HCAs also have a responsibility to say if they are unsure of what they have been asked to do. Ultimately they are accountable for any actions that they take. However, the onus of responsibility lies with the nurse delegating the task to ensure that the person undertaking the task has the necessary knowledge and skills to do this effectively.

This example demonstrates collegial relationships between the team members and a valuing of people based on mutual understanding of roles and authority, and an acceptance of responsibility.

## Developing professional competence

There is a move towards competency-based learning and assessment in nursing in practice, but what does professional competence actually mean? 'Professional' is defined in the dictionary as highly skilled. Nurses' values and beliefs about their job will impact on what they believe to be professional. For me, professional nursing practice is about being patient-centred, working therapeutically, working as part of a team and having a clear understanding of the responsibility and accountability that are associated with the work.

Competence means having the ability or authority to do what is required. In nursing today it appears to be about using initiative, seeking help appropriately and accepting accountability for work. Historically, good nurses 'coped'. Johns (1996) argues that this encourages a facade of competence and may discourage nurses from seeking appropriate help.

The learning domains referred to earlier — of becoming patient-centred, being therapeutic with patients and families, giving and receiving feedback and coping with work in ways which sustain therapeutic action — all contribute to professionalism.

At times it can be inappropriate to pass on knowledge. For example, you are working with a student nurse who is in their final year, and has had little experience of administering drugs to patients. You decide that it would be a valuable learning experience for the student to shadow you doing the drug round a couple of times with a view to them being able to undertake this role under supervision in the future, and ultimately helping the student develop their professional competence in preparation for when they qualify.

This is an appropriate action to take with the student. But it would be inappropriate to offer the same opportunity to an HCA because the task of medication administration does not fall within the HCA role. You would be assisting a colleague to develop in an area outside their sphere of professional responsibility.

# IMPLICIT CONCEPTS

We will now move on to explore the concepts implicit in Clause 14.

## Authority

Authority is defined as the power or right to give orders and make others obey or take specific action, or a person with specialised knowledge. Power is frequently seen as a rather unpleasant characteristic but it does have many positive aspects.

Power and influence go together and power may be legitimate in the form of authority, that is, if there is some official backing, for example your ward manager, who has the authority to ask what you are doing. People can have power through various routes — position, knowledge, personality and resources. All power types exist within nursing. To work within Clause 14 requires nurses to exercise their power in both covert and overt ways, for example through persuasion and skilled interpersonal skills, through non-cooperation, and through authority in relation to position.

# Other implicit concepts

Concepts of managing team working, role modelling/leadership, giving and receiving feedback are key to working within Clause 14. They all relate to interdisciplinary collaboration and working in a collegiate way. There needs to be willingness to participate in shared planning and decision making, with people seeing themselves as members of a team and contributing to a common product or goal. This should be done while respecting the unique abilities of each profession within the team (Collucio and Maguire, 1983).

Collegiality is essential for collaboration, but is a fundamentally different concept. It is a unique condition among members of a definable professional work group, which aims to advance the profession itself, with the ultimate goal broader than the one pursued in collaboration (Hansen, 1995). It has four characteristics:

- non-hierarchical relationships;

- group cohesiveness;

- interpersonal exchanges and collaboration;

- coordination and cooperation when making and implementing decisions.

Both collegiality and collaboration contribute to productive working relationships. One cannot develop another's professional competence without first recognising and respecting differing professional contributions and that everyone is working towards a common purpose. This may all seem obvious but there is a long history of conflict between some health care professionals, particularly nurses and doctors, embedded in social, economic and professional issues.

Cavanagh (1991) uses the work of Ma (1984), who identified categories of conflict within nursing, including:

- difference in values;

- difference in role expectations;

- difference in perception;
- lack of communication.

# CONCLUSION

How each of us perceives Clause 14 will to some extent depend on our personal world view and the world views that influenced our own socialisation as practitioners. The aim of this chapter is to get nurses to think about themselves and their practice in relation to Clause 14. To take this thinking a step further requires a development of reflective ability, as it is only through reflection on action that our reflective ability in action is enhanced (Schon, 1983). This means nurses not only maintaining, but also continually developing their practice in relation to the concepts discussed.

## References

Benner, P. (1984) *From Novice to Expert: Excellence and power in clinical nursing practice*. Menlo Park, California: Addison-Wesley.

Benner, P., Tanner, C. (1987) Clinical judgement: how expert nurses use intuition. *American Journal of Nursing*; 87: 1, 23-31.

Carper, B. (1978) Fundamental patterns of knowing in nursing. *Advances in Nursing Science*; 1: 1, 13-23.

Cavanagh, S. (1991) The conflict management style of staff nurses and nurse managers. *Journal of Advanced Nursing*; 16: 10, 1254- 1260.

Collucio, M., Maguire, P. (1983) Collaborative practice becoming a reality through primary nursing. *Nursing Administration Quarterly*; 7: summer, 59-63.

Hansen, H.E. (1995) A model of collegiality among staff nurses in acute care. *Journal of Nursing Administration*; 25: 12, 10-20.

Hardy, M.E. (1974) Theories, components, development and evaluation. *Nursing Research*; 23: 2, 100-107.

Johns, C. (1993) Professional Supervision. *Journal of Nursing Management*; 1: 1, 9-18.

Johns, C. (Ed) (1994) *The Burford NDU Model: Caring in Practice*. Oxford: Blackwell Science.

Johns, C. (1995) Achieving effective work as a professional activity. In: Schrober, J.E., Hinchcliff, S.M. (Eds) *Towards Advanced Practice: Key concepts for health care*. London: Arnold.

Schon, D. (1983) *The Reflective Practitioner. How professionals think in action*. San Francisco: Jossey Bass.

Walker, L., Avant, K. (1994) *Strategies for theory construction in nursing* (3rd Edition). New York: Appleton and Lange.

# Clause 15: A touch of bribery?

## Jacqueline Docherty

> '...refuse any gift, favour or hospitality from patients or clients currently in your care which might be interpreted as seeking to exert influence to obtain preferential consideration.'

There is a lack of clarity about the meaning of 'obtaining preferential consideration'. Presumably it implies that patients or clients (and even friends or relatives of those receiving care) feel it may be appropriate to offer some kind of reward in the hope of securing more or better care. This could be considered tantamount to a bribe even in its most subtle form. To think the unthinkable, patients may even believe such action is necessary to receive the routine care which society believes they are entitled to by right.

This notion of influencing access to more or better care is echoed in guidance from the General Medical Council, which states that as a member of the medical profession a doctor must 'act in the patient's best interests when making referrals and providing or arranging treatment of care. So you must not ask for or accept any inducement, gift or hospitality which may affect or be seen to affect your judgment.' (GMC, 1995).

The key to interpreting the clause in the UKCC Code is linked both to the size of the gift or favour and to the intention, which may be either overt or covert. On the face of it, accepting a box of chocolates or a small token of gratitude appears harmless, but nurses need to be aware of the implications and inherent dangers behind such a gesture and the degree to which they are able to influence access to more or improved care for patients.

## ACCESS TO SERVICES

Why, in a country that has had a National Health Service free at the point of delivery for over 50 years, should patients and their relatives or carers feel the need to try to exert influence in this way? In the western world society is expected to have an ethical obligation to ensure equitable access to health care for all; health care being the relief of suffering, preventing premature death, restoring functioning, increasing opportunity, providing information and education about an individual's condition, and empathy and compassion (Aroskar 1987).

However, because health needs and desires are virtually limitless, every health care system faces some form of scarcity and not everyone who needs a particular form of health care can get it. The need and demand for health care is growing faster than the resources for providing it. The main reasons are an increasingly ageing population, a rise in patient expectations and advances in new technology and knowledge. NHS allocation occurs by several means, including queuing and the use of restrictive criteria for services. Rationing has been linked to limited resources, crisis management and the setting of priorities in the health care budget. Increasingly the media takes up the cases of those who are denied access to health care resources. One example was the leukaemia sufferer known as Child B and later revealed as Jaymee Bowen, who in 1996 was denied a treatment because her local health authority, Cambridge and Huntingdon, refused to fund it.

An increasingly evidence-based health care culture may be seen as a means of assisting health policy, clinical and managerial decision-making, while providing a rational basis for identifying and defending such decisions within the public arena. However, resource allocation decisions taken at a macro level often have little apparent relevance to people trying to deal with the day-to-day reality of clinical practice and patient interaction, and this is where most nurses rely on their values, morals and ethical principles to assist them.

# THE MEANING OF ETHICS

Ethics and morality are concerned with good and right and being good and right. While morality tends to focus on the individual aspects of this, ethics relates to social good. This can be expanded to include questions about the right and wrong of given actions. Ethics may be defined as 'the philosophical study of moral conduct and reasoning' (Sparkes, 1991), in which moral conduct may be seen to be set within a framework that has four levels: moral judgments, moral rules, moral principles and moral thoughts. However, good and right do not stand alone, they have to be put into practice.

Every person concerns themselves with ethics at one time or another, and its study is not solely for those within an academic ivory tower. It is acutely relevant to nurses who have to deal with issues of information, consent, treatment and care, as well as choices regarding resource allocation of time, people, equipment or support, every day. We encounter many situations that raise ethical issues and it can be difficult to give an absolute yes or no about the intrinsic moral worth of particular incidents or situations. Ethics can provide a way of thinking rationally about situations but cannot offer universal answers.

We all experience and interpret events from our own perspective, and notions of good and right are largely personal. To help overcome this most societies rely on rules to indicate and influence moral reasoning. Kendrick (1993) says the main problem with rules-based dictums is that their absolute form does not allow for the consideration of consequences. For example, although we may agree 'Thou shalt not kill' is a precept by which we should all live, we condone and indeed encourage such behaviour in times of war. For the practising clinician ethical and clinical knowledge should be inseparable. Ethical principles relating to patients' rights and autonomy must be translated into everyday clinical behaviour.

# NURSING ETHICS AND THE DUTY OF CARE

Nurses, midwives and health visitors have a duty of care to each patient. This is underpinned by the positive principle of beneficence (to do good), balanced with the maxim of non-maleficence (to do no harm). The latter ideal is frequently moderated when the potential gain arising as a result of an action (or harm) is set against the perceived or short-lived disadvantage of the action. Examples include giving a patient a pain-relieving injection, which causes temporary discomfort, but will be beneficial over a number of hours; and more contentiously, perhaps, nurses helping to administer electroconvulsive therapy (ECT).

Nursing ethics are grounded in the idea of caring. Care is defined as the alleviation of vulnerability, the promotion of growth and health, the facilitation of comfort, dignity or a good and peaceful death, mutual realisation, and preservation and extension of human possibilities in a person, a community, a family, or a tradition (Benner et al, 1996). The various models of nursing used within today's health care setting are based on specific values, each of which stresses particular aspects of care. Ideally, underpinning each model should be the five components of caring identified by the Canadian nurse-philosopher Roache (1987). These are:

- compassion;

- competence;

- confidence;

- conscience;

- commitment.

While it is true that each aspect may exist independently they tend to come together in their most coherent and powerful form when primary nursing is being practised.

Nursing is interested in human needs related to health and illness, in healthy lifestyles, in coping with activities of daily living, in adjustment to illness, in feeling pain and suffering and in dying. Raatikainen (1989) identifies that when interacting with the patient the nurse can either strengthen or weaken the patient's individuality, integrity, self-determination and personal growth, depending on to what extent and how he or she gives freedom to the patient. Patients may express individuality by giving presents as a token of recognition for a job well done, as a reflection of shared experiences or endeavours, or as acknowledgment of friendship, empathy and care in a difficult situation. However, care must be taken to ensure that influence or coercion are not brought to bear where patients feel the need to reward staff.

# PATIENTS AND PROFESSIONAL AUTONOMY

The notion of patients as fully independent and self-governing beings, or indeed nurses as truly autonomous practitioners, is to some extent spurious. Autonomy is inevitably linked to power. People are said to be autonomous by the extent to which they are able to control their own lives, and to some degree their own destiny, through their own faculties. Harris (1985) refers to four key 'defects' through which an individual's autonomy may be undermined and diminished. These are defects in:

- the person's ability to control either their desires or actions or both;

- the person's reasoning;

- the information available to them, and on which they base their choices;

- the stability of the person's own desires.

Some situations diminish a person's autonomy, particularly illness, psychological impairment, physical or mental disability. Illness can make people confused, weak or fearful.

Caring and taking responsibility for another human being and respecting their individuality requires knowledge and understanding of that person. The promotion of shared responsibility is easily disregarded if the nurse lacks the skills required for a democratic, cooperative working relationship but instead merely seeks to do things for the patient. This may be so particularly where a task-centred approach to nursing care is pursued. Nurses may be seen as powerful 'doers' whom patients (or relatives) may seek to influence through the giving of money or presents.

A recent example was the district nurse manager who was dismissed after agreeing to take money from a patient's wife and using it for a staff tea kitty (O'Dowd, 1998). Nurses over a three-year period had apparently accepted between £60 and £90, allegedly given in the hope that they would treat the woman's sick husband kindly. Although the nurse involved won her unfair dismissal claim she was not reinstated by the trust on the grounds that she had breached both the UKCC Code and the trust's own policy in regard to accepting and reporting gifts.

## POWER RELATIONSHIPS

This issue of nurses as powerful beings who can grant or withhold care is highly significant. We should not be aiming for power over others, but power with others. Patients may feel powerless since their access to health care professionals is carefully controlled, particularly in the NHS. They do not always understand how health care organisations work, which puts them at a disadvantage in being able to pursue their own interests. Health care professionals, on the other hand, are or at least appear familiar with the way their organisation operates. They tend to speak a specialist jargon which is difficult for others to understand. This is just as true of other professions. Remember the first time you tried to buy a computer or a mobile phone and the bewildering discussion that no doubt took place.

But this feeling of imbalance and powerlessness becomes even more acute in relation to health and future well-being. Communicating information in a clear and concise manner helps patients begin to make real choices for themselves, which in turn can positively affect outcomes valued by them. Routine regimes can reduce the patient's feeling of power. Examples include: requiring patients to wear night clothes during the day even when they are physically able to be up and about; the tendency for conversations with professionals to take place when the patient is lying down; and the impression of authority and power that wearing uniforms can convey.

Health care professionals also have power because they control access to tests and treatment. They have the ultimate sanction in admitting or limiting access of friends and family within a hospital or nursing home setting. And the system can appear to close ranks to protect its own members in the face of patient or relative complaints.

The notion of equality means that everybody should have the same opportunity to receive health services and nursing care. Although the help given to each patient or family may differ, it should be of equal quality. The time and skills devoted to the care given will depend primarily on the type and amount of care that person needs. Where services are free of charge, many assume equality is upheld and there are no regional differences in provision. But inequality does exist, albeit in a more insidious form which is harder to detect. The more affluent and articulate are able to demand services for themselves and their families, while those who are inarticulate and disadvantaged for whatever reason tend to remain passive recipients of a level and standard of care that is decided by others. Little wonder then that some patients and relatives may feel the need to try to influence or redress the balance in more subliminal ways, through the use of gifts or hospitality.

## THE NURSE AS THE PATIENT'S ADVOCATE

Nurses are often hailed as 'the patient's advocate', and indeed the UKCC, in *Exercising Accountability* (UKCC, 1989), envisages the role of patient or client advocate as an integral and essential aspect of good professional practice. But advocacy has also been accused of promoting professional discord, of being both paternalistic and an unwarranted interference in the autonomy of others. Bird (1994) highlights two factors that place the nurse in the role of patient advocate. They are:

- The power relationship within the health care system is unequal, with the formidable might of the medical profession and to a lesser degree managers and budget holders on the one side, and the ill, vulnerable person on the other.

- The nursing profession, on the other hand, tends to regard each patient as an individual with a mind that requires as much attention as the body. This is evidenced in nursing's approach to holistic and individualised patient care planning.

The case for the nurse as advocate still has to be proved and nurses should resist rushing to claim the moral high ground here. As Melia (1994) points out 'at best the activity of the nurse as advocate is likely to resemble benevolent paternalism on the part of the nurse and trusting acceptance on the part of the patient'. Nurses frequently derive power from being seen as experts within their chosen field. Expert power is a social power that a person brings into a relationship, through education, knowledge, skills and experience. Within certain situations people may exercise power by withholding or giving information. Patients rely on nurses to report their observations about their condition to others in an impartial way. And sometimes patients may seek to influence this professional relationship through the use of gifts. However, more often patients see such gifts as a sign of appreciation of the attention they have been given.

## Paternalism versus genuine choice

Acting in the best interests of patients is consistent with manifesting respect for individuals. But problems may arise when concern for the welfare of others takes place from the perspective of paternalism or moralism. Paternalism is the belief that it can be right to order the lives of others for their own good, irrespective of their own wishes or judgements, that is, 'nurse knows best', while moralism is the belief that it can be right to order the lives of others so that 'morality' may be preserved.

The problem for all those who care about others is how to reconcile respect for their free choice with real concern for their welfare, particularly when their choices are or appear to be self-destructive. Health education and the promotion of a healthy life style are all aspects of current nursing practice, but what happens when a patient chooses to ignore such advice? Do we reward the 'good', while seeking to punish the 'bad' through informal means such as saying: 'Terry can have an extra visitor since he's stuck to his diet today.' And what happens if this slips into: 'Terry can have a bath tonight since he gave us a box of chocolates yesterday'?

Respect for a person is shown through concern for their welfare and regard for their wishes. Normally these two dimensions complement each other, but sometimes there are tensions between them, for instance if patients are perceived as being responsible for their own health problem — examples include liver failure brought on as a result of prolonged alcohol abuse, drug taking and unprotected sexual activity leading to HIV and AIDS, and accidents arising through drunk driving. Nurses need to be cautious about applying value judgments to such situations since any notion of responsibility for outcomes will be influenced by issues of causality, control and foresight.

How nurses view and react to patients is important. Research by Olsen (1997) found that when acute care patients perceive their nurse to be empathetic they are less depressed, anxious and angry.

In another study of nurses caring for patients labelled either as difficult, neutral or ideal, Carveth (1995) found that while patients perceived as difficult received the same amount of nursing care, the care was less supportive than that given to others. In such situations how would those patients labelled difficult seek to redress the balance — through dialogue and discussion, modified or changed behaviour or the use of influence and leverage promoted by present-giving?

## Nurses' perceptions

Every human relationship is coloured to a certain extent by transference. Everyone projects both positive and negative parts of themselves on to others, and is aware of both positive and negative aspects of other people. In the nurse-patient relationship, it is not just the patient who does this. We are, after all, only human and as nurses bring with us elements of our past into the work situation. We need to be aware of these aspects of self in order to maintain appropriate boundaries in the nurse-patient relationship and relate to patients as a whole rather than as 'objects'. Research by Menzies-Lyth (1970) shows that viewing patients as 'objects' means nurses experience both 'good' and 'bad' feelings about them. To cope with these divergent feelings and reduce the resulting anxiety and distress, nurses tend to restrict contact with the patient by retreating into a system of task allocation.

Given that nurses frequently have to make decisions about the allocation of scarce resources, how do they go about deciding in a ward of 20 patients who is cared for first and on what basis? Is it needs-based or influenced by patronage?

Nurses are frequently placed in a position of responsibility and power over patients, and they have a duty not to abuse this. Over the past decade the emphasis has increased on treating the patient in a holistic manner and as a partner in care. By encouraging patients to discuss their thoughts and feelings, often regarding intimate and sensitive issues, the likelihood increases of patients feeling vulnerable. If personal boundaries become too relaxed, the patient may become open to the possibility of intrusion and invasion.

## A HOME FROM HOME?

In some settings personal and professional boundaries may become even more marked, particularly where the care setting becomes or seeks to replicate the patient's home. Those it can happen to include, for example, young chronically sick people, those with learning disabilities or those in elderly health care settings. It can place a further burden on health carers. Nurses come to symbolise the 'significant other' in the lives of many of these patients, who may consider very seriously what the nurse expects of them. As a result, patients may moderate their behaviour in accordance with nurses' preferences.

A study of 140 nursing students in 1987 found that the students preferred caring for patients who were cheerful, dependent and communicative (Baer and Lowery, 1987). Evidence suggests that when patients are liked by staff, they receive more therapeutic effort and are more likely to be rated as improved (Doherty, 1971 in Hall, 1983).

The damaging effect of hospital life in the care of elderly people is well documented. Admission to hospital may mean clients relaxing their independent habits as nursing staff take over more care and responsibility. This can lead to nursing staff encouraging dependence-related behaviour. The loss of privacy in an enforced community, having to share rooms with other people, and the noise and general disturbance which so often accompanies communal living, can be very distressing for patients, as can the loss of identity inherent in leaving friends, family and even belongings behind. Hutt (1980) highlighted the needs of elderly people: 'They want to be wanted, as contributing members of society and for themselves. Above all, they want to be loved and not merely tolerated as recipients of disinterested care, grudgingly given'.

It is small wonder, therefore, that patients in this situation welcome and want to reward staff who treat them as individuals, encourage achievement and who seek through collaborative partnerships to involve them in goal identification and attainment. Friendships with nurses who treat them in a humane and caring manner, who 'adopt' them as a quasi-family member or who simply show them some kindness within the confines of a busy working day are understandable. But care must be taken to ensure that this type of recognised and therapeutic interaction does not spill over into the realms of seeking tangible rewards from the patients concerned. Unfortunately, enough horror stories about nurse abuse of patient trust are reported in the nursing press — through the withholding of care and treatment or indeed inflicting either mental or physical abuse — to warrant that we as professionals remain vigilant and take appropriate action if we suspect such practice in others.

Campaigning group the Prevention of Professional Abuse Network (POPAN) has identified maltreatment ranging from emotional abuse, including breaches of confidentiality and bullying, to sexual and physical abuse. In a recent incident a nursing home sister was struck off for telling staff not to feed elderly patients, and was also found guilty of verbally abusing patients and 'inappropriate bandaging' (O'Dowd, 1998).

Along with the UKCC Code, nurses should be aware of and familiar with their organisation's policies and approach to issues of 'whistleblowing' and should know what systems exist to encourage staff to report any sign of abuse without fear of reprisal.

Within my own trust, King's College Hospital, staff are made aware at induction of such policies and told that an openness code exists to support staff when faced with such situations.

The trust also has a clear policy regarding registering gifts, hospitality or other favours. This is particularly important where patients and their nurses may build up friendships which last beyond and outside the normal working situation. Many of us are familiar with the case of the district nurse sacked as a result of being left money and furniture in a former patient's will (Casey, 1997).

The nurse in question won her case for unfair dismissal because she received the gift after the patient was dead and no longer in her care. However, the fact that she did not disclose the bequest was a deciding factor in the trust's decision to proceed with disciplinary action leading ultimately to dismissal. Of course, patients are free to leave anything to anybody in their wills, but professional people would need to prove beyond reproach that there had been no hint of coercion on their part, and this may be contested by relatives of the deceased.

The need to ensure public confidence both in the service and in professional probity is even more acute and should be further strengthened as a result of changes to be brought about by the introduction of clinical governance, as outlined in *A First Class Service, Quality in the New NHS* (DoH, 1998). Clinical governance is the framework through which NHS organisations are accountable for continuously improving the quality of their services and safeguarding high standards of care by creating an environment in which excellence in clinical care will flourish. The underpinning structure for this is clear and transparent professional self-regulation, which places on each of us the requirement to act in an honest and trustworthy way in our dealings with patients and the general public.

# CONCLUSION

Deep down, nursing rests on human empathy and respect for human needs in situations where the patient or client is very vulnerable. The key aspect of professional and social ethics is where people consider what they morally, ethically or legally ought or ought not to do. To a large extent, the source of ethics and our moral reasoning is found in codes, guidelines, national and local policies, personal moral opinion, current debates, religious tenets and the law.

In difficult situations, however, there is often a request for the right answer or for a clear indication as to the right thing to do. Codes and policies can provide help and guidance since, by keeping to them, people can be seen to be acting within agreed parameters. Nevertheless, in some situations this approach may have to be modified since there is often no black or white answer, merely increasing shades of grey. The best way forward may be to err on the side of caution, to refuse tactfully but firmly to accept gifts or favours, and to adopt the approach of Jiminy Cricket and 'always let your conscience be your guide'.

# References

Aroskar, M.A. (1987) The interface of ethics and politics in nursing. *Nursing Outlook*; 35: 6, 268-272.

Baer, E.D., Lowery, B.J. (1987) Patient and situational factors that affect nursing students' like or dislike of caring for patients. *Nursing Research*; 36: 5, 298-302.

Benner, P., Tanner, C.A., Chesla, C.A. (1996) *Expertise in Nursing Practice. Caring, Clinical Judgement and Ethics.* New York: Springer Publishing Company.

Bird, A.W. (1994) Enhancing patient well-being: advocacy or negotiation? *Journal of Medical Ethics*; 20: 3, 152-156.

Carveth, J. (1995) Perceived patient deviance and avoidance by nurses. *Nursing Research*, 44: 3, 173-178.

Casey, N. (1997) Editorial. Some interesting issues for nurses about that grey area of gifts. *Nursing Standard*; 11: 32, 1.

Department of Health (1998) *A First Class Service — Quality in the New NHS.* London: The Stationery Office.

Doherty, J. (1971) Cited in Hall, B.A. (1983) *Mental Health and the Elderly.* New York: Grune and Stratton.

General Medical Council (1995) *Good Medical Practice.* London: GMC.

Harris, J. (1985) *The Value of Life. An introduction to medical ethics*. London and New York: Routledge.

Hutt, A. (1980) The over eighties — a new explosion in care — health prospects for the old. *Royal Society Health;* 4: 120-123. Cited in: Kenny, T. (1990) Erosion of individuality in care of the elderly people in hospital — an alternative approach. *Journal of Advanced Nursing;* 15: 5, 571-576.

Kendrick, K. (1993) Understanding ethics in nursing practice. *British Journal of Nursing;* 2: 18, 924-925

Melia, K.M. (1994) The task of nursing ethics. *Journal of Medical Ethics;* 20: 1, 7-11.

Menzies-Lyth (1970) *The Functioning of Social Systems as a Defence against Anxiety*. London: Centre for Applied Social Research. Cited in: Briant, S., Freshwater, D. Exploring mutuality within the nurse-patient relationship. *British Journal of Nursing;* 7: 4, 204-206, 208-211.

O'Dowd, A. (1998) Nurse wins tea-kitty dismissal case. *Nursing Times;* 94: 44, 8.

O'Dowd, A. (1998) Sister removed from the register for telling staff not to feed residents. *Nursing Times;* 94: 32, 10.

Olsen, D.P. (1997) When the patient causes the problem: the effect of patient responsibility on the nurse-patient relationship. *Journal of Advanced Nursing;* 26: 3, 515-522.

Raatikainen, R. (1989) Values and ethical principles in nursing. *Journal of Advanced Nursing;* 14: 2, 92-96.

Roach, M.S. (1987) *The Human Act of Caring*. Revised edition. Ottawa: Canadian Hospital Association.

Sparkes, A.W. (1991) *Talking Philosophy. A Workbook*. London: Routledge.

UKCC (1989) *Exercising Accountability*. London: UKCC.

# Clause 16: Eliminating the bias

**Patricia Black**

> '...ensure that your registration status is not used in the promotion of commercial products or services, declare any financial or other interests in relevant organisations providing such goods or services and ensure that your professional judgement is not influenced by any commercial considerations.'

The prime importance of Clause 16 is to ensure that the interests of patients and clients are paramount and that nurses will not allow commercial interests to influence their professional judgement. The caring environment, including departments, wards and information areas, should be free of commercial promotions or anything not conducive to recovery and rehabilitation.

The clause is not intended to prevent practitioners using their registration on notepaper or business cards when it is clear to potential customers that the nurse is involved or working for a particular commercial organisation. The aim is to prevent others, not so qualified, promoting themselves as a registered practitioner for commercial gain.

In justifying public trust, nurses must always be aware of the ways in which their professional qualifications may be exploited, and whether they could influence patients, particularly those in vulnerable groups such as people with learning difficulties. Nurses' clothes, whether uniforms or the mufti worn by staff in paediatric and mental health units, should not carry any advertising as this can imply endorsement of a product or supplier.

## LEGAL ISSUES

Apart from the Code, there are many other guidance circulars warning staff against accusations of impropriety or breaching the principle of impartiality, including the Scottish Home and Health Department (1989); National Audit Office (1991); Standards of Business Conduct for NHS Staff (NHS Executive, 1993) and the NHS Executive's EL(94) (1994).

Nurses must observe a basic principle that in dealing with members of the public who are either ill or relatives in distress, they must at all times be seen to be honest, scrupulously impartial and above suspicion. The Prevention of Corruption Acts 1906 and 1916 prevent public service staff from obtaining any kind of inducements from anyone they have official dealings with. Nurses who breach these provisions are liable to prosecution and disciplinary action. The 1916 Act creates a presumption of corruption, and prosecution will follow if it can be proved that consideration, gifts or money have been exchanged by a person holding or seeking to hold a contract with a public body. Anybody involved in such activity, who holds qualifications from a statutory body, may be removed from that body.

Nursing staff in all areas may often have the opportunity to accept a gift, such as a pen or notepad linked to a promotion by a manufacturer or supplier, which is obviously not an inducement to buy or take out a contract. However, even something so apparently innocuous can make the nurse feel an obligation to that supplier, which may affect their impartiality and professional integrity. It also brings into play a feeling of dissonance for the nurse. Describing this conflict of interest, Festinger (1964) writes:

> *The individual experiencing dissonance will either discount or ignore the inconsistent information, reinterpret or reappraise the inconsistent information to bring it in line with consistency, or actively seek out*

*additional supporting information to reinforce the currently held attitude and belief system.*

When trusts and organisations invite tenders for a service, their Standing Financial Instructions must have a notice informing contractors of the consequences of engaging in any corrupt practices involving members of the trust or staff in the organisation. A clause should also be included allowing the trust or organisation to cancel and recover losses if the contractor is found offering inducements to staff members.

Nurses in several areas are now purchasers or hold their own budgets and should follow the principles issued by the Institute of Purchasing and Supply relating to confidentiality, competition, business gifts and hospitality. The principles are as follows:

- **Confidentiality:** confidentiality and accuracy of information received in the course of duty should be respected and never used for personal gain. Information given to patients should be true and fair and never designed to mislead.

- **Competition:** while bearing in mind the advantages to the nurse's employing organisation of maintaining a continuing relationship with a supplier, any arrangement which might, in the long term, prevent effective operation of fair competition should be avoided.

- **Business gifts:** gifts should not be accepted, other than items of very small intrinsic value such as business diaries or calendars.

- **Hospitality:** modest hospitality is an accepted courtesy of a business relationship. However, the recipient should not allow themselves to reach a position where they might, or might be deemed by others, to have been influenced in making a business decision as a consequence of accepting hospitality. The frequency and scale of hospitality accepted should not be significantly greater than the recipient's employer would be likely to provide in return.

# ETHICAL ISSUES

For many nurses the only way to pay for courses or further education such as a degree is to seek outside sources of funding. In the current cash-strapped climate of the NHS, nurses are unlikely to receive full or even partial funding for a designated course or degree. The RCN issues a long list of organisations and professional bodies that will help with fees but even if the applicant is deemed suitable, often it can take up to a year or more to sanction funds. Some also require practitioners to take an examination at designated times of year, which may clash with the course the nurse is seeking to fund.

In seeking or accepting financial help from commercial companies, nurses must not put themselves under any obligation which would appear to influence the purchase of equipment, products or drugs. When accepting an invitation to attend or speak at a conference, nurses must ensure it is not sponsored wholly by one company. The nurse could be accused of favouring the products of one company over comparable products from other firms. If junior staff attend conferences where travel and hospitality is paid for by a commercial company, managers should ensure that the hospitality is commensurate with the level of staff attending.

In large trusts and organisations, companies may offer to underwrite research costs or supply an expensive piece of equipment. Research projects, irrespective of their funding source, have to be submitted to the local ethics committee, which will consider the proposed form of funding and whether the sponsoring company is receiving preferential treatment. When seeking funds to develop service areas, managers must be sure this will not restrict the department's freedom to purchase from the most advantageous source in the future.

Nurses must declare any financial interests with any supplier who intends to seek a contract with their trust or organisation. This includes holding a post as a consultant to a firm that may be an interested party. A typical situation where an accusation of bias could be levelled is where the sister of an elderly care ward discharges patients to a convalescent home owned and managed by her husband.

If an outside agency such as the media offers a practitioner a fee in return for their experience and expertise, the nurse must discuss it with their manager before any commitment is given. Any outside work must not impinge on the nurse's full-time NHS employment. But the nurse is entitled to accept payment for any work in the media, publishing or teaching, which takes place outside work hours.

The Standards of Business Conduct for NHS Staff (NHS Executive, 1993) includes a checklist urging managers to:

▶ ensure that all staff are aware of the Guidance HSG(93)5;

▶ develop a local policy and implement it;

- show no favouritism in awarding contracts (such as to a business run by employees, ex-employees and their friends or families);

- include a warning against corruption in all invitations to tender;

- consider requests from staff for permission to undertake additional outside employment;

- receive rewards or royalties in respect of work carried out by employees in the course of their NHS work and ensure that such employees receive due rewards;

- ensure receipt of rewards for collaborative work with manufacturers and pass on to participating employees;

- ensure acceptance of commercial sponsorship will not influence or jeopardise purchasing decisions;

- refuse linked deals whereby sponsorship of staff posts is tied to the purchase of particular products or supplies from particular sources;

- avoid excessive secrecy and abuse of the term 'commercial in confidence'.

# MARKETING

Considering all the legal and ethical pitfalls of promoting commercial goods and services, including the possibility of being de-registered, it seems strange that a nurse should want to get involved.

For many nurses mixing the commercial and vocational world causes anxiety and distress. When goods and services arrive on the ward or in the community, nurses often do not query who made the decision to purchase a particular brand, where it came from, and importantly, how much it cost. Yet knowledge of the commercial market-place and purchasing can help nurses to enhance their skills, especially when innovations are being introduced in a clinical setting.

Yet many nurses have shown that if they market themselves properly and are aware of the commercial world, they can put their expertise to good use, either as consultants or as independent specialists.

Most nurses probably think of marketing as meaning the advertising or selling of products or services. But the American Marketing Association defines it as 'the process of planning and executing the conception, pricing, promotion, and distribution of ideas, goods and services to create exchanges that satisfy individual and organisational objectives' (Belch, 1993).

Marketing can also be described as a process where people gradually become favourably disposed toward a new idea or product. But whichever definition is used, studies show that nurses reveal little awareness of the use of marketing strategies in the promotion of products or in marketing themselves (Brown, 1992; Bircumshaw, 1990). Nurses who have a position as budget holders for a speciality inevitably have to deal with commercial companies trying to persuade them to buy their products.

# CASE STUDY

Maureen is a stoma care specialist who holds her own budget and makes the decision on what stock should be held for the acute sector. She sees several representatives every month from different companies all trying to sell her comparable goods. She is in a unique position to influence the other nurses in areas where she has patients, and therefore could be seen as a marketeer, with the other staff as consumers. She is able to target her market, the ward staff, and use marketing strategies to enhance staff adoption of the product.

Maureen has to decide how the ward staff will view the new product, considering complexity, advantage over other products and ease of use.

One useful guide is Rogers' diffusion of innovation theory and marketing principles (Landrum, 1998). Through this, nurses can achieve marketing objectives for marketing themselves or marketing a new product or innovation to help their patient group or nurse colleagues.

Things Maureen must consider in relation to a new product include:

> There should be observable patient improvement through the use of this product.

> The price should reflect the quality of the product and not be higher than that which would be acceptable in either the ward or specialist's budget.

> The distribution of the product — it should be easy to obtain.

> Whether each patient will have their own stock while in hospital.

> The way the product will be promoted and what publicity will be available for the ward staff and other patients who might find this product is the best for them.

# HEALTH PROMOTION

In many areas of health promotion sponsorship pays for patient information leaflets, for example nutrition leaflets produced by the food industry. Particularly prevalent are the baby food leaflets on weaning produced by the baby food companies. One health educator's study found that unless a commercial point was being made, many baby leaflets did not state the nutrient quantity (Hodges, 1993).

Non-commercially produced leaflets mentioned that commercially produced foods were a possible food source. But leaflets produced commercially pushed the brand names of their own products and many did not mention the use of fresh food for weaning.

Although commercial companies do not set out to deliberately mislead in their literature, there are concerns about what the company leaves out. Can health professionals trust the literature that is available from the commercial sector, especially when they are dealing with vulnerable groups? Should there be an unbiased body that supplies and prints literature of this kind so that the patient is able to make a fully informed choice? While it seems a good idea, who is going to pay? It is unlikely that cash-strapped health authorities will cough up.

Nurses need to think about whether commercial material can be altruistic or whether the sponsor has a hidden agenda.

Another example of a vulnerable group being given commercially sensitive goods is mothers who have just given birth in hospital. The maternity department often has boxes of various products donated by commercial baby food companies to hand out. Does this tell the mother that the hospital endorses the products in the box?

Similarly, the first stoma bag that the patient is introduced to and uses with no problem will usually be the product with which the patient remains while they have a stoma. And consequently stoma care nurses face constant pressure from company representatives to recommend their product to patients.

# DISEASE MANAGEMENT PACKAGES

Disease management packages (DMP) attract considerable attention from the pharmaceutical industry, which sees this area as a way of extending its activities beyond drug development to health care management and organisation. These packages propose a long-term relationship between commercial pharmaceutical companies and the appropriate NHS body. The term originated in the USA, where pharmaceutical companies have been active in building partnerships with major managed care organisations. It is not clear whether disease management offers advantages to the NHS or society in general (Drummond, 1997).

Many diseases, especially chronic ones, may need life-long health care, and DMP will require a nursing-care component. Many aspects of health care management have been incorporated into the NHS, but the health care that patients receive is not universal across the country.

Nurses in the primary and secondary sectors are active contributors to health care management. Funding for these posts often comes from the commercial sector.

Inevitably the motives in partnerships such as disease management are unlikely to be altruistic, and it is important that patients have access to best practice and that packages do not preclude this option.

In using DMPs, restrictions on prescribing may lead to a compromise in patient care. The answer is to ensure that contracts in disease management packages contain a statement that allows the health care professional to use a different product if necessary.

A recent example occurred when the government tried to restrict the number of eczema products available. The National Eczema Society and the relevant pharmaceutical companies worked together to overturn the proposal on the basis that it infringed patient choice.

Costing of equipment and appliances also needs to be equated into packages. Patients in the community who are being cared for by district nurses can be denied treatments that are more efficacious because the treatments are not on FP10 (prescribable by a GP from the Drug Tariff).

Such treatments include wound cavity dressings and four-layer bandage systems used to treat venous leg ulceration. These problems would have to be addressed by DMPs. Any commercial company offering to provide specific disease management should have relevant previous experience, and generic disease management should not be used as it does not recognise the need for specialist input.

The issue is whether DMPs are just a vehicle for the pharmaceutical industry to become more involved in patient care or a way for the industry to stay afloat and continue with its increasingly difficult role of discovering and researching drugs. Burns (1996) suggests that ultimately the judgement of the industry on DMPs will be based on whether they increase profits. The NHS has a more difficult judgement to make. Practitioners have to ask if they are in the patients' best interests, and whether they compromise their professional role.

# SPONSORSHIP

Commercial sponsorship schemes are a fact of life in today's NHS. Some involve the employment of nurses, midwives and health visitors and the most widely written about in the UK over the last nine years is the scheme for sponsorship of stoma care posts in NHS community and hospital trusts.

Sponsorship and its future pitfalls were first highlighted by Black (1990) in a resolution at the RCN Congress, calling for Council to examine health care agencies entering into sponsorship arrangements with private companies. These agencies were urged to abandon arrangements where the independent judgement of nurses would be compromised.

To determine this, nurses need to ask themselves whether sponsorship would still give the patient a choice of products and freedom to choose. They need to consider how their professional development could continue and what would happen to their original contract of employment, pension rights, annual leave and long-term job prospects. They also need to consider the consequences if a sponsoring company decided to pull out of the contract at any time, as the trust may have no obligation to re-employ the nurse.

Black (1992) considers the ethical questions for nurses and managers put in this invidious position. Interested sponsorship opens a Pandora's box as it is explicitly linked with increasing the sales of a particular product or service.

In return for sponsoring the post, the company expects the nurse to present its product to patients as the preferred prescription option. Since 1990 sponsorship has grown rapidly in the speciality of stoma care, with about 60% of stoma care nurses now in sponsored posts (Black, 1997). Many companies adopt a 'back-door' method when approaching management or supplies departments, circumventing the stoma care nurse who may know nothing of the possibility of the post becoming sponsored. The stoma care nurse holding a hospital or district-wide budget for appliances is the most influential person for a sponsoring company to target. It costs about £1,500 a year to keep a patient with a permanent stoma in appliances. Therefore a hospital performing 100 new stomas a year is an exciting prospect for a company. Because the numbers of these patients is fairly static there is a constant fight among the commercial appliance companies for the larger share of this cake.

If sponsorship for any community or trust nursing post becomes a possibility, ethical decision-making can help with understanding the consequences of such a choice. Managing finance and care prudently within the NHS so that it is concentrated on the patient rather than the bureaucrat should be the key for managers when considering a sponsored post (Small, 1989). The decision whether or not to accept commercial money for a nursing service should be based on a framework with quantifiable answers:

- As a nurse manager, Clause 16 of the Code should be uppermost in your consideration and you should ensure that your own professional judgement and that of your nurses is not influenced by any commercial consideration.

- Sponsorship agreements should not take place in a shroud of secrecy in the hope of avoiding criticism or without the consent of the participating nurse.

- Although legislation does not specifically exist, stating that the patient's needs must always be put before commercial considerations, the ethical implications involved in the practice of nurse sponsorship may have serious consequences relating to care.

- Should a long-term relationship with a company be accepted when the company is seeking some sort of exclusive supply agreement or preferential use of its own products?

- Arrangements which appear to give preferential treatment of a company or its products or effectively exclude competitors are likely to infringe UK and European competition law.

- Any initiative which might impair clinical responsibility or inappropriately influence a clinician's choice raises issues of responsibility and accountability for individual patient care.

▷ Any decision to move to direct sponsorship of nursing posts should rest very firmly in the concern that care of the patient group should be determined by need rather than commercial interest.

▷ Guidelines on commercial sponsorship of nursing posts should be observed (RCN, 1994).

Any nurse registered with a statutory body is personally accountable for their practice and the clauses in the Code of Professional Conduct are mandatory, not optional, and therefore become an essential part of professional nursing practice.

# References

Belch, G.E., Belch, M.A., (1993) *Introduction to advertising and promotion: an integrated marketing communications perspective* (2nd Ed). Alabama: Homewood Irwin.

Bircumshaw, D. (1990) The utilisation of research findings in clinical nursing practice. *Journal of Advanced Nursing*; 15: 11, 1272-1280.

Black, P. (1990) RCN Congress 1990 — Quest for Quality. *Stoma Care Forum Newsletter*; 10: 2, 1.

Black, P. (1992) Pandora's profits. *Health Service Journal*; 102: 5320, 31.

Black, P. (1995) Management Review — Sponsorship in Stoma Care. *British Journal of Health Care Management*; 1: 13, 654-657.

Brown, R. (1992) Managing the 'S' curves of innovation. *Journal of Consumer Marketing*; 9: 61-72.

Burns, H. (1996) Disease management and the drug industry: carve out or carve up? *Lancet*; 347: 9007, 1021-1023.

Drummond, M. (1997) *Disease Management: who needs it? Discussion Paper 152*. York: Centre for Health Economics, NHS Centre for Reviews and Dissemination.

Festinger, L. (1964) The motivating effect of cognitive dissonance. In Harper, R., Christansen, C., Hunka, S. *The Cognitive Processes: Readings*. Englewood Cliffs, NJ: Prentice Hall, 509-523.

Hodges, C. (1993) A healthy balance. *Nursing Times*, 89: 14, 44-45.

Landrum, B. (1998) Marketing Innovations to Nurses, Part 2: Marketing's Role in the Adoption of innovations. *Wound, Ostomy, and Continence Nursing*; 25: 5, 227- 232.

National Audit Office (1991) *National Health Service Supplies in England*. London: HMSO.

NHS Executive EL (94)94 (1994) *Commercial approaches to the NHS regarding disease management packages*. Leeds: NHS Executive.

NHS Executive (1993) *Standards of Business Conduct*. Leeds: NHS Executive.

Royal College of Nursing (1994) Guidelines on Commercial Sponsorship of Nursing Posts. *Issues in Nursing and Health;* 9. London: RCN.

Scottish Home Office (1989) *NHS Circular (1989)(GEN)32*. Edinburgh: Scottish Home and Health Department.

Small, N. (1989) *Politics and Planning in the NHS*. Buckinghamshire: Open University Press.

# Recommended reading

Tschudin, V. (1994) *Ethics. Conflicts of Interest*. Harrow: Scutari Press.

Black, P. (1995) Management Review — Sponsorship in Stoma Care. *British Journal of Health Care Management*; 1: 13, 654-657.

# Appendix 1: Code breakers: the professional disciplinary process

## Irene Heywood Jones

The nursing profession can best secure public trust and confidence by making it clear that it will censure those practitioners who fall short of expected standards. The UKCC's mandatory function as the profession's self-regulator requires it to investigate allegations of professional misconduct and unfitness to practise. It does this with the clear remit to protect the public and maintain the safety and well-being of patients under the care of registered practitioners.

If a lay person fraudulently poses as a registered practitioner, they are subject to the 1997 Nurses, Midwives and Health Visitors Act and face criminal charges for false representation. As they are not on the register, this would be a matter for the criminal courts, not the UKCC. Employers must always check the PIN registration details of prospective employees with the UKCC, as a number of bogus practitioners are detected each year.

However, while the term 'registered nurse' is a protected title, it is not illegal to call yourself a nurse. There is some concern that employers, particularly in nursing homes, are keen to call all their care staff 'nurses', confusing patients and relatives who may believe they are being cared for by qualified nursing staff.

Almost half the UKCC's funding is devoted to professional conduct business. The process is backed by law and the professional conduct committee (PCC) has the power to remove a practitioner from the register with immediate effect. The policing of standards and the performance of practitioners is the responsibility of the profession itself. Nurses can best assess and appreciate the circumstances facing the nurse respondent and are best able to judge if misconduct has occurred. All complaints must be examined rigorously and peer evaluation must ensure that it serves the public interest.

The regulatory body can assess the nurse's actions by using its own guidelines for standards of practice within the profession and by referring to the UKCC Code, which acts as a benchmark. As Reg Pyne, in his preface to a book on nursing competence explains (Kershaw, 1990): 'It is important to note that the UKCC, having given practitioners advice as to what it expects of them, now uses exactly that advice as a backcloth against which to consider complaints alleging misconduct in a professional sense against individual practitioners.'

# THE PROFESSIONAL DISCIPLINARY PROCESS

Following a brief overview of the mechanisms that control the professional disciplinary procedure we shall explore issues surrounding this process which are important to the profession.

## Preliminary proceedings committee

All complaints made to the UKCC — between 800-1,000 a year — alleging professional misconduct or unfitness to practise are brought before the preliminary proceedings committee (PPC). This committee is made up of Council members (and may include lay practitioners and representatives from the consumer panel), which has been nominated by health care consumer groups, such as MIND, MENCAP, AIMS and community health councils.

The hearing is held in private and initially sifts through the cases to see if they warrant further investigation. Around 60% of cases are closed at this stage. Documentary evidence is sought about the allegation, together with statements from the complainant and the practitioner, with perhaps a report from the UKCC solicitor and input from a professional officer.

These will provide the basis for consideration by the PPC, which has the power to:

- close the case;

- issue a formal caution;

- refer to the health committee;

- refer to the professional conduct committee.

## Professional conduct committee

The professional conduct committee (PCC), which normally comprises five members, holds a full open public hearing. At least three PCC members will also be UKCC Council members and one person is selected from the consumer panel. It is a legal requirement, and makes sense for a fair hearing, that at least one of the committee members has expertise in the same area of practice as the respondent, and that member may need to be drawn from the practitioner panel.

A legal assessor attends the hearing to advise on points of law and the admissibility of evidence, but is not party to the decision-making. The Council has the power to subpoena witnesses and compel them to attend a PCC hearing.

The practitioner is given formal notice to attend the hearing and is invited to bring a friend, which could be a welfare adviser from the Nurses' Welfare Service (NWS). They may also elect to have a representative, usually an official from a trade union or professional organisation, or a solicitor or barrister. If the practitioner chooses not to attend, the hearing will continue in their absence and they will be advised of the decision.

The facts of the incident are gathered through statements from the respondent, the complainant and witnesses, perhaps with evidence from an independent witness to get a greater understanding of the context in which the event occurred.

The committee must first decide if the facts are proven. If the answer is 'no', then there is no case to answer and no further action is taken.

If the facts are proven, the committee then decides if they constitute professional misconduct. This is considered within the context of the incident and not in isolation, because other factors may have a bearing on the reasons for the nurse's behaviour.

If the committee decides that misconduct did occur, a mitigation stage follows. Evidence and references may be given on behalf of the respondent outlining their previous good conduct, professional history and exemplary practice and may include a report from an NWS welfare adviser. Testimonials supporting the respondent are welcomed but anyone writing one must declare that they understand the reasons behind the request and the context in which their evidence is being given. The committee may also consider any undue personal or professional pressures which have since been resolved.

All this will help the committee decide whether to:

- take no action;
- administer a formal caution;
- postpone judgement on certain conditions;
- remove the practitioner from the register;
- refer to the health committee (HC).

## Health committee

A case may be referred directly to the health committee where there is concern that the practitioner may be unfit to practise due to physical or mental illness. Just as anyone can allege misconduct, so they can allege concern for the public if practice is compromised due to illness.

A practitioner may also be referred during proceedings of the PPC or PCC if the committees' members feel this is the more appropriate avenue. A panel of screeners — a group of Council members — will consider the documentary evidence and, if they wish to pursue this route, can refer the nurse to a specialist medical examiner. Based on the examiner's report the screeners may then decide to refer the case to the HC, which may refer it back to the PPC or PCC if illness is not considered to be a contributory factor.

If the practitioner's fitness to practise is seriously impaired by illness and the public is endangered, then the HC can remove them from the register.

The self-regulatory mechanism allows for the possibility that illness, rather than incompetence or malice, could be the cause of professional misconduct. The most common problems relate to drug and alcohol abuse and mental illness.

Where health issues are chronic or enduring, it is obviously preferable for the service and the individual practitioner if this situation is confronted at an early stage. If these problems can be safely addressed and managed locally there may be no need to involve the UKCC.

## MAKING A DECISION

When misconduct in a professional sense has been proved, the PCC has a number of options to decide the future of the practitioner, which are underpinned by prime regard for the protection and safety of the public.

At the mitigation stage there may be evidence putting the act of misconduct into the context of the practitioner's professional background and character. Someone with an exemplary history is unlikely to be treated harshly for one slip. However, other factors must be considered, such as repetition of poor practice, intentional and planned abuse, concealing errors and the inability to admit or learn from the problem.

The practitioner's laxity may be due to personal, domestic or money worries, which were temporary and have now been resolved and mean the nurse is safe and competent to practise again.

On occasion the UKCC may publicly admonish management for putting a practitioner in an impossible working situation where an accident was bound to happen. In these cases pressure of work, unacceptable practices or poor supervision suggest the deficiencies lie with the system and not the individual, who has been effectively scapegoated. The UKCC can make a statement to the management and probably would not allow the individual nurse to suffer in these circumstances.

Nurse managers are also registrants and can therefore be held accountable in their managerial sphere of responsibility for not upholding the UKCC Code. They must address situations where inadequacies and lack of investment may compromise patient care and jeopardise the personal and professional safety of individual workers. They must report concerns, both verbally and in writing, to the appropriate authority, even when it may be obvious that no action will be taken. Failure to make these concerns known breaches the Code.

They should copy and keep contemporaneous documentary evidence, as it may be used later in the practitioner's defence against allegations of misconduct and to demonstrate that they did all they could to alleviate the problems.

## No action

Even if misconduct is proven, the committee may take into account the circumstances of the case and any mitigating evidence and decide no further action is needed.

## Formal caution

The committee can decide to issue a formal caution to remind the practitioner of the standards they are expected to adhere to and also some advice on their future conduct. The misconduct finding is held on the practitioner's record for five years and is disclosed to any prospective employer, member of the public making an enquiry, or at any subsequent PCC hearing.

## Postponement of judgement

The committee can postpone a judgement and ask the practitioner to fulfil certain criteria or provide further information and references at an agreed later date. Postponement commonly occurs where there are drug administration or record-keeping errors, and a period of supervised practice is needed.

The nurse may need further training and supervision before being allowed back to unsupervised practice. If the judgement is postponed, the practitioner will be called before the PCC again so it can reconsider the case and see that any conditions have been met before making a final decision.

## Removal from the register

On average about 100 practitioners are struck from the register each year. This takes immediate effect and is announced by the committee chairman publicly at the hearing. The nurse leaves stripped of their registration status, and unable to work in their chosen profession.

The sanction of deregistration does not prevent the nurse from working in a caring capacity. It is the most obvious employment option for an ex-nurse to be taken on as an auxiliary, possibly in a hospital, a nursing home or in social care. Employers must be extremely careful not to use the skills of an experienced deregistered nurse in a way that goes beyond the remit of their current status.

## Rehabilitation and restoration

A practitioner who wants be restored to the register at a later date (not usually before 12 months have elapsed) will need to show evidence of good conduct during that time. There are about 25 such applications a year, although most are unsuccessful.

At a hearing of the restoration PCC the practitioner must demonstrate that:

- they understand and accept the reason for the removal;
- they have taken appropriate action, such as counselling, to address problems;
- they have worked in a related field of care for a significant period of time and demonstrated exemplary standards;
- the application is supported by impeccable references from the current employer and, if appropriate, a medical practitioner.

At times, restoring practitioners to registration can cause an outcry. One controversial case in 1983 was that of nurse Yuen How Choy from East Sussex, convicted of raping a former psychiatric patient in her own home. He was removed from the register in 1986, but applied for restoration and was eventually restored in 1996, on the basis of favourable references from employers. However, it was subsequently found that he had lied to his employers. The RCN mounted a High Court challenge to the UKCC decision to restore him.

The UKCC is alerted to the unsuitability of restoring some practitioners to the register, even if from a legal standpoint they have paid their debt to society. However, the Council has no legal right to impose life bans from the register. But steps are now in place to ensure practitioners removed from the register for serious criminal offences will not be reinstated if this is likely to undermine public confidence in the profession. This has been achieved by strengthening the restoration proceedings. Measures include creating a separate committee with separate meetings, and including two consumers alongside Council members on the restoration PCC.

## INTERIM SUSPENSION OF REGISTRATION

One of the drawbacks of the disciplinary mechanism is the delay taken in addressing the complaint, although the sifting role of the PPC has helped to speed up the process. The gathering of evidence and the convening of a PCC hearing involves a detailed and lengthy process and a nurse accused of hazardous practice can legally work as a registered practitioner during this period. They retain the nurse's registration status until the PCC decides otherwise, because the practitioner is 'innocent until proved guilty'. This means that even if their employer has suspended them, they can take work elsewhere, for example with an agency.

However, the PCC is allowed to suspend somebody from the register in the interim if the public is clearly exposed to an unacceptably high level of risk. This power is invoked when a practitioner is charged with a serious criminal offence, such as murder, rape or child pornography, and is waiting to go to court. Interim suspension, which is reviewed every three months, may also be imposed where there are doubts over a nurse's fitness to practise on health grounds.

## WHO CAN COMPLAIN?

Anyone can complain to the UKCC about misconduct or unfitness to practise by any registered nurse, midwife or health visitor. This includes colleagues, patients, or any member of the public.

Of course, the person needs to know of the existence of the complaints mechanism, where to address the complaint and have sufficient evidence to support their claim. The UKCC does not accept anonymous complaints.

The complainant must offer factual evidence and credible witnesses to support their allegation, as required by any legal process. The UKCC must be careful of malicious allegations against practitioners by colleagues or patients that cannot be substantiated.

The complaints procedure does not apply to other carer employees, nurses in training, health care assistants, auxiliary or support staff working alongside the professional practitioner.

There is no time limit for making a complaint, although a long delay will obviously make an investigation difficult as it will be harder to gather reliable evidence.

There can be complaints from the following:

▸ **Patients** — Patients and their relatives usually complain to the practitioner's employer in the first instance. Just how many members of the public know of the existence of the statutory body called the UKCC is debatable. Unfortunately, its presence is often only noticed when adverse disciplinary proceedings reach the press. The Royal College of Nursing and Unison receive more media exposure than the UKCC. Some nurses on the register even believe the RCN is their statutory body.

The UKCC is trying to publicise its role with patient leaflets on its functions and how to complain. A poster also displays the wording of the Code of Professional Conduct.

▸ **Public** — Nurses must respect confidentiality both on and off duty. A member of the public may make a complaint if they overhear a conversation on a bus or train, witness poor practice on a ward or questionable behaviour in general.

▸ **Colleagues** — Health care professionals, or non-professional staff, can complain about a practitioner. It is not easy to make a complaint about a colleague or to challenge a team member, and the whistleblower may have real fears of reprisal and victimisation. This is especially true when there is evidence of institutionalised sub-standard behaviour that has been tolerated by others who feel unable to challenge the status quo.

Complaints often come from newly employed nurses or those who have recently qualified. They may face accusations of being too idealistic. However, they are acting courageously and selflessly, in the best interests of patients, while other more compliant professionals who fail to report poor standards are breaching the Code.

▸ **Employers** — Employers and managers who complain about a practitioner on their staff must appreciate that the UKCC can only consider activities directly affecting the protection of the public, as opposed to breaches of employment contract, unless these affect quality of care. An employer must alert the UKCC to any possibility of misconduct or unfitness to practice, even if the practitioner concerned has left their employ. It is a professional indiscretion for employers to know that they are jeopardising the well-being of patients elsewhere by failing to voice their concerns.

## CRIMINAL COURTS

The police and court officials are automatically required to notify the UKCC if a practitioner is found guilty of any criminal offence, even if it results in a suspended sentence, fine or community service. This also applies when the person has been found guilty but has been given a conditional discharge or a probation order. If a conviction is obtained overseas, the UKCC must get an official certificate of conviction or the statement witness of an investigating officer, or evidence to support the verdict, to ensure the same standards of proof as required in this country were applied in the overseas case.

Where a nurse is found guilty of a criminal offence it will be at the PPC's discretion, with perhaps a referral to the PCC, to decide if this activity also amounts to professional misconduct, in the light of current conventions of behaviour.

Obviously crimes such as murder, drug dealing, and sexual abuse pose a danger to the public. But many nurses do not realise that if they are found guilty of a less serious crime that seems to have no bearing on their nursing role, such as non-payment of Council Tax or a motoring offence, it will still be reported to the UKCC by the police or courts. This can have an unexpected effect on their professional life — a nurse is truly a nurse 24 hours a day.

## THE FULL FORCE OF LAW

The UKCC complaints and disciplinary mechanisms are backed by law because it represents the profession in relation to the safety and protection of the public. Practitioners on the register are covered by the 1997 Nurses, Midwives and Health Visitors Act and Parliament has conferred substantial powers of self-regulation on the UKCC. Disciplinary hearings have a legal formality, with a solicitor representing the UKCC and usually one for the respondent.

By holding the proceedings in public, in various parts of the UK, the UKCC demonstrates its own accountability and openness. In a progressive move, the UKCC now allows members of the public from the consumer panel to contribute to the deliberations of the PPC, the PCC and restoration PCC. Hopefully in future this will also apply to the HC. The consumer representative must not be a registrant of the UKCC.

The decisions of the PCC and HC can be subject to further legal scrutiny. The High Court can consider appeals on the grounds of procedure, though only the UKCC can decide whether misconduct has occurred.

The government is reviewing the area of regulation throughout the profession and, while it is likely to endorse the self-regulatory function, it wants this to be more open, accountable and responsive. It is also looking at the possible regulation of health care assistants in the future.

## INTRACTABLE INCOMPETENCE

One of the areas currently being addressed by the UKCC is the notion of the incompetent practitioner. This involves dealing with evidence of sustained unsatisfactory performance, which would institute remedial measures or lead to removal from the register if the public is at risk. In many cases a practitioner is referred to the UKCC with allegations which question their actual competence, rather than any single act of omission or commission that may constitute misconduct. A procedure which detects and deals with incompetence early on may prevent harm to a patient that would finally bring the practitioner before the PCC.

The nurse being 'carried' by the team, who is given selected duties because in reality they are not considered up to standard, is a familiar phenomenon. Managers have a responsibility to address this locally and not let practitioners struggle on, especially in a professionally dangerous fashion, when clinical supervision and appropriate professional development could possibly help.

## WHAT MISCONDUCT?

There are a number of recurring themes of misconduct that reach the UKCC:

- physical, verbal or sexual abuse of patients;

> stealing from patients;

> failure to care for patients, or maintain an acceptable environment of care for managers and employers who are also registrants;

> deliberately concealing unsafe practice, falsifying records and failing to maintain proper records;

> failing to administer medicines correctly, often made worse by trying to cover up the mistake.

A worrying proportion of nurses reaching the disciplinary process are male. Although men only make up 9% of the register, 48% of respondents in PCC hearings are male (UKCC, 1998). Staff who work in elderly care and nursing homes feature in many complaints of misconduct, possibly resulting from frustration, repetitive heavy work, low morale, and desensitisation to patients as individuals, together with poor professional opportunities. In a perverse way the highlighting of poor care may result in positive change in these environments. For in the past bad practice was simply tolerated and no one dared to speak out.

Second-level nurses also appear more frequently before the PCC. This may be a reflection of poor management with the practitioner assigned greaterresponsibility than they should be shouldering, only to be admonished for their failings.

## PROTECTION NOT PUNISHMENT

The profession's previous statutory bodies used the term 'disciplinary committee' — a harsh and admonishing term with a punitive connotation. The UKCC abandoned it in favour of 'professional conduct committee', combined with the guidance of the Code of Professional Conduct. This more compassionate stance towards professional practitioners is supported by the possible option of restoration following rehabilitation, the recognition of health issues through the use of the health committee and involvement of the Nurses' Welfare Service.

The NWS is a social work agency which helps practitioners facing the professional disciplinary machinery. At a time of extreme anxiety and profound concern for their future and their personal and professional standing, it can be comforting for the practitioner to gain support from this specialised service.

The NWS is an independent body, part funded by the UKCC and a number of charities. It may seem strange that the statutory body charged with censuring practitioners also offers care and support to them when they face disciplinary action.

When the PPC sends a letter to the practitioner inviting a statement about the allegations of misconduct it encloses a leaflet explaining the NWS's role. This also occurs if they face a medical examination over concerns about fitness to practise due to illness. In addition, practitioners come into contact with the NWS if they are brought before the disciplinary machinery following a court conviction, and the service has many parallels with the probation service.

Practitioners may avail themselves of the service, which is free and confidential. Once the practitioner has given written consent, the welfare adviser of the NWS can have access to case documents.

Together with a personal interview these documents enable the adviser to provide the necessary assistance. The adviser may prepare a social background report which can be offered in support of the practitioner's case at the mitigation stage of the PCC.

The committee respects a report from the NWS and understands its remit. As an independent professional social work report it will contain details of the practitioner's personal circumstances, but will in no way collude with callous or reckless behaviour or an unrepentant attitude. Above all, the welfare adviser is able to demystify the workings of the disciplinary machinery, hopefully to make it less daunting.

If the practitioner is removed from the register and needs to make a life away from nursing, the welfare adviser continues longer-term support. The practitioner receives assistance and sound and realistic advice from the service, should they later apply for restoration.

It is commonly felt that the nursing profession does little to care for its own members. So it is encouraging to know that the NWS provides a cushion of support at a time of extreme anxiety for practitioners, when their future is being held in the balance.

# References

Kershaw, B. (1990) *Nursing Competence. A Guide to Professional Development.* London: Edward Arnold.

UKCC. (1998) *Annual Report of the UKCC 1997-1998*. London: UKCC.

## Recommended reading

Heywood Jones, I. (1990) *The Nurse's Code*. London: Macmillan Press.

Pyne, R. (1998) *Professional Discipline in Nursing, Midwifery and Health Visiting* (3rd ed). London: Blackwell Scientific.

# Appendix 2: The sixteen commandments: a modest proposal

## Martin Vousden

If you are a Christian, your life in all its variety and glory is governed by 10 commandments, but if you are a nurse, midwife or health visitor you need 16 commandments in the Code of Professional Conduct. So what is all that about then? Why is being a nurse so complicated?

Well actually it isn't, or at least I don't think so. It is my belief that the Code is an overwritten, clumsy, repetitive piece of work which is not always easy to understand and sets an impossibly high standard for practitioners to attain. And I am not the only one who believes the Code could do with a good editor. Paul Chapman, a professional officer with Unison, thinks it could be distilled to the following 37 words:

- Safeguard and promote interests of patients;
- Only work within your competence;
- Be a good team member;
- Maintain and develop your knowledge/skills;
- Keep confidentiality;
- Report dangers;
- Help develop other staff;
- Refuse gifts;

- Don't advertise;
- Respect ethnic beliefs.

Not bad as far as it goes, but in truth, doesn't everything else stem from those first six words, 'safeguard and promote interests of patients'? For example, would you be safeguarding and promoting the interests of patients if you did not 'report dangers', 'respect ethnic beliefs', 'maintain and develop your knowledge/skills' or 'only work within your competence'? Good try, Paul, but no coconut.

I think the Code could be reduced to the phrase: 'Always do your best, and do nothing to hurt patients.' There you have it, a Code of Conduct in 10 words.

So that's it then, we can all go home now.

Well, maybe not. The UKCC will no doubt think this is not quite the ticket and, in fairness, so will a number of nurses. Sadly, we sadly live in age where quantity is mistaken for quality so, instead of substituting my own Code, why not simply abbreviate and simplify the one with which we have been saddled by the UKCC.

**Clause 1: '...always act in such a manner as to promote and safeguard the interests and well-being of patients and clients.'**

As a critic of the Code, this is the most difficult clause to make a substantial argument against because pretty much all of the rest of this frightening document stems from here and this is virtually the Code in its entirety. However, it could still be edited.

For example, the first word 'always' is redundant. If it read: 'Act in such a manner...' then the always is assumed and implicit. But that phrase 'act in such a manner' has the ring of bureaucratic pomposity and is, in fact, also superfluous to requirements. Likewise, later this clause talks about the 'interests and well-being' of the people for whom you care, but can you think of any examples when interests and well-being are not the same? If something is in your interests, it will promote your well-being, and vice versa.

Incidentally, does it need to keep mentioning patients and clients? Surely either word is interchangeable and refers to patients, clients, service users, customers, friends, family, relatives, pets and anyone else for whom we might have professional responsibility.

I therefore suggest that this clause would mean the same, and be much shorter, if it read:

**'Promote and safeguard the well-being of clients.'**

**Clause 2: '...ensure that no action or omission on your part, or within your sphere of responsibility, is detrimental to the interests, condition or safety of patients and clients.'**

Frankly, after Clause 1 this whole sentence is unnecessary. If you are going to 'promote and safeguard the well-being of clients' then it stands to reason that you will not, by action or omission, do something, or allow something to be done that is detrimental to the interests, condition or safety of patients and clients. First, the bit 'on your part' is not needed because, if something is in 'your sphere of responsibility' it will include acts carried out by you. Preferably, that 'sphere of responsibility' stuff should be replaced by 'for which you are responsible'. This more clearly covers any act carried out by you or by someone else on your instructions or under your control.

I also have problems with the bit which says 'is detrimental to the...' because I think that is the same as the words 'damages' or 'harms'. So the clause could read:

**'Ensure that no action for which you are responsible will harm, or potentially harm, clients.'**

**Clause 3: '...maintain and improve your professional knowledge and competence.'**

Short, sweet and to the point. Cannot be improved.

**Clause 4: '...acknowledge any limitations in your knowledge and competence and decline any duties or responsibilities unless able to perform them in a safe and skilled manner.'**

The first objection to this clause is a practical one. To 'acknowledge any limitations in your knowledge and competence' you must first be aware that you have a deficiency in these areas. It's that old conundrum of 'how do you know which are the things that you don't know?'

The answer is: 'I don't know.'

That last word, 'manner' is also a bit of a worry. I always prefer to use 'way' in these sort of situations. It is much shorter, means the same and, to some minds at least, rolls off the tongue just that tiny bit more easily.

Equally, where do the words 'duties and responsibilities' differ? Also, the words 'safe and skilled', while not meaning the same, are an unnecessary pairing here because if you cannot do something in a skilled way, the chances are that it will not be safe. As with Clause 1, the second part makes the first redundant. Therefore, an alternative wording might be: 'Decline any duties unless you are able to perform them in a skilled way.' However, because this sounds negative, it would be even better to say:

**'Carry out only those duties which you can perform in a skilled way.'**

**Clause 5: '...work in an open and cooperative manner with patients, clients and their families, foster their independence and recognise and respect their involvement in the planning and delivery of care.'**

Oh dear, this really is a bit of a mess isn't it? The ambition behind this clause seems to be to involve a patient's loved ones in the care you deliver, although mention is made only of 'families', so if you are gay, or living with someone in a heterosexual relationship, you can presumably be ignored with impunity. For many of us the strongest relationships in our lives concern people with whom we do not have a 'family' tie — such as friends, lovers and partners. The UKCC probably shies away from the phrase 'loved ones' because, while accurate, it does not sound official or bureaucratic enough for such an important document. Nevertheless, the UKCC is right to avoid that horrible American import 'significant others'.

It would be difficult to work in a cooperative way if you were not 'open', and our old friend 'manner' makes an unwelcome reappearance, along with his mate 'patient'. It is also difficult to see how a nurse, no matter how skilled and dedicated, could foster the independence of families. It is a laudable ambition to encourage patients to take an active part in their treatment and rehabilitation so they are not merely passive recipients of care, but how you are supposed to do the same with their families is a bit of a mystery. I suggest it is rewritten to say:

**'Encourage clients to be independent and involve their loved ones in their care.'**

**Clause 6: '...work in a collaborative and cooperative manner with health care professionals and others involved in providing care, and recognise and respect their particular contributions within the care team.'**

My thesaurus suggests that tautology means pleonasm (sounds nasty), reiteration, repetition, wordiness, verbosity and verbiage. In other words, using two, or several words when one will do. What is the difference between collaborative and cooperative, and how can you be one without the other? Ditto with recognise and respect – if you don't see or recognise something it becomes mighty difficult to respect it. We also have the phrase 'health care professionals and others involved in providing care', which surely means 'all those providing care'. Alternative wording:

**'Work collaboratively with all those providing care.'**

**Clause 7: '...recognise and respect the uniqueness and dignity of each patient and client, and respond to their need for care, irrespective of their ethnic origin, religious beliefs, personal attributes, the nature of their health problems or any other factor.'**

You are no doubt seeing a pattern emerge, as that increasingly familiar double act 'recognise and respect' hove once more into view, establishing themselves as the Morecambe and Wise of the Code (although slightly less funny). This opening passage would be just as clear if the first two words were deleted. Clause 7 goes on to list the sorts of things you should respect, such as ethnic origin but here alarm bells started ringing at UKCC headquarters in Portland Place. You can imagine the conversation:

'So what sort of things should nurses recognise and respect in their patients?'

'Well, ethnic origin, obviously, we don't want any racist nurses.'

'Certainly, and how about religious beliefs?'

'Oh, absolutely, we must encourage religious tolerance.'

'But what about the awkward, unlikeable and unpopular patients. There's been a lot of research into them and apparently some nurses tend to avoid them?'

'Good point, but we can't say "unpopular patients", that would be open to interpretation, so why not use the words "personal attributes?"'

'Well, we could, but isn't an attribute a positive thing, a virtue or quality?'

'Yes, you might be right. But I can't think of another phrase right now so let's stick with it for the time being. What else should we include?'

'I think we should discourage nurses from making a negative judgement because of the nature of the patient's illness — they might disapprove of a gay man with AIDS, for example, or an unmarried woman who is pregnant, or a smoker with emphysema.'

'Quite right. You know, I'm getting a bit worried. We could list all the things that a nurse might disapprove of but you can guarantee that as soon as the Code is published, we'll remember another one. Or someone will write in and say, "You forgot about people who have sex with gerbils, or are overweight, or support Arsenal or something."'

'Mmm. What we need, then, is a catch-all phrase that covers every eventuality, like that bit in a job description that says, "And any other duties which you might be called on to perform."'

'I've got it. Why not say, "Or any other factor"?. That should cover everything.'

'Excellent. Fancy a pint?'

Of course, if you are going to use the phrase 'any other factor' you do not need the word 'other', you could simply say 'any factor' and forget about listing a few examples. At heart, it seems that this clause is trying to ensure that nurses do not allow their personal prejudices to cloud the care they give, so it could read:

**'Give equal care to all clients.'**

**Clause 8: '…report to an appropriate person or authority, at the earliest possible time, any conscientious objection which may be relevant to your professional practice.'**

Bit of an odd one this because the implicit suggestion is that you are allowed to have, and act upon, a conscientious objection. Yet we all know that, with the notable exception of abortion, where a Roman Catholic nurse may refuse to participate on religious grounds, you are not allowed to opt out of care simply because you disapprove in some way.

In mental health, for example, there has long been a view that nurses should be able to have nothing to do with electroconvulsive therapy (ECT) if they choose — on the grounds that it constitutes a physical assault (as do many medical procedures), has damaging, possibly permanent unwanted effects and no one knows how it works. This view has received short shrift from both employers and the UKCC, and at least one nurse has been sacked in the past for taking a principled stand against the treatment.

Therefore, if you are not allowed to withdraw care because of a conscientious objection, and we already know from Clause 7 that your care has to be given equally to all patients, no matter what you think of them, what would be the point of reporting your views to a higher authority?

And while we are on the subject, what is the difference between an appropriate person or authority? In this instance, the appropriate person, your line manager for example, is an agent of your employer, and therefore the same thing. So the appropriate person is also the appropriate authority, or at least its representative.

And what about this phrase 'relevant to your professional practice'? What else is it going to be relevant to? You presumably would not report a conscientious objection on the grounds that it offended your taste in music or didn't match the curtains.

The bit about doing your reporting 'at the earliest possible time' also seems odd, the unspoken message being that, if these words were not included, nurses would wait weeks, months or even years to report a conscientious objection. If we followed that line of thought through to its logical conclusion, the same words could be applied to almost every clause in the Code. For example, Clause 4 says, in part: 'Acknowledge any limitations in your knowledge and competence…' yet should surely say: 'Acknowledge any limitations in your knowledge and competence *at the earliest possible time*' if this principle of speediness is so important. Alternative wording:

**'Make known any conscientious objection.'**

**Clause 9: '…avoid any abuse of your privileged relationship with patients and clients and of the privileged access allowed to their person, property, residence or workplace.'**

If you avoid abusing your privileged relationship with patients and clients, you would, inevitably, avoid abusing the privileged access you have to their person. So one alternative wording could be: 'Do not abuse your privileged access to patients, their person, property, residence or workplace.' This would seem to cover things like stealing from someone's home, or bedside locker, or in some other way taking advantage of their vulnerability in the relationship — such as having sex with a psychiatric patient who has become inappropriately (perhaps) attracted to you as a professional carer. So the alternative wording becomes:

**'Do not abuse your privileged access to clients, their person, property, residence or workplace.'**

**Clause 10: '…protect all confidential information concerning patients and clients obtained in the course of professional practice and make**

disclosures only with consent, where required by the order of a court or where you can justify disclosure in the wider public interest.'

I wonder how a nurse might gather confidential information about patients other than 'in the course of professional practice'. Presumably it is possible that you might, for example, be in a pub with a patient's relative and hear something about the patient. But if you passed that information on to somebody who does not have a right to know, you would be in breach of the Code anyway because you would not be acting in the patient's best interests.

Surely the motive behind this clause is to respect privacy and not divulge to any outside, or irrelevant party, information you discover as part of your nursing duties. If so, it is surely enough to say 'respect patient confidentiality'. The way in which you may gather confidential information is immaterial, the key point is that you should not pass it on, other than in the examples given. Also, what is the difference between 'public interest' and 'wider public interest?' Suggested wording:

**'Respect client confidentiality, except where disclosure is required by a court order, or justified in the public interest.'**

**Clause 11: '...report to an appropriate person or authority, having regard to the physical, psychological and social effects on patients and clients, any circumstances in the environment of care which could jeopardise standards of practice.'**

**Clause 12: '...report to an appropriate person or authority any circumstances in which safe and appropriate care for patients and clients cannot be provided.'**

Clause 11 needs to be read with Clause 12, because the two cover very similar ground, which is why they have been analysed in the same chapter earlier in this book. Because of uncertainty about the differences between Clauses 11 and 12 I wrote to the UKCC and asked for clarification. The UKCC replied: 'Clause 11 covers the general well-being of patients and clients and talks about standards being jeopardised; impaired might be another good word. In other words, care can be delivered but the highest standards may not be attainable because of A, B or C.

'Clause 12 seems to go one step further in that it is not about impairment or the general well-being of patients; instead it is about circumstances in which safe or appropriate care absolutely cannot be provided. It is more definite in its degree of certainty that care cannot be provided.'

So that is that cleared up. Except for me it wasn't. I read the above several times and now think I understand it. There should be one combined clause which reads: 'Report to an appropriate person or authority, having regard to the physical, psychological and social effects on patients and clients, any circumstances in the environment of care which could jeopardise standards of practice, or any circumstances in which safe and appropriate care for patients and clients cannot be provided.' Finally, would 'unsafe care' be appropriate care? I think not. So, why not edit it to read:

**'Report to an appropriate person any circumstances which could jeopardise standards of practice, or in which safe care cannot be provided.'**

**Clause 13: '...report to an appropriate person or authority where it appears that the health or safety of colleagues is at risk, as such circumstances may compromise standards of practice and care.'**

This is probably the muzziest, fuzziest and most awkwardly written clause of the lot. It is ungrammatical, poorly constructed and you have to read it several times just to make sure that it really does read as badly as it first appears. That word 'where' just does not fit, and the whole thing would be improved if it read: 'Report to an appropriate person any circumstances where it appears...'

And as for that last bit, how clunkingly literal can you get? It seems to come from the school of the bleedin' obvious to say that if the health and safety of your colleagues is at risk, patient care might be compromised. And why the repetition of practice and care? Choose either one, it doesn't really matter and delete the other, the clause still makes perfect sense — or as much sense as it is ever going to make.

It is also very unclear where this clause actually differs from 11 and 12. Those two, as we have already established, focus on the environment of care and I can see nothing in Clause 13 that has not already been covered by Clause 12. If, as Clause 12 tells you, to report 'any circumstances in which safe and appropriate care for patients and clients cannot be provided', then you will report any situations in which 'the health or safety of colleagues is at risk'. The whole thing is entirely unnecessary and smacks a little of desperation on the part of the UKCC.

'How many clauses do we have then?'

'So far, 12.'

'Excellent, then I suggest we print it and go home for a well-earned rest. Unless, that is, you fancy a pint?'

'Sure do, but I'm not convinced we've got enough clauses.'

'What's wrong with 12, then?'

'I don't know, but this is going to be the definitive code of conduct for over half a million people. And it is going to be published in all sorts of books and magazines and things. And we've got enough paper to print it on four sides.'

'Fair point, well made.'

See what I mean? Frankly, there's not much can be done with this dog's dinner except to ditch it, but if the UKCC does insist on having something that specifically mentions colleagues, the alternative wording could be:

**'Report to an appropriate person any situation in which the health or safety of colleagues is at risk.'**

**Clause 14: '...assist professional colleagues, in the context of your own knowledge, experience and sphere of responsibility, to develop their professional competence, and assist others in the care team, including informal carers, to contribute safely and to a degree appropriate to their roles.'**

This is another lulu, especially the bit that says: 'Assist professional colleagues, *in the context of your own knowledge, experience and sphere of responsibility*, to develop their professional competence...' (my italics).

So who else's knowledge, experience and sphere of responsibility can you use but your own? This is like that old standby so beloved of barristers, who like to say to witnesses: 'Please tell the court, in your own words...', which begs the response: 'Who else's words would I use?' The last bit doesn't help much either because if people did not contribute 'to a degree appropriate to their roles' then they would not be contributing safely. But what are they contributing to? — making the ward tea, sweeping the floor, hanging the Christmas decorations or simply to the good atmosphere that exists where you work?

The motive behind this clause would appear to underline poet John Donne's notion that no man is an island. It is not enough to make sure of your own good practice, you must bear responsibility also for the practice of everyone else who comes in contact with the patient. So let's just say so, with the alternative wording:

'Help colleagues develop their professional competence, and assist others, including informal carers, to contribute safely to client care.'

**Clause 15: '...refuse any gift, favour or hospitality from patients or clients currently in your care which might be interpreted as seeking to exert influence to obtain preferential consideration.'**

That's easy — alternative wording: 'Don't take bribes.' Okay, that is not exactly what it means but as it stands you could, for example, take gifts, favours or hospitality from a patient's relative, or anyone else who was trying to influence you. You could also take gifts, favours or hospitality from a patient who has been discharged, or gone to another ward. This sets up the delightful prospect of the following exchange:

Patient: 'You've been so good to me nurse that I would like to give you this handsome Cartier watch; it's pure gold, diamond encrusted and worth £27,000.'

Nurse: 'Mr Radcliffe, that's so kind of you but I couldn't possibly accept. Why don't I visit you at home tomorrow, after you have been discharged, and you can give it to me then.'

In fact, this area is covered by Clause 7, which we concluded should read: 'Give equal care to all clients.' If you lived by this philosophy, you would not accept bribes or any other gift, favour or hospitality. Which might inevitably make you wonder about those boxes of chocolates or bunches of flowers that patients and their loved ones like to donate to individual nurses or staff teams.

However, in UKCC-land all is not as it seems because, if you read this passage closely it does not say, in effect: 'Refuse anything that might influence your preferential consideration,' it says: 'Refuse anything which *might be interpreted* as seeking to influence preferential consideration' (my italics). Therefore, the UKCC appears to be saying that you should avoid people thinking you are being bribed, rather than you should avoid being bribed.

However, if we accept that the rationale behind this clause is to stop bribery, the alternative wording could be:

**'Do not accept any gift, favour or hospitality that will influence your nursing care.'**

**Clause 16: '...ensure that your registration status is not used in the promotion of commercial products or services, declare any financial or**

other interests in relevant organisations providing such goods or services and ensure that your professional judgement is not influenced by any commercial considerations.'

Back to bribery again, especially the second part. But what is considered to be 'promotion' of products or services? Shouldn't that clause read: 'promotion of commercial products or services, *from which you stand to benefit*' (my italics) because all nurses will have favourite products, which they will recommend if asked?

And what is wrong with promoting goods or services anyway? I would argue that nurses have a duty to promote those which will do the job best. What they should not do, of course, is promote a product which they think is rubbish, for financial gain. That phrase 'in the promotion of' is beloved of bureaucrats everywhere and actually means 'to promote'. Therefore, 'the promotion of commercial products...' becomes 'to promote commercial products'. It's already beginning to read just a tad easier.

You are also supposed to 'declare any financial or other interests in relevant organisations providing such goods or services', but what exactly does this mean, and to whom are you supposed to make the declaration? When you go for a job interview, are you obliged to declare that you have a few shares in 3M Health Care, and therefore cannot use that company's Micropore tape, even though you may think it is the best one around? Or what if your husband or wife is employed by Johnson and Johnson, and you therefore have a very real financial interest in that organisation — it's contributing well over half of your family income — are you supposed to mention this to every patient you nurse?

The Code only applies to nurses on the register so the first few words of this clause are absolutely unnecessary. Suggested wording:

**'Do not promote commercial products or services from which you stand to benefit and ensure that your professional judgement is not influenced by commercial considerations.'**

We now have a Code of Professional Conduct that reads:

- Promote and safeguard the well-being of clients.
- Ensure that no action for which you are responsible will harm, or potentially harm, clients.
- Maintain and improve your professional knowledge and competence.
- Carry out only those duties which you can perform in a skilled way.

- Encourage clients to be independent and involve their loved ones in their care.

- Work collaboratively with all those providing care.

- Give equal care to all clients.

- Make known any conscientious objection.

- Do not abuse your privileged access to clients, their person, property, residence or workplace.

- Respect client confidentiality, except where disclosure is required by a court order, or justified in the public interest.

- Report to an appropriate person any circumstances which could jeopardise standards of practice, or in which safe care cannot be provided.

- Report to an appropriate person any situation in which the health or safety of colleagues is at risk.

- Help colleagues develop their professional competence, and assist others, including informal carers, to contribute safely to client care.

- Do not accept any gift, favour or hospitality that will influence your nursing care.

- Do not promote commercial products or services from which you stand to benefit and ensure that your professional judgement is not influenced by commercial considerations.

Alternatively, as I suggested at the beginning, you could have just one sentence, which reads:

**'Always do your best, and do nothing to hurt patients.'**

No, on reflection that is far too simple.

Of course, now that the formal review of the statutory bodies has been completed, and it looks as if the UKCC and national boards are going to be unified into a single body, it is possible that we may have a real opportunity to see a re-written Code. The new statutory authority could act decisively by giving the major policy document governing practitioners a significant, and long overdue, overhaul.

Oh, and a large pink pig has just flown past my window.

# Useful addresses

United Kingdom Central Council for Nursing,
Midwifery and Health Visiting

23 Portland Place,
London W1N 4JT.
Tel: 0171 637 7181

Royal College of Nursing
20 Cavendish Square,
London W1M 0AB.
Tel: 0171 409 3333
RCN Direct — 0345 726 100

Royal College of Midwives
15 Mansfield Street,
London W1M 0BE.
Tel: 0171 312 3535

Community Practitioners' and Health Visitors' Association
40 Bermondsey Street,
London SE1 3UD.
Tel: 0171 367 6800

UNISON
1, Mabledon Place
London WC1H 9AJ
Tel: 0171 388 2366

Community and District Nursing Association
Thames Valley University
8 University House
Ealing Green
London W5 5ED
Tel: 0181 231 2776

Nurses' Welfare Service
16/18 Strutton Ground,
London SW1P 2HP.
Tel: 0171 222 1563

# Index